NATION, NATIONALISM
and the
PUBLIC SPHERE

Thank you for choosing a SAGE product!
If you have any comment, observation or feedback,
I would like to personally hear from you.

Please write to me at **contactceo@sagepub.in**

Vivek Mehra, Managing Director and CEO, SAGE India.

Bulk Sales

SAGE India offers special discounts
for purchase of books in bulk.
We also make available special imprints
and excerpts from our books on demand.

For orders and enquiries, write to us at

Marketing Department
SAGE Publications India Pvt Ltd
B1/I-1, Mohan Cooperative Industrial Area
Mathura Road, Post Bag 7
New Delhi 110044, India

E-mail us at **marketing@sagepub.in**

Subscribe to our mailing list
Write to **marketing@sagepub.in**

This book is also available as an e-book.

NATION, NATIONALISM and the PUBLIC SPHERE

Religious Politics in India

Edited by
AVISHEK RAY
ISHITA BANERJEE-DUBE

Los Angeles | London | New Delhi
Singapore | Washington DC | Melbourne

First published in 2020 by

SAGE Publications India Pvt Ltd
B1/I-1 Mohan Cooperative Industrial Area
Mathura Road, New Delhi 110 044, India
www.sagepub.in

SAGE Publications Inc
2455 Teller Road
Thousand Oaks, California 91320, USA

SAGE Publications Ltd
1 Oliver's Yard, 55 City Road
London EC1Y 1SP, United Kingdom

SAGE Publications Asia-Pacific Pte Ltd
18 Cross Street #10-10/11/12
China Square Central
Singapore 048423

Published by Vivek Mehra for SAGE Publications India Pvt Ltd. Typeset in 10.5/13 pt Bembo by Zaza Eunice, Hosur, Tamil Nadu, India.

Library of Congress Cataloging-in-Publication Data

Names: Ray, Avishek, 1985-editor. | Banerjee-Dube, Ishita, editor.
Title: Nation, nationalism, and the public sphere: religious politics in
   India / [edited by] Avishek Ray and Ishita Banerjee-Dube.
Description: New Delhi, India: SAGE Publications India Pvt Ltd; Thousand
   Oaks, California, USA: SAGE Publications, Inc., 2020. | Includes
   bibliographical references and index.
Identifiers: LCCN 2020014964 | ISBN 9789353883805 (hardback) | ISBN
   9789353883812 (epub) | ISBN 9789353883829 (adobe pdf)
Subjects: LCSH: Religion and politics--India.
Classification: LCC BL2015.P57 N38 2020 | DDC 322/.10954--dc23
LC record available at https://lccn.loc.gov/2020014964

ISBN: 978-93-5388-380-5 (HB)

SAGE Team: Amrita Dutta, Satvinder Kaur and Rajinder Kaur

Contents

Acknowledgements

Working on this book has been an enriching and pleasurable experience. We have learnt a lot from the detailed and insightful analyses on a variety of themes provided in the chapters. Our sincere thanks to the contributors for making this teamwork possible and worthwhile.

Our gratitude extends to the SAGE editorial and production team for their competent and professional support throughout this project. We thank Amrita Dutta of SAGE, in particular, for answering our innumerable queries and concerns unfailingly with patience.

This book has immensely benefited from the invaluable technical and research support rendered by Luis Gamaliel Quiñones Martínez and Parijat Goswami and the incisive feedback and suggestions from Saurabh Dube and Neha Gupta.

We also thank the anonymous reviewers whose well-considered reports have substantially enhanced the quality of this book.

Introduction

Nation, Religion, Identity— Crisscrossing Concerns

Ishita Banerjee-Dube and Avishek Ray

'Religion', in its constructed and essentialized as well as empirical and experiential dimensions, has turned the table upside down on initial and enthusiastic expectations of the secular-modern by stubbornly refusing to disappear from private domains and the public arena. Indeed, over the past three decades, it has acquired remarkable salience by becoming a crucial element in cultural nationalisms that 'reify' history and 'aestheticize politics' in the name of 'authenticity' and 'culture' (Bannerji 2000, 1), where 'culture is collapsed into 'civilization' and 'civilization' into religion as a kind of patrimony' (Ahmed 2000, 16). Such enduring presence and resurgence of religion in politics in distinct parts of the globe at different moments have occasioned serious and erudite reflections by scholars not just on the many meanings of the religious and the secular but also on their variable and contingent configurations, their application as universal categories by the colonizing West, and their discrete apprehensions.

Scholarly reflections have resulted in the excavation of the genealogy of 'religion' in order to lay bare its gradual construction as an essentialist, trans-historical phenomenon beginning with the separation of religion and politics (the church and the state) in a few societies of Western Europe at a particular historical juncture, and sustained and bolstered by influential definitions in disciplines such as anthropology (Asad 1993, 27–54). They have also led to careful delineations of the secular as 'a central, modern, epistemic category', secularism as a world-view, and secularization as 'an analytical conceptualization of modern world-historical processes' (Casanova 2009, 1049). While Talal Asad and Jose Casanova, two leading scholars who have critically analysed the secular, coincide in accepting the secular as an epistemic category, Casanova views secularism as a worldview, and Asad sees it as a political doctrine of Euro-America with far greater force than a worldview. It is an ideology that 'presupposes' new concepts of religion, ethics and politics and the imperatives such concepts entail (Asad 2003, 1–2). And it is precisely the divergent perceptions and apprehensions of the implicit imperatives of the secular that have produced a variety of responses to secularism including its rejection as a 'Western' doctrine in some societies of the Middle East and elsewhere and an assertion by the advocates of secularism that despite its parochial roots the doctrine has universal applicability (Asad 2003, 2).[1]

THE RELIGIOUS AND THE SECULAR

It is important to unpack the concerns and arguments of the debates outlined above. First, they arose in the wake of actual historical and sociopolitical occurrences in various societies that reaffirmed the signifi-cance of religion in the public, political sphere. Second, the analytical distinction made by scholars between the three jumbled empirical enti-ties of the secular, secularism and secularization allows an understanding of the conditions that made possible the emergence of the secular as an episteme and of notions that underlie it, and indicate the happen-ings and aspirations that occasioned the consolidation of secularism as a redemptive worldview/ideology. By formally separating the spheres of the religious (the church and the ecclesiastical) from the 'secular' (the state, economy, science and art) in the 'early-modern' period, secularism as an ideology/worldview—accompanied by secularization as a plural process—is taken to have slowly transformed the dominance

---

[1] Asad is referring to the work of Charles Taylor (1999). A more detailed and intricate argument of Taylor is contained in Taylor (2008). Indeed, the literature is copious. For a productive understanding, see the many writings of and debates between Talal Asad (1993, 2003) and Jose Casanova (2009).

and influence of the religious/ecclesiastical in politics and public life into an autonomy of the secular, signalling thereby a break with the 'medieval' or the pre-modern and the onset of the modern. It is in this sense that secularism has been widely acknowledged as a liberating force that made possible the transition to modern contemporary societies by breaking loose the grasp of 'religion' (Casanova 2009, 1050). Third and finally, these incisive analyses do not only question the universality of the 'universal' categories of the religious and the secular but also insist on the necessity of paying close attention to empirical contexts since differing contexts conduce diverse experience and understandings that power disparate processes of secularization and distinct configurations of 'secular' democracies resulting in varied manifestations of religion in the public sphere. In other words, they prompt us to question the assumptions that take pre-constructed understandings of the secular and its prevalence in 'modern' democracies as axiomatic. It bears mention here that scholars have indicated that the 'liberation', inaugurated by secularism, has come at a cost, particularly in societies of the non-West, where the religious and the secular were muddled in ways that made such a clear separation difficult (Bhargava 1998). For Nandy (1997a), who clearly demarcates the modern and the 'non-modern', secularism has been a pretext for de-indigenization and de-culturation. Together, the analyses also encourage serious contemplation of what constitutes 'religion' in contemporary societies.

An attention to contexts indicates that it was possibly the 'Iranian Revolution'—often termed the 'Islamic Revolution' of 1978–1979— that occasioned a serious rethinking of the widely acknowledged separation of the religious and the secular in state policies and public politics. This revolution, it is worth recounting, brought monarchy to an end through a coming together of clerics, leftist forces and popular upheaval. Mohammad Reza Shah (Pahlavi) of Iran had sought to legitimize his regime on a programme of 'modernization' and appeals to patriotism poised on the strategic support of western allies, particularly the United States, and propped up by state repression. If the predominant US presence occasioned a 'conservative' backlash that spoke in the name of saving Shia Islam, the Shah's repressive policies and economic turmoil brought students and workers with disparate but broad leftist ideologies together with the clerics. A collective belief in a 'primordial' Iran as a 2,500-year-old 'nation' with several shared elements made this curious and unusual combination possible (Aghaie 2014, 187–188).[2] As a consequence, an 'Islamic republic' was proclaimed at the end of the 'Revolution'. A 'religious' republic that was primarily Iranian: an anachronistic combination that disrupted the tidy separation of the religious and the political as well as their categorization as 'non-modern' and 'modern'.

NATION, CULTURE, POLITICS

Significantly, the Islamic Revolution ceased to be an 'anomaly' and soon became a major theme in international politics as peoples in different countries began to express a longing for 'indigenous' alternatives to 'secular' Western politics that had religion and culture as key components (Juergensmeyer 1993, 2008).[3] The upsurge of 'ethnic' and other cultural 'nationalisms' that led to the disintegration of powerful, multi-nation states such as the Soviet Union, Yugoslavia (and Czechoslovakia) in the early 1990s, urged a close scrutiny of the relation between the state and its institutionalized nationalism with other loyalties and modes of identification among different sections of a heterogeneous population that contravened the 'nationality' policies and politics of these states (Ludden 1996, 2). Nationalism came under close scholarly scrutiny; influential theories of the nation (and nationalism) emphasized how they were imagined and constructed on the basis of some common markers that generated a sense of belonging and sharing (Anderson 2006; Chatterjee 1986, 1993; Gellner 1983). The mutual imbrications of nationalism and 'ethno-nationalism' were also carefully considered (Connor 1994). In addition, formidable formulations of the intimate links between nation, nationalism and racism underscored the contradictions that lie at the very core of the nation and its diverse history, and nationalism as an ideology that often deploys racism as an integral component to uphold and legitimize the 'integrity of the

---

[2] We thank Kamal Soleimani for referring us to this and other publications on Iran and the Islamic Revolution.

[3] Instead of taking issues with 'religious nationalism' as something that pertains to the Islamic, Hindu, Buddhist and Zionist worlds, Juergensmeyer (2008) looks at 'religious nationalism' from the perspective of its proponents to examine the problems of secular nationalism.

nation' internally and externally. The reciprocity of nationalism and racism in turn is sustained by the increasing dominance of the order of nation-states over other social formations (Balibar 1988).

Explorations of how and why nations were fashioned and sustained were accompanied by analyses of the materiality of nations: the vital 'social force' of nationalism and religion that accounted for the efficacy of these 'cultural constructs' in everyday lives (van der Veer and Lehman 1999, 3). These studies revealed the inadequacy of the 'conventional dichotomies' of social theory poised on an 'ideological a priori distinction' between national imagination and religious imagination, and indicated how national and religious loyalties, instead of being rivals and mutually exclusive, can combine to shore up loyalty to the imagined community (Aghaie 2014; van der Veer 1994; van der Veer and Lehman 1999).

Anthony D. Smith (2000, 792) added greater force to this argument by underscoring that the nation is best understood as a 'sacred communion of citizens', a 'felt and willed communion' of peoples who 'assert a particular moral faith and feel a common ancestral affinity'. Not only does such a felt and willed 'sacred' moral community confer cohesiveness on the nation, it also shores up its self-confidence and exclusivity, a fact that has important implications for the global interstate order of 'national-states'. Adopting a Durkheimian approach, Smith marked out the function and significance of the symbolic, the ideological and the political components of the nation, nationalism and national identity to affirm that most national identities are 'suffused and underpinned' by a belief in the sacred that often result in a politicization of religion and a 'messianization' of the people (Smith 2000, 795; 1991, 2001 [2010]). He untangled the levels of the 'official', the 'popular' and the 'sacred' in the imbricated relation between religion and national identity, to delineate the sacred markers that contribute to the constitution of the nation as a 'sacred communion' of an imagined community of the dead, the living and the to be born in an upward linear trajectory of time, a community that is not just 'imagined' but 'felt and willed' (Smith 2000, 800–810). This formulation effectively overturned the ideas of the secular nation replacing religious, primordial and ethnic identities.

Combining a reading of the evolution and interaction of nationalism and capitalism, scholars of the Marxist vein have offered a distinct and important analysis of the materiality of nations by analysing their 'class character' (Desai 2008b; Patnaik 2016). They disagree with the thesis that nation–states have become less relevant under regimes of neoliberalism and globalization in the last quarter of the 20th century. Far from disappearing, nations and nationalisms took on a different form. The 'developmental nationalisms' of the third quarter of the century got transformed into 'cultural nationalisms' that are flagrantly neoliberal and frame their cultural politics in terms of religion, ethnicity and culture, where culture is taken to be 'pre-given, static and original' (Desai 2008a, 648; Patnaik 2016).

Apart from underlining the problems with the antinomies of the 'modern', these studies, by closely examining the recent growth of cultural nationalisms the world over, have demonstrated the hollowness of the binaries of religion and politics, the religious and the secular and of the innately secular nature of modern nations, urging a serious probe of our own orientations and approaches to social worlds and politics.

NATIONALISM AND NATIONAL IDENTITY

The 'nation-state' is often argued to be an overtly restrictive projection of a model derived from the Western European experience onto the non-West where it may not apply.[4] Likewise, the religious categories in India, before the colonial intervention, were neither watertight nor mutually exclusive. Among the families in undivided Punjab, for example, it was not uncommon to raise one child as Sikh and another as Hindu. Even today, many Indians who practice non-Indic faiths (Christianity, Judaism and Islam) observe many Hindu practices and beliefs; and, conversely, many Hindus include icons of Christ, Mary, Buddha and Muslim mystics in their personal shrines, and visit Muslim

---

[4] It is germane here to recall Partha Chatterjee's (1993, 5) famous rejoinder to Anderson's (2006 [1983]) influential formulation on nationalism: 'If nationalisms in the rest of the world have to choose their imagined community from certain 'modular' forms already made available to them by Europe and the Americas, what do they have left to imagine?'

or Christian pilgrimages and observe non-Hindu festivals (Nandy 1997b). The colonial imperative of trying to know India through an 'episteme' that sought to enumerate, classify and govern it produced what Bernard Cohn (1996) calls the 'colonial forms of knowledge', which objectified and categorized India in discrete ways and assigned all groups a 'role' in the sociological drama. As a result, by the time nationalism and the nationalist struggle for independence grew, certain epistemic categories—for example, the census-driven heuristics of (religious) majority–minority—had unwittingly become an element of nationhood. It bears pointing out in this context that the various articulations in (re)casting social and cultural identities—the myriad and nuanced ways in which identities continue to be engendered and reinforced—within the framework of (post)colonialism—have always yielded hybrid configurations.

Tagore (2002 [1917], 115) in his rebuttal of nationalism writes, 'India never had a *real* sense of nationalism' (emphasis added). It was rather 'follow[ing] the West in its acceptance of the organised selfishness of Nationalism' (Tagore 2002 [1917], 21). Yet, evident in his assertion is an imaginative articulation of 'India' counterpoised against the West. Beyond any modular approach, it is therefore pertinent to consider the cultural impulses in the disjunctive temporalities and multiple vernacular iterations of nation(alism). Notwithstanding the 'political correctness' in maintaining that there is no one Indian-ness,[5] vernacular iterations of territorially fantasized cultural connections and flows, indeed, have existed since the 'pre-modern' times (Bandyopadhyay 2006; Eck 2013). Consider, after Bandyopadhyay (2006), the three instances of (a) the *Satipeethas*, (b) the sites for *Kumbhmelas* and (c) the four *Mathas* founded by Sankaracharya.[6] This 'sacred geography', for example, predates the 'modern' cartographic imagination of India and

---

[5] India's Sanskritic past, Spivak (1990, 39) contends, is too Indic; the name 'India' was mistakenly given by Alexander, Hindustan by Islamic conquerors, and Bharat is reminiscent of a mythic king.

[6] *Satipeethas* are religious shrines erected on the sites where, according to 'Indian' mythology, parts of Sati's (goddess) corpse had fallen. *Kumbhmelas* are quasi-religious fairs organized since antiquity, rotationally in different 'Indian' cities based on the celestial configuration and 'Indian' calendrical systems. The *Mathas* refer to the four monasteries—located at Joshimath (in North India), Puri (in the

illustrates the inefficacy of the modular approach or the modern(ity)/ tradition dyad as analytics, when it comes to understanding nationalism in the context of India.

More to it, one has to seriously consider the conceptual (in)congruity in the Indian languages, leading to interferences in utilization of 'foreign' concepts which may have apparently translatable 'Indian' term(inologie)s, but with totally different content/context(s). For example, think of the vernacular expressions: *swaraj* (cf. Gandhi, K. C. Bhattacharya), *deshabhiman, swadeshprem, deshbhakti, swadeshchetana, swajatyabodh* and so on. Are these synonymous and conceptually congruent with 'nationalism'? Or, because they emerge from different conceptual–cultural universes, do they gesture towards an alternative understanding of nation(hood)? However, during the current political regime—one that tacitly plays on the dialectics of the majority–minority to achieve religious mobilization—the scope of any alternative understanding of nation(hood) is increasingly shrinking. The immense problem in how the political dissenters in contemporary India are being dismissed as 'minorities', or worse still, outrightly labelled as 'secessionists', 'antinationals' and so on—*empty signifiers, though*—in the statist idiom is illustrative of the nature of the problem.

Whether with respect to the nationalist or the anti-national, nationalism, in the statist discourse, is typically understood as neat, coherent and uniform—barely leaving any room for alternative imagination! This brings us to the problem of separating 'good' nationalism from 'bad' nationalism. How do we politically account for the classificatory practice that, for example, deems the Indian or the African National Congress 'good' (in view of their antipathy towards the British) but the Czarist or the Ottoman obsession with the nation 'bad'? Is this a difference in degree—the extent of fervency in one's allegiance with the nation—than in kind? For instance, what renders an ideologue of 'Indian' (civic/civilizational) nationalism a 'good' nationalist but that

---

east), Shringeri (in the south) and Dwarka (in the west of 'India'—founded by Shankaracharya roughly between mid-8th and early 9th centuries.

of territorial–regional (ethnic) nationalism a 'secessionist'[7]? Raymond Williams (1985, 214) astutely observes the complexity in

> separating **national feeling** (good) from **nationalist feeling** (bad if it is another's country, making claims against one's own), or ... **national interest** (good) from **nationalism** (the asserted national interest of another group). The complexity has been increased by the usually separable distinction between **nationalism** (selfish pursuit of a nation's interests as against others) and **internationalism** (co-operation between nations). [bold in the original]

Perhaps, nationalism, as Plamenatz (1976) and Scruton (1990) suggest, cannot be 'essentially' good or bad. It is rather the nature of the 'intervention' of the state—the 'constructivist' aspect involved therein—that makes nationalism appear good or bad.

It is with reference to the shift away from a positivist approach to a constructivist approach that the recent religious mobilizations in the context of Indian nationalism have to be understood.[8] South Asia in general and India in particular offer illuminating examples of how the social force of a religious–cultural imagination blends easily with imaginings of a territorially grounded powerful political nation in the persuasive projection of an intimate association between national pride and cultural roots in Hinduism bolstered by the discourse of Hindutva.

---

[7] Think of the Gorkhaland movement in India in this context.

[8] The positivist historian believes that 'historical processes were a *natural* process and therefore required a scientific method to interpret it' (Collingwood 1962, 100 [emphasis added]). The positivist teleology, thus, renders the nation-state naturalized. For the constructivist, however, historical processes, and by extension nation-states, are but sociopolitical constructs manoeuvred to appear as natural. Along the same lines, Sumit Sarkar (2003) reminds us: 'History is not primarily about isolated "facts" or details. It tries to select, arrange, analyse and explain them through narrative patterns which are diverse, open to change, often mutually conflicting.... A bit of information about the past becomes a historical "fact" only within a particular narrative, which would be based on a set of hypotheses or frame of analysis. In a sense, then, it is "constituted" by the latter.' Anderson (1998, 2006), Breuilly (1982), Chatterjee (1993), Hobsbawm (1991), Gellner (1983) and Smith (1986), among others, have highlighted the different aspects of sociocultural craftedness that go into the making of nationalism.

This imposing combination of the religious–cultural–political with the national–territorial has conferred a unique significance and authority on parties of the Hindu Right in the public political sphere over the past three decades (Hansen 1999).

In his important and sensitive study published in the wake of the first success of the Hindu Right to form a government at the Centre, Thomas Blom Hansen had commented on the 'relative ease' with which the Hindu nationalist discourse had fitted in with the most authorized discourses on India and the authorized discourses on politics and culture in the post-colonial world (Hansen 1999, 5). This was because Hindu nationalism in India owed its shaping to 'public culture', the 'public space' in which a society and the individuals and communities it is composed of, 'imagine, represent, and recognize through political discourse, commercial and cultural expressions, and representations of state and civic organizations' (Hansen 1999, 4).

Two decades later, the Hindu Right appears to reign supreme in India. More than ever before, the Hindu nationalist aspiration to transform Indian public culture into a disciplined national culture premised on a supposedly superior Hindu past, and India into a strong Hindu *rashtra* (state) where citizens are moved by *bhakti* (devotion) to the *rashtra* appears to have gained great provenance. The return to power for a second term by a government at the Centre under Narendra Modi—a Rashtriya Swayamsevak Sangh *pracharak* who rose to political prominence in Gujarat—consequent, to a large extent, upon a trust in Modi as the man of the hour and a national hero, tends to vindicate the Indian population's belief in and support for a strong, unified, intolerant nation-state as India's way forward in the international order and a world increasingly dominated by multinational corporations.

A convoluted yet successful amalgamation of nation and culture shored up by an increasing assertion of the demographic dominance of the Hindus have resulted in a majoritarianism that openly and confidently rejects consensus based on a recognition of and respect for plurality and heterogeneity. The indistinct but palpable Hindutva, which is meant to inhere in all true Hindus—autochthonous residents of a 'sacred' father land (*pitrubhumi*)—has found wide acceptance among large sections of the vast urban and rural middle and lower classes that believe in an avowal of Hindu majority and cultural pride as the way to India's national and international glory. To them, the veritable problems of a huge and heterogeneous democratic nation appear to have been occasioned by a negligence of Hindu cultural roots.

The gradual transformation of the idea of the majority in Indian democracy from one being based on 'consensus' to one based on numbers, in particular of members of 'religious' communities, has been evident in an unstated yet palpable consensus among political parties on the 'Hindu vote' from the turn of the 21st century. This unproblematic consensus together with a shift towards a 'religious Right' has fostered a reconfiguration of the Hindu majority as 'democracy', and of Hinduism as the most tolerant of religions turning the 'secular' into a false, anti-Hindu construct (Vanaik 2017, 246), and conferred on parties of the Hindu Right an astounding electoral success.

As a result, democratic politics of electoral representation has occasioned the triumph of an undemocratic and aggressive Hindu nation-state. Never before in the history of independent India have 'racism' and intolerance been flaunted in the name of 'national integrity' and national identity with greater confidence. This vexed yet palpable state of affairs call for a close and careful consideration.

NATION, IMAGININGS, RELIGION

This book tracks the interface of the religious and the political and their jumbled articulations in varied manifestations of national imaginings and nationalism in India from different perspectives and orientations. Traversing the early 20th century to the present, it traces the distinct and overlapping elements and sentiments that went into the making of the 'national' and continue to sustain it in distinct ways. Such consciousness and the social force of the elements straddle the religious and the political, the regional and the linguistic, race and ethnicity, travel and tourism, film and media, space and community, and culture, demography and majoritarian consciousness through analyses that range from the historical, ethnographical, literary, legal and political to those of architecture, cinema, media and space. Together, the book offers insights into the material and the symbolic, the ideological, the 'sacred' and the political components of nation and nationalism.

The first two chapters by a veteran scholar (Juergensmeyer) and a young academic (Khan) complement each other by examining the impact of the internalization of colonial policies and politics by elite reformers, and political leaders in India, and by reformers, legal practitioners and feminist activists in Pakistan. Their incisive analyses comment on the enduring ramifications of such internalization in perceptions of the religious–traditional and the secular–modern in projections of the nation in these post-colonial states. While Juergensmeyer highlights the consequences of the paradoxical coexistence of the absence of a common perception of what constitutes the 'religious' and/or a 'national community' among marginal communities of late 20th-century India with the acceptance by Indian elites and political leaders of a clear separation of the 'religious' and the 'secular-political', the 'majority' and the 'minority', and the 'modern' and the 'traditional' in contemporary India, Khan dwells at length on the problems related to the acceptance and deployment of 'Western' categories that view Islamic law through texts, instead of practices and interpretation. She urges a surpassing of the tradition/modern binary and an attention to 'traditional' scholars in order to effect laws that are gender sensitive and based on the experience of discrimination and hierarchy by women.

Chapters 3, 4 and 5 trace the emergence and consolidation of nationalist imageries and a sense of belonging to and serving the cause of a nation, often conceived as Hindu. Nijwahan's careful reading of the new genre of travel writings in Hindi published in a well-known journal in the first half of the 20th century unpacks the dual purpose they served: that of establishing a standardized Hindi as a language of literary expression and of evoking an inchoate yet palpable sense of the territorial expanse and the grandeur of the 'nation'. Ghosal focuses on the consciously majoritarian concerns of sections of the 'Hindu elite' to show how, by the beginning of the 20th century, colonial policies of categorization and classification had consolidated and made them acceptable terms of public, political discourse. A combination of race, religion and numbers had come to uphold the notion of the Hindus as a superior race and authentic inhabitants of India, whose dwindling numbers were causing great concern. Through her exploration of the Lakshminarayan Birla temple inaugurated in Delhi in 1939, and the project of temple building undertaken by G. D. Birla, a close associate of Mahatma Gandhi, Hartig argues that the temples were built to contribute to the political project of nation-building and infuse it with a 'Hindu' religious mentality. The temple, with its unorthodox, eclectic architectural style, came to embody a visible symbol of 'modern' aspirations and contributed to the shaping of the national and religious identity of an emergent nation.

Kapoor and Sharma move our attention to the present and to the lived and experiential dimensions of faith in Chapters 6 and 7, respectively. Kapoor's sensitive study of a 'cosmopolitan' Guru-led faith movement, The Art of Living Foundation, reveals that despite its global reach and adherents, the foundation's activities within India invoke and give expression to a primordial Hindu (Vedic) community that sustains cultural nationalism. Sharma offers an incisive ethnography of a *gaushala* (cow-shelter) that unpacks the existence of gendered hierarchies and discriminatory practices in the valorized Hindu nationalist cause of the protection and conservation of the cow as the nation's mother.

In Chapters 8, 9 and 10, Chatterjee, Mitra and Alvarado Becerril open a vista to the colourful worlds of social media, film and television. Chatterjee tries to understand the electoral success of the Hindu Right (and cultural nationalism) by turning her attention to Prime Minister Narendra Modi as the 'national hero' and man of the hour, a cult figure whose populism inspires devotion among his *bhakts,* devotees, who become 'true' Indians and serve the cause of the nation through devotion to Modi. Mitra reads the words and world of a super-hero of 'Bollywood', Shah Rukh Khan, to cull out the multiple and contingent meanings of being a 'cosmopolitan' citizen of a 'minority' community and of belonging to the nation in films and real life. Alvarado Becerril's exploration of contemporary televisual debates in top news channels draws our attention to the role of these channels in constantly constructing and sustaining notions of what/who constitutes the 'true' national and nationalist that sustain Hindu nationalist categorizations of national and anti-national, patriot and traitor while they provide a feel of 'deliberative' democracy to participants and viewers.

Finally, in the last chapter, Gogoi offers an anthropological account of the making and unmaking of a cultural landscape among the Dimasa community of the North-East, by tracking the developmental imperatives of the modern state that encroach upon spatial notions of the 'sacred' of marginal communities, and force them to reconfigure their relation with space and faith.

Taken together, the chapters, different in approach, method and focus, point to the multifarious elements that constitute and detract from the 'nation' and the 'national', and underscore the mixed articulations of the religious, secular, cultural and political. They offer valuable insights on the interface of religious nationalism and the spatialization of the nation-state that enable the territorialization of religion, on the perceptions and experience of the imbricated concepts of religion, political, secular, national that result in reinforcement of 'tradition' and feed into the ethos of nationalism. In sum, this book aims to illustrate the crisscrossing identities of the religious, the secular, the cultural–civilizational and the political—the interstitial spaces—while overturning the neat boundaries and throwing the belief in them into disarray.

REFERENCES

Aghaie, Kamran Scot. 2014. 'Islamic-Iranian Nationalism and Its Implications for the Study of Political Islam and Religious Nationalism'. In *Rethinking Iranian Nationalism and Modernity*, edited by Kamran Scot Aghaie and Afshin Marashi. Austin, TX: University of Texas Press.

Ahmed, Aijaz. 2000. 'Nationalism and Globalisation'. Occasional Papers Series: 4. Department of Sociology, University of Pune.

Anderson, B. 1998. *The Spectre of Comparisons: Nationalism, Southeast Asia, and the World*. London: Verso. First published in 1983.

———. 2006 [1983]. *Imagined Communities: Reflections on the Origin and Spread of Nationalism*, London and New York: Verso.

Asad, Talal. 1993. *Genealogies of Religion: Discipline and Reasons of Power in Christianity and Islam*. Baltimore, MD: Johns Hopkins University Press.

———. 2003. *Formations of the Secular: Christianity, Islam, Modernity*. Stanford, CA: Stanford University Press.

Balibar, Etienne. 1988. 'Racismo y nacionalismo'. In *Raza, Nación y Clase*, edited by Etienne Balibar and Immanuel Wallerstein. Madrid: IEPALA.

Bandyopadhyay, D. 2006. 'The Pre-colonial Imagined Boundaries'. Adhir Chakroborty Memorial Lecture, delivered at the Centre for Archaeological Training and Research, Govt. of West Bengal, India on 8 December 2006.

Bannerji, Himani. 2000. *The Dark Side of the Nation: Essays on Multiculturalism, Nationalism and Gender*. Toronto: Canadian Scholars' Press Inc.

Bhargava, R. ed. 1998. *Secularism and Its Critics*. New Delhi: Oxford University Press.

Breuilly, J. 1982. *Nationalism and the State*. Manchester: Manchester University Press.

Casanova, Jose. 2009. 'The Secular and Secularisms'. *Social Research* 76 (4): 1049–1066.

Chatterjee, P. 1986. *Nationalist Thought and the Colonial World: A Derivative Discourse?* London: Zed Books.

———. 1993. *The Nation and Its Fragments: Colonial and Postcolonial Histories*. Delhi: Oxford University Press.

Cohn, B. 1996. *Colonialism and Its Forms of Knowledge*. Princeton, NJ: Princeton University Press.

Connor, W. 1994. *Ethnonationalism: The Quest for Understanding*. Princeton, NJ: Princeton University Press.

Desai, Radhika. 2008a. 'Conclusion: From Developmental Culture to Nationalisms'. *Third World Quarterly* 29 (3): 647–670.

———. 2008b. 'Developmental and Cultural Nationalisms in Historical Perspective'. *The Asia-Pacific Journal, Japan Focus* 6 (6). https://apjjf.org/-Radhika-Desai/2791/article.html

Eck, Diana L. 2013. *India: A Sacred Geography*. New York: Harmony.

Gellner, E. 1983. *Nations and Nationalism*. Oxford: Oxford University Press.

Hansen, Thomas Blom. 1999. *The Saffron Wave: Democracy and Hindu Nationalism in Modern India*. Princeton, NJ: Princeton University Press.

Hobsbawm, E. 1991. *Nations and Nationalism Since 1780: Programme, Myth, Reality*. Cambridge, UK: Cambridge University Press.

Juergensmeyer, Mark. 1993. *The New Cold War? Religious Nationalism Confronts the Secular State*. Berkeley and Los Angeles: University of California Press.

———. 2008. *Global Rebellion: Religious Challenges to the Secular State, from Christian Militants to al Qaeda*. Berkeley and Los Angeles: University of California Press.

Ludden, David. 1996. 'Introduction'. In *Making India Hindu: Religion, Community, and the Politics of Democracy in India*, edited by David Ludden. New Delhi: Oxford University Press.

Nandy, Ashis. 1997a. 'The Twilight of Certitudes: Secularism, Hindu Nationalism and Other Masks of Deculturation'. *Alternatives: Global, Local, Political* 22 (2): 157–176.

———. 1997b. 'Facing Extermination: A Report on the Present State of the Gods and Goddesses in South Asia'. *Manushi: A Journal about Women and Society* 99: 5–19.

Patnaik, Prabhat. 2016. 'Nationalism, Hindutva, and the Assault on Thought'. *Marxist* 32 (1). https://cpim.org/content/nationalism-hindutva-and-assault-thought

Plamenatz, John. 1976. 'Two Types of Nationalism'. In *Nationalism: The Nature and Evolution of an Idea,* edited by Eugene Kamenka, 22–36. London: Edward Arnold.

Sarkar, Sumit. 2003. 'The Limits of Nationalism'. *Seminar.* 522. https://www.india-seminar.com/2003/522/522%20sumit%20sarkar.htm

Scruton, R. 1990. 'In Defence of the Nation'. In *Ideas and Politics in Modern Britain,* edited by J. C. D. Clark, 53–86. London: Palgrave Macmillan.

Smith, Anthony D. 1986. *The Ethnic Origins of Nations.* Oxford: Blackwell.

———. 1991. *National Identity.* Reno: University of Nevada Press.

———. 2000. 'The Sacred Dimension of Nationalism'. *Millennium: Journal of International Studies* 29 (3): 791–814.

———. 2010 [2001]. *Nationalism: Theory, Ideology, History.* Cambridge: Polity Press.

Spivak, Gayatri C. 1990. *The Post-colonial Critic: Interviews, Strategies, Dialogues.* New York: Routledge.

Tagore, R. 2002 [1917]. *Nationalism.* Madras: Macmillan India.

Taylor, Charles. 1999. 'Modes of Secularism'. In *Secularism and Its Critics,* edited by R. Bhargava, 31–53. Delhi and New York: Oxford University Press.

———. 2008. *A Secular Age.* Cambridge, MA: Harvard University Press.

Vanaik, Achin. 2017. *The Rise of Hindu Authoritarianism: Secular Claims, Communal Realities.* London: Verso.

van der Veer, Peter. 1994. *Religious Nationalism. Hindus and Muslims in India.* Berkeley and Los Angeles: University of California Press.

van der Veer, Peter and Harmut Lehman. 1999. 'Introduction'. In *Nation and Religion: Perspectives on Europe and Asia,* edited by Peter van der Veer and Hartmut Lehman. Princeton, NJ: Princeton University Press.

Williams, Raymond. 1985. *Keywords: A Vocabulary of Culture and Society.* New York: Oxford University Press.

Chapter 1

The Clash of Religious Politics in India

Mark Juergensmeyer

Years ago, when I began my research into religion and society in North India, I had difficulty translating the term 'religion'. I found that no single term for this English word and the singular idea it implied existed, at least not traditionally, in any Indian language. When I tried to discuss this concept in rural Punjab, I found that instead of one term for religion, there were many terms that described different aspects of religiosity—*qaum*, a word that means 'nation' or 'community'; *mazhab*, which means 'beliefs'; *dharma*, the term often used by missionaries to describe religion, which means ethical law or moral order; and *panth*, which means a fellowship of faithful believers. Someone who wore the *qaumik* turban of Sikhs could ascribe to traditional Hindu *dharmic* values and follow a Muslim *pir* as part of a local *panth*. It is this fluid religiosity that Gandhi would describe as a universal quest for truth, and that Rabindranath Tagore would characterize as 'the religion of man' (Tagore 1931).

How this fluid religiosity in India became hardened into fractious communalism and became highly politicized is an interesting and contested story. Consensus places its development in the late British colonial period. The rise of new moneyed classes both urban and rural and the need to stake a claim in emerging arenas of political competition serve to stoke the fires of communal identity. How these social and political forces combined to create communalism is a matter of historical debate and contemporary significance (Chandhoke 2019; Chandra 1984; Das 1994; Hasan 2019; Pandey 2012; Singh 2011). One of the more intriguing suggestions is that the European Enlightenment's idea of religious social identity was transplanted onto the South Asian context by the British, who saw India's political landscape in communal terms.

THE EUROPEAN ORIGINS OF INDIA'S RELIGIOUS POLITICS

In an interesting book, *Enlightenment in the Colony*, Aamir Mufti (2007) argues that the British helped to invent not only the English language's idea of religion in India but also the European concept of religious minorities. Mufti's point is that although Muslims in South Asia were in the numerical minority over the centuries ever since Moghul rule brought Islam to the subcontinent, they did not think of themselves as minorities. Nor were they treated as minorities within a society that was unselfconsciously pluralistic. As I have mentioned, the traditional Indian society was one of religious fluidity, encompassing a variety of religious communities. The tradition that we know as 'Hinduism' has been a congeries of different sects and lineages of teachers and teachings that vary widely from one another (Hawley 1991). Muslims, Sikhs, Christians, Jains and other religious communities fit easily into this pattern of religious diversity.

According to Mufti, the process of secular nation-building in Europe has gone hand in hand with the conceptualization of a national culture that marginalizes some religious and ethnic communities in the process of creating the idea of a unified national culture. In doing so, the by-product of this nationalist paradigm is the invention of the notion of 'minorities' as a problem. The paradigmatic case in Europe is the 'Jewish question', in which Jews do not fit into the idea of cultural consensus in emerging modern national communities. Adolf Hitler's infamous 'final solution' to the Jewish problem was an attempt at cultural and physical extermination. Alternatively, the

British solution at the end of World War II was to help create the modern state of Israel as one that would provide a national homeland for the Jews.

Mufti argues that this idea is transported to South Asia where both British and Indian nationalist leaders identified the national culture with Hinduism. They imagined that, as in European nations, the national culture of India should be part of one homogeneous religious entity. This way of thinking makes Muslims a minority, and like the Jews in Europe, they create a problem for the building of a modern national community. In Mufti's examination of the literature in Britain as well as the literature produced by Indian writers in English, Hindi and Urdu languages, he finds that this notion of Muslim-minority identity as a problem creeps into writing about nation-building in the subcontinent in the 19th and 20th centuries. No surprise, then, that Jinnah—the urbane, London-trained leader of the Muslims—as well as the cosmopolitan Nehru would think of India's nation-building as one of homogeneous cultural unity in a way that would naturally exclude minorities such as Muslims. Nehru's 1946 book, *Discovery of India,* chronicles his own self-discovery of the unity of India's past, implicitly a cultural as well as political unity. No wonder that Jinnah thought that his Muslims would be uncomfortable in such a nation, and no wonder, also, that the British Viceroy, Lord Mountbatten, would instinctively understand the logic of having a separate nation for a nation-sized minority. The formation of Pakistan became for South Asian Muslims what the creation of Israel had been for European Jews.

The idea of the modern nation-state is a part of the world's inheritance from the European Enlightenment, in which religion plays a somewhat paradoxical role. While Enlightenment thinkers such as John Locke regarded political institutions as secular—free from the taint of religious influence—they thought of the culture of a national community as unified, a unity that often involved common religious beliefs. According to the Berkeley sociologist, John Lie (2004), in an arresting book, *Modern Peoplehood,* the concept of a national community, or 'peoplehood', is one of the major constructs of the Enlightenment's understanding of modernity. The modern nation is inconceivable, Lie argues, without it.

According to Lie, the whole notion of a modern nation rests on the notion that there is such a thing as naturally occurring, geographically configured communities of people united by a common culture. The agreement at the Peace of Westphalia in 1648 indicated that a nation's religion should be in conformity with the state, and ever since there has been a tacit assumption that culture—including matters of ethnicity, language and religion—is a criterion for a homogeneous national community. Lie says that this concept is problematic even in European and other Western countries where increasingly large immigrant communities from other parts of the world are changing the character of national societies. But it is even more problematic in non-Western areas of the world—including South Asia—where often deep divisions have existed between the ethnic and religious communities of regions that come to be defined as nations. Often, in fact, the boundaries of these new nation-states were drawn hastily by retreating European colonial powers without much attention to the ethnic makeup within them. The subsequent attempts to create homogeneous national communities in regions of Africa, South and Southeast Asia, and the Middle East, argues Lie, have sometimes led to ethnic cleansing, the disenfranchisement of minorities and, in extreme cases, genocide.

But at the same time that the very notion of a national community needed the glue of culture, including religion, to hold it together, the Enlightenment concept of the political apparatus of the modern state was supposed to be free from religion. The state was supposed to be secular. This dichotomy between religion and secularism as two separate spheres of social reality was something that emerged as a part of the Enlightenment thinkers' views of the world. It made it possible to think of religion as something that could be encapsulated into a limited area of social and cultural influence, leaving the public sphere of governance free from religious influences. In a monumental work, *A Secular Age,* the Canadian philosopher Charles Taylor (2007) has shown how the secular idea has taken on various dimensions, from a simple division between the authority of church and state to a whole way of thinking about human relationships to the cosmos. Secularism, according to Taylor, has its own ideological character.

It is this ideological character of secularism that is the concern of Talal Asad (2003) in a challenging book, *Formations of the Secular:*

Christianity, Islam, Modernity. Asad argues that secularism is an ideology that creates its own notion of 'religion' as something that can be encompassed in a limited arena within the public sphere. It is a notion that does not apply easily to many parts of the world, including the Islamic world, and one might argue that it does not work well in South Asia either.

My own contribution to this discussion is found in my co-authored introduction and an essay in the book *Rethinking Secularism,* which is the product of a multi-year series of workshops on the topic involving Taylor, Asad and several other scholars, including Rajeev Bhargava, Jose Casanova, Craig Calhoun and myself.[1] My argument is that the imagined difference between secular and religious spheres of culture has created the conditions in which extreme religion and extreme secularism vie against one another. France, for example, can proclaim its national culture free from the taint of religiosity while Iran and Israel revel in their Muslim and Jewish national identities. Many of the movements that are thought of as terrorist in the 21st century, from the Muslim Islamic State to the Christian Militia and the Buddhist militants of Southeast Asia, are propelled by the desire to surmount the secular nationalism of their regions with religious nationalist visions of their own. The very idea that there are differences between secular and religious notions of society has created political tensions.

NEHRU'S VISION OF A SECULAR AND SOCIALIST SOCIETY

Even though it may have not been part of the lexicon of South Asian thinking traditionally, the idea of secularism arrived in South Asia along with European concepts of nationalism and democratic politics as a part of the accompanied baggage of British colonial rule. Both Jinnah and Nehru bought into the European idea that national communities were formed with a homogeneous culture. They also accepted the Enlightenment notion that national governments should be secular— free from the influence of sectarian bias or religious authority. To Jinnah, this meant that South Asian Muslims constituted a distinct nation within the subcontinent, and this warranted their being granted a

---

[1] For details, see Calhoun, Juergensmeyer, and van Antwerpen (2011).

semi-autonomous region, or failing that, their own separate nation-state of Pakistan. But the dapper Jinnah, ever dressed in a European-style business suit, was insistent that the government of the new Pakistan would be similar to European states, that is, secular.

Nehru also accepted the European notion of a culturally homogeneous nation with a secular government, but he interpreted both of those concepts somewhat differently than Jinnah had. Nehru's description of India's cultural unity in the *Discovery of India* seemed to be very Hindu to many Muslims, but Nehru thought of it as Indic—not narrowly Hindu but a part of a united cultural tradition. He did not think that it privileged Hindu or any other set of religious beliefs. In his mind, Indian culture embraced Islam as well as Hinduism. His notion of secularism, therefore, was not just a matter of keeping religious influences out of government but also treating all religious communities equally and in a fair-minded way. It was precisely for this reason that Nehru thought that the Muslims should be a part of India and not separate from it.

In fact, neither Jinnah nor Nehru's European notions of national culture and secular government had much connection to traditional ways of thinking about religion and politics in India's history. The concept of a national community is non-existent in India's early history, as it was in most societies, including European ones, before the 18th century. There were caliphs and kings, princes and emperors, who ruled on the basis of power, not the consent of the governed. Even so, however, they were expected to uphold certain moral standards in their conduct of governing. In traditional India, there is the notion that kings are expected to come from military castes that have their own ethical codes of conduct. Moreover, the king of a realm is expected to rule on behalf of *dharma,* the moral order that undergirds all of society. The image that is presented in ancient scriptures is that of a king upholding the 'white umbrella' of moral righteousness over the people. But these rulers are not in any narrow sense religious.

The same can be said of the Mughal rulers, a lineage of Muslim emperors who reigned over much of the subcontinent from roughly the 16th century through the middle of the 19th century. Though a quarter of the Indian population converted to Islam during this period, and Muslim holy sites were often privileged over Hindu ones, the imperial rule was hardly a theocratic state. One of the greatest Mughal rulers, Akbar, in the latter half of the 16th century created his own court religion that was dismissive of orthodox Islam and meant to be compatible with all faiths. Famously, Akbar is said to have welcomed theologians and thinkers from all religious persuasions to enter into philosophic discussions in his chambers.

British colonial rule was secular, of course, but the colonial government maintained an ambivalent relationship to the hordes of Christian missionaries who had the run of India during its rule. Many of the British officers regarded them as a nuisance. But others regarded them as an extension of the civilizing influence of the British rule. Christian hospitals and educational institutions were especially welcomed as efforts to serve Indian society and bring the benefits of Western civilization to South Asian shores.

Hence, the inheritors of British rule in South Asia—Nehru and Jinnah—carried on this tradition of secular government with a benign, but wary, attitude towards religious authorities and organizations. Each regarded religious extremists and true believers as potentially dangerous. But each also regarded religion, as an ingredient of the cultural homogeneity that made India and Pakistan distinctive national communities, to be absolutely essential.

HINDU AND MUSLIM NATIONALISM IN INDEPENDENT INDIA

The trajectory of religious politics in India and Pakistan after independence in 1947 is different from what either Nehru or Jinnah expected. In both cases, religion burst out of the confines in which they thought it had been contained, as elements of a homogeneous national culture, into direct participation in politics.

In Pakistan, successive political leaders increasingly found religion to be a useful rallying point for national unity. It also provided a built-in network of support from Muslim religious authorities and activists. Perhaps, no political leader in Pakistan did more to pander to conservative Muslim support than Muhammad Zia-ul-Haq, who led the country from 1977 to 1988 after instituting a coup against his mentor, Zulfikar Ali Bhutto. Zia established shari'ah law, outlawed marginal and heretical religious movements, and codified Muslim customs into law. Though the numbers of votes gained by Muslim religious parties in Pakistan have consistently been very small, since the time of Zia, their influence in the government has been disproportionately large.

One legacy of the Zia regime has been the covert Pakistani support for extremist Muslim political movements in Afghanistan. First, the Mujahadeen and then the Taliban movements have been secretly supported by elements of the Pakistan military and intelligence services. The ideas of the Taliban are related to the Deoband Muslim reform movement in South Asia that attempted to purify and standardize the teachings and practices of Islam. This was interpreted by groups such as the Taliban in a rigid and uncompromising way. The movement was not only an agent of religious standardization; however, it became the political wing of the Pashtun tribal community, large numbers of which were within Pakistan's own western borders. Mollifying the Taliban, then, was a way of currying favour with the critical Pashtun community.

At the same time that Pakistan was developing a more strident Muslim political posture, religious nationalism was also surfacing within India. In some ways, the emergence of the Bharatiya Janata Party (BJP) was the re-emergence of a religious strand of Indian nationalism that extended back to the early part of the 20th century. One of the early voices for Indian independence came from Vinayak Damodar Savarkar, who founded the *Hindu Mahasabha* and advocated a concept of Hindu culture, which he called *Hindutva*, as being the basis of Indian national identity. He once entered into a debate with Mohandas Gandhi over the efficacy of using violence in the struggle for India's freedom.[2] Despite Savarkar's efforts, Hindu nationalism was not a major element

---

[2] The debate between Gandhi and Savarkar directly preceded the writing of Gandhi's book *Hind Swaraj, or Indian Home Rule*, which was undoubtedly influenced by the debate. For my discussion of the incident, see Juergensmeyer (2007).

in India's nationalist movement. After independence, several political parties took up the banner of support for Hindu causes, notably the Jan Sangh, but it was not until the 1990s that a new movement of religious consciousness led to spectacular political successes for the BJP.

The BJP was officially launched in 1980 out of the remnants of previous Hindu-oriented political parties (Graham 2007). It did not gain strength, however, until the 1990s with the events that led up to the attack on a Muslim mosque said to be located on the sight of the birthplace of the Hindu god Ram in the town of Ayodhya. Religious activists associated with the sectarian Hindu organizations, the Vishwa Hindu Parishad and the Rashtriya Swayamsevak Sangh, championed the destruction of the mosque in order to liberate the grounds on which an ancient Hindu temple was said to have been located, a temple that marked the holy site of the god Ram's birthplace. Although archaeologists questioned the authenticity of the assertion, and many questioned whether a spiritual entity such as a god actually had a birthplace, the site became a matter of religious contention, fuelled by political rhetoric. It was the secular Congress Party, after all, that allowed the mosque to continue to exist on that spot. Though the Indian government said that it was protecting the site in the name of secularism—which in India meant the equal protection of all religious communities—the BJP political response was that the Congress's position was 'pseudo-secularism', which in fact masked the privileging of minority communities, such as Muslims, over the interests of Hindus. (Even after the creation of Pakistan, the numbers of Muslims remaining in India were 15 per cent of the population, enough to constitute a significant electoral base of votes, and a reason for politicians to curry the Muslims' favour.)

In 1992, a mob of over a hundred thousand angry Hindus convened in Ayodhya, attacked the mosque with improvised tools, and rendered it to dust. The BJP capitalized on this sentiment of Hindu nationalism and employing Savarkar's concept of Hindutva as the bedrock of Hindu nationalist culture, launched a series of political campaigns. The elections brought the BJP into positions of power in the legislatures of several states, and from 1998 to 2004 they were the dominant party in a national coalition that ruled India, and the BJP leader, Atal Bihari Vajpayee, became India's prime minister. The 2014 elections brought the BJP back into power, and the former chief minister of Gujarat, Narendra Modi, was installed as the prime minister of the country, who was resoundingly re-elected in 2019. If one considers the BJP to be a movement of religious nationalism, it quite likely has had the largest following of any such movement in world history—it has claimed a membership as large as 110 million. It has also been one of the most politically successful movements.

THE SIKH ATTEMPT TO CREATE A RELIGIOUS STATE

In the 1980s, a sizeable section of the young Sikh population in the rural areas of the northwest Indian state of Punjab became embroiled in a violent confrontation with the Indian government. My own interests in this troubling situation were both intellectual and personal, since for some years I had studied the interrelation between religion and politics in South Asia, and I had a special interest in Punjab. I had lived and taught in this area of India for several years and knew the Sikhs to be a generous and tolerant community. So, the explosion of religious politics in Punjab was, for me, something that was not just intellectually interesting but also personally disturbing. I returned to the region to try to understand why this spiral of violence had emerged, and what religion had to do with it.

What I expected to find is what journalists and political observers often tell us they find in such situations that these are cases where religion has been politicized by wily politicians out to use the innocence of religion for political purposes. It would be a case of the politicization of religion, they would claim. That was not, however, what I found. When I returned to the Punjab and listened to recordings of the sermons of the Sikh leader, Sant Jarnail Singh Bhindranwale, and talked with his supporters, I found a different message.[3] Bhindranwale was a rural preacher who spoke with the conviction of someone who knew the details of his religious heritage. He said that the great battles of Sikh

---

[3] A discussion of the Sikh movement based on my interviews with Sikh activists may be found in Juergensmeyer (2017, 109–127).

history were being repeated in the present day. Like then, the present confrontation was 'a struggle ... for our faith, for the Sikh nation, for the oppressed' (Bhindranwale 1983, 2). The enemy that concerned Bhindranwale, however, was not a force from legendary history, but something much closer at hand: the secular government of then Prime Minister Indira Gandhi. She so infuriated Bhindranwale that he did not even use her name. 'That woman born into a house of Brahmins', he would sputter. She was responsible for the sorry state of affairs in which the Sikh community found itself.

Rather than politicizing religion, Bhindranwale was religionizing politics. He was bringing a contemporary political conflict into the high proscenium of religious drama. The confrontation between his group of angry Sikhs and the Indian government was not just a clash of political views, it was war. And more than war, it was cosmic confrontation, the battle of good versus evil, right against wrong and religion against anti-religion. Bhindranwale would recount the great battles of Sikh tradition, the heroic sacrifice and martyrdom of early Sikh leaders when confronted with the military force of the Moghul Empire, and by implication suggest that those legendary times were alive once more. He and his followers saw their own struggle in grand historical terms; it was a transhistorical conflict of order versus chaos. They saw themselves engaged in not just a political conflict but also a defence of the whole of Sikh culture and civilization. For these reasons, they were willing to kill to defend their position. And they were willing to die for it.

The Sikh uprising in the 1980s, though violent and dramatic, was not the only time that Sikhs had been politically active in the Punjab. In the 1960s, for instance, another Sikh leader, Sant Fateh Singh, threatened to immolate himself in a vat of boiling oil on the roof of the Akal Takht, one of the main buildings in the precincts of the Harmandir Sahib, also known as the Golden Temple, which is the Sikhs' central shrine, located in the city of Amritsar. Sant Fateh Singh never carried out his threat, but the demands of the moment were met. The Indian state of Punjab was carved into three states, so that in the smaller state of Punjab that remained, Sikhs were in the majority. It was a concession by the central government that was intended to solve the Sikh problem once and for all.

This turned out not to be the case. The Sikh militancy in the 1980s was, in some ways, a repeat of the early movement, but it was also significantly different, in at least two ways. It was more strident, more violent, and its vehemence was aimed against the secular state. The aim was not just to secure more political power for the Sikh community but to reject the secular authority of the Indian government. Hinduism as a religion was not the target, even though some Hindu leaders were seen as cooperative with the state's position and, therefore, worthy of attack in the eyes of the Sikh militants. The explicit goal was to reject the legitimacy of the secular state. Though there was a controversy within the movement as to what should replace it, many Sikhs who supported the movement thought that its success would lead to the creation of a new religious nation. The proposed new Sikh state was dubbed Khalistan—the land of the Sikh community, the Khalsa. Bhindranwale, the most prominent spokesperson for the movement, said that he was neither for nor against the idea of Khalistan. But clearly, he and his followers wanted a new political order, one that would be based on religion rather than secularism.

It may seem preposterous that a religious community could claim the status of nationhood. Where could the Sikhs have gotten such a remarkable idea? The European Enlightenment model of the nation-state presumes a stance of secular detachment from religion. And, yet, for the Sikhs, examples of religious nationalism were close at hand. They needed to look no further away than the rise of Hindu nationalism in India and Muslim nationalism in the country that formed the western borders of Punjab, Pakistan.

THE INVENTION OF A MODERN MUSLIM NATION

Perhaps the most momentous political event in South Asia in the 20th century was not independence and the withdrawal of British rule, but the political partition of the subcontinent into two rival states: India and Pakistan (Pandey 2001). Perhaps even more striking, the retreating colonial rule of Great Britain consciously participated in the creation of a new national entity based on religion, a Pakistan based on Muslim identity. This event has done more to spur the notion of religious politics—and the possibility of a religious state for Sikhs, Hindus, and Buddhists in the subcontinent—than anything else in recent history. How could the secular government of Britain have allowed such a thing?

It is not clear that partition had to happen. There had not previously been a strong groundswell of support for a Muslim-dominated state. Although there were some lone voices calling for an independent Muslim state earlier in the 20th century, notably by the poet, Muhammad Iqbal, which he expressed in the 1930 meeting of the Muslim League. But most leaders in the League desired a semi-autonomous region in a united India, and according to one historian, Ayesha Jalal (1994), Jinnah raised the issue of an independent Pakistan largely as a threat, a kind of bargaining chip to gain what he really wanted, a semi-autonomous state.[4] Jinnah's rival Muslim organization, the Unionist Party in Punjab, was adamantly opposed to secession. Interestingly, the most articulate voices from the religious right were also opposed to the idea of a separate Muslim state. Maulana Abul Ala Maududi, the best-known Muslim political thinker in the region, adopted a position much like that of Said Qutb in Egypt. Maududi regarded the Western concept of the nation-state to be non-Islamic, and feared that a secular state, even one comprised largely of Muslims, would be antithetical to the religious community of devout Muslims. Eventually, Maududi joined Pakistan after it was created, and helped to form a new Muslim political party, the Jamaat-e-Islami, which continues today to be a voice for Muslim interests in Pakistan.

So, if there was no huge demand for a separate Muslim Pakistan in the subcontinent, where did the idea come from? One might argue that it came from the Muslim political tradition over the centuries, but that is not quite true either. Although Muslim history is full of

---

[4] For another book-length perspective, see Stanley Wolpert (2006), who places much of the blame for the partition and the careless drawing of boundaries between the two states on the British Viceroy Lord Mountbatten.

strong political leaders, caliphs who led armies and empires, there is not really a precedent for the modern idea of a religious nation-state. In fact, the idea of the nation-state—the notion that there is such a thing as a natural national community in a geographical region that supports a state apparatus which is responsible to it—is a foreign idea. Specifically, it is a European idea, and as I mentioned earlier it was the European idea of national community—and the role of religious affiliation within it—that was exported by the British to the emerging Pakistan and India and, for that matter, to a better part of the rest of the world.

INDIA'S RELIGIOUS POLITICS IN THE GLOBAL ERA

By the end of the second decade of the 21th century, most of the movements of religious politics in India were still alive. The BJP had been reaffirmed in the 2019 elections and remained strong in pockets of support throughout the country. The Khalistan movement in Punjab had been crushed, but Sikh political influence continued to dominate the electoral politics of the state. Perhaps more importantly, the rise of religious politics in India found parallels in similar movements throughout the South and Southeast Asia regions.

In Pakistan and Bangladesh, Muslim political parties have become more entrenched, and in some regions of Pakistan, the extremism of Muslim political groups has led to violent confrontations and acts of terrorism. Some of these, from Mumbai to Delhi and Kashmir, have also affected India. The Taliban rebounded from its defeat in the invasion of the US coalition forces in 2001 and asserted a major role in Afghan politics. The Taliban and its affiliates, such as the extremist Haqqani network, have controlled much of the Pashtun and other tribal regions of western Pakistan.

Elsewhere in South Asia, religious politics have also emerged at the turn of the 21st century, often in surprising places. Although one does not often think of Buddhism as a religious culture that supports political activism and violence, strong movements of religious politics have surfaced in several of South Asia's Buddhist nations. In Sri Lanka, Buddhist monks supported movements resisting the government's concessions to Tamil Hindus and Christians in the northern portion of the country, claiming that Sri Lanka should be a Sinhalese Buddhist state. Prime Minister Bandranaike was assassinated by a Buddhist monk. After the failure of the Tamil succession movement, the ideology of Buddhist purity in Sri Lanka was behind attacks on Muslims, leading to major riots in 2014 and 2018. These attacks are led by monks associated with a Buddhist extremist group, the Bodu Bala Sena, though many Buddhist monks have also denounced the assaults on Muslims and protected them and their mosques in Sri Lanka.

In the tiny Himalayan kingdom of Bhutan, the longing for a Buddhist state was realized. An almost theocratic alliance among the monarchical, monastic and elected branches of power in Bhutan led to an enormous amount of government support for Buddhist institutions and sites, and established a rigid code of behaviour that mandated that all citizens wear traditional clothing and maintain their homes in traditional styles. Non-Buddhist Nepalese Hindus were forcibly removed from Bhutan, an act of ethnic cleansing that expelled 15 per cent of Bhutan's population. Many of these exiled ethnic Nepalese were driven into refugee camps in India and Nepal.

In other parts of South Asia, Buddhism has been an instrument of protest and revolt. In the country of Myanmar, formerly known as Burma, Buddhist monks were at the forefront of protests against the autocratic military rule. After the military junta was officially dissolved in 2011, the country has been racked with anti-Muslim violence, directed especially at the Rohingya minority that live near the border of Bangladesh. A fiery Buddhist monk, Ashin Wirathu, has been blamed for fanning the flames of ethnic hatred. He is the most well-known spokesman for the '969 Movement'—named after the nine special attributes of the Buddha, the six distinctive features of his teachings and the nine characteristics of monks—which was formed to defend the purity of Burmese Buddhist culture against its alleged adulteration from outside influences, primarily Muslim. Hence, it is widely regarded as an anti-Islamic hate movement. The violence against the Rohingya minority, however, has been supported by the government, with some of the most vicious attacked conducted by military raids on Rohingya villages.

In Tibet, monks protesting the loss of cultural autonomy and the steady increase of Han Chinese presence in the region clashed with the Chinese military. Often, despite the Dalai Lama's admonition to adopt only non-violent tactics, Tibetan Buddhist monks were aggressors in the conflict. From the Chinese perspective, the Tibetans challenged the notion of China's sovereignty. From the Tibetan perspective, China was attempting to undercut the national cultural integrity of Tibet. A similar dynamic has been unfolding in the Xinjiang region of western China where Uyghurs feel their traditional culture and their Muslim faith is under attack by the increasing attempts of the Chinese government to unify their region both culturally and economically with the rest of China. In 2019, the Chinese government's erection of 're-education camps' to house huge numbers of Uyghurs and purge them from their traditional Muslim culture and practices has led to the accusation of cultural genocide on the part of Han Chinese. The old issue of the role of religion in defining a national community was once more the central issue in both of these cases, as it has been in the Middle East, Africa, Europe and the United States.

The reason why it is valuable to look at religious politics in India within the wider context of strident new religious political movements elsewhere in South and Southeast Asia and around the world is to acknowledge that the Indian developments are part of a global phenomenon. They are not alone.

These movements of religious politics persist, somewhat paradoxically, in the global era of the 21st century. It is a period in world history in which transnational forces challenge national institutions and communities, and in which the very notion of the nation-state as the prime unit of world political order is being reassessed. A critical aspect of contemporary globalization is the de-nationalization of demographic communities. Today everyone can live everywhere, and they often do. It is a phenomenon that affects the established societies of Europe as well as emerging nations of South Asia. For instance, in a time when a large percentage of the French population consists of non-Christians born in the Middle East and elsewhere, and an equally large number of French live abroad, the notion of a French national community has become a subject of grave concern. Everywhere the question is debated about what a distinctive national community in an era of globalization can be.

Religion is often part of these political discussions. And it can also be a factor in the immigrant communities' responses to their situations. Often their defensiveness is expressed in a heightened sense of their own cultural awareness. In some cases, the sense of alienation that immigrants experience is overcome by identifying with a struggle for a religious or ethnic nationalism back home. Paradoxically, the support for such movements can be even stronger in the diaspora than in the homeland. This was often the case with the Sikh Khalistan movement, which was monetarily supported by the Sikh communities in the United States and the United Kingdom, where the symbols of the movement were created. The first currency printed in the name of Khalistan, for instance, was minted in England. The BJP also received widespread support from the Hindus living abroad, and I was told by Lal Krishna Advani, one of the BJP leaders, that he relied on sources of funding from expatriate Indian Hindus living in such places as Houston, Los Angeles and Washington DC. Both sides of the struggle in Sri Lanka were supported by Sri Lankans living abroad, especially in the United Kingdom, where Sinhalese Buddhists supported one side and Sri Lankan Tamils supported the other.

The global diaspora of ethnic and religious communities has also created something of a global backlash. New right-wing movements of angry Christians in the United States and Europe have targeted the Middle East Muslim community in the United States and asserted the importance of a homogeneous ethnicity and religious culture in affirming their European and American national communities. In Hungary, Sweden and the Netherlands, new political movements have attempted to marginalize immigrant communities and assert the primacy of traditional notions of ethnic nationalism. In some cases, this hostility has been aimed not only at the immigrant communities, but also at secular governments that protect them. The European and American religious nationalists blame their own secular governments for their indifference to matters of religion, and also for their active toleration of an ideology of multiculturalism that welcomes and supports the ethnic and religious diversity of a society impacted by new immigrant communities.

Often the voices of support for such right-wing protests are strident; occasionally, their political strength is substantial; and on some tragic occasions, the rhetoric moves some desperate extremists to violent actions, even terrorism. In a sad incident in Christchurch, New Zealand, in 2019, Brenton Tarrant, an angry young Australian, attacked two mosques during Friday prayers, killing 51 and wounding a similar number. His manifesto indicated his admiration for Anders Breivik, the Norwegian who attacked the summer camp of a political party pledged to multiculturalism. Like Breivik, Tarrant thought that his efforts would keep European ethnic culture from going into Muslim control. A similar attack in the United States in 2012 was aimed at a Sikh gurdwara in the suburbs of Milwaukee, where a member of a racist anti-Christian subculture killed seven, including himself. The killer, Wade Michael Page, thought he was preserving a pure American culture in the face of multicultural globalism. Ironically it was Sikhs—who in the 1980s were attacking the secular state of India to create their own religiously pure homeland—who were the targets of this Christian terrorist in America who saw them as a problem in his own notion of national purity.

It is understandable that religion plays a role in responding to the challenges of the global era, not only because it provides a form of symbolic empowerment to people who feel marginalized by the great impersonal transnational forces of social change, but also because it responds in very basic ways to the insecurities of the era.[5] Globalization raises three fundamental questions, the question of *identity*, who are we as a people in the public order; the question of *accountability*, who is in charge and who can we trust; and the question of *security*, how can we be safe?

Traditional religion provides answers to all three of those questions. It provides a sense of religious identity that is often combined with national identity to shore up the notion of a national culture. It gives a sense of accountability and authority through traditional religious law and leadership that project an aura of unassailable certainty. And it offers a secure haven of religious community and divine protection that comfort in times of social and political peril. All of these factors are

---

[5] I explore these issues further in Juergensmeyer (2008).

elements in the rise of religious politics in India, as they are elsewhere in the world.

Thus, the Indian experience with religious politics—interesting in its own right—also is instructive about the rise of religious politics globally in recent decades. Secularism as an ideology has not been seen as a neutral actor; it seems, neither in South Asia nor in other parts of the world where religious politics have often emerged as a response to what is perceived to be attempts to remove traditional aspects of religious culture from the public sphere. Hence, the rise of religious politics in India tells us much about this particular moment of late modernity, where it may well be not so much a passing fancy as a bellwether of new postmodern and postsecular identities and new forms of imagined transnational publics in a shifting global order.

REFERENCES

Asad, Talal. 2003. *Formations of the Secular: Christianity, Islam, Modernity*. Stanford, CA: Stanford University Press.

Bhindranwale, Jarnail Singh. 1983. 'Two Lectures on July 19, 1983 and September 20, 1983', translated by Ranbir Singh Sandhu. Dublin, OH: Sikh Religious and Educational Trust.

Calhoun, Craig, Mark Juergensmeyer, and Jonathan van Antwerpen, eds. 2011. *Rethinking Secularism*. New York, NY: Oxford University Press.

Chandhoke, Neera. 2019. *Rethinking Pluralism, Secularism, and Tolerance*. Delhi: SAGE Publications.

Chandra, Bipan. 1984. *Communalism in Modern India*. Delhi: Har Anand Publications.

Das, Suranjan. 1994. *Communal Riots in Bengal, 1905–47*. Delhi: Oxford University Press.

Graham, Bruce Desmond. 2007. *Hindu Nationalism and Indian Politics: The Origins and Development of the Bharatiya Jana Sangh*. Cambridge. London: Cambridge University Press.

Hasan, Mushirul. 2019. *Legacy of a Divided Nation: India's Muslims since Independence*. London: Routledge.

Hawley, John Stratton. 1991. 'Naming Hinduism'. *Wilson Quarterly* 15: 20–22.

Jalal, Ayesha. 1994. *The Sole Spokesman: Jinnah, the Muslim League, and the Demand for Pakistan*. Cambridge: Cambridge University Press.

Juergensmeyer, Mark. 2007. 'Gandhi vs. Terrorism'. *Daedalus* 136 (1): 30–39.

———. 2008. *Global Rebellion: Religious Challenges to the Secular State*. Berkeley, CA: University of California Press.

Juergensmeyer, Mark. 2017. *Terror in the Mind of God: The Global Rise of Religious Violence.* 4th Edition. Berkeley, CA: University of California Press.

Lie, John. 2004. *Modern Peoplehood.* Cambridge, MA: Harvard University Press.

Mufti, Aamir. 2007. *Enlightenment in the Colony: The Jewish Question and the Crisis of Postcolonial Culture.* Princeton, NJ: Princeton University Press.

Pandey, Gyanendra. 2001. *Remembering Partition: Violence, Nationalism and History in India.* Cambridge: Cambridge University Press.

———. 2012. *The Construction of Communalism in Colonial North India.* Delhi: Oxford University Press.

Singh, Radhir. 2011. *On Nationalism and Communalism in India.* Delhi: Aakar Publications.

Tagore, Rabindranath. 1931. *The Religion of Man.* London: MacMillan.

Taylor, Charles. 2007. *A Secular Age.* Cambridge, MA: Harvard University Press.

Wolpert, Stanley. 2006. *Shameful Flight: The Last Years of the British Empire in India.* New York, NY: Oxford University Press.

Chapter 2

Women's Rights between Modernity and Tradition
'Modernizing' Islam

Tabinda M. Khan

During the late 18th and early 19th centuries, East India Company's judges relied on a handful of English translations of juristic (*fiqh*) commentaries used in Mughal courts to extract what they perceived to be 'rules' of Islam and combined them with common law reasoning. Case precedent, hierarchical courts and all-India legal digests fixed these 'rules' in place. They tried to understand religion through texts, rather than ongoing interpretation and practice, due to an 'Orientalist textualist' approach to Indian society, which saw it as 'static, timeless and spaceless' (Cohn and Singer 1968, 8). Both Muslim and Hindu 'traditions' were incorporated into the legal system of a modern state through epistemological assumptions, and institutional structures, that were at odds with how traditional scholars interpreted religion and how their followers practised it in society. While this led to the 'reification' of Indian caste on the one hand (Cohn and Singer 1968, 8), it led to the 'stagnation' of *sharia*, on the other hand (Kugle 2001)—not necessarily due to an intrinsic incapability for change but due to the need of a modern state for 'uniform' and 'standardized' rules. The changes wrought by the colonial state coincided with movements within Hinduism and Islam to 'modernize' religion, through a 'rational' interpretation of primary texts, and by overthrowing the authority of traditional scholars. By the 20th century, these transformations in colonial state and society, in addition to the Enlightenment binaries absorbed from imperial liberalism, created the perception among the modern-educated Indian middle class that 'modernity' and 'tradition' were intrinsically opposed, with modernity signifying 'change' and tradition signifying 'stagnation', despite the fact that it was the modern state that had stripped religious traditions of their internal mechanisms of change (Hallaq 2009).[1]

In this chapter, I will explain how this process led middle-class reformers in Pakistan to justify 'modernizing' Islamic law, without giving the *ulama* (traditional Islamic scholars) reasons 'internal' to their tradition, as tradition itself was viewed as 'stagnant' and the *ulama* as 'obscurantist'. Pakistani women's rights groups collaborated with reformers and made these laws unassailable symbols of their move-ment. Not only were these reforms questionable from the perspective of democracy, religious freedom and feminism (as middle-class women presumed to speak for 'all' women), but the theological controversy they generated precluded a conversation on structural judicial and police reforms that could substantively protect women. I will apply the concept of 'internal' or 'reciprocal' reasoning from moral and political theory to explain why these reforms were branded 'un-Islamic' by the Deobandi *ulama* and Jamaat-e-Islami and consider whether Pakistan's women's rights movement would benefit from disassociating itself from such projects, in favour of religious pluralism, as feminists like Flavia Agnes have urged the Indian women's rights movement to do.[2]

Theorists of deliberative democracy, such as Amy Guttmann and Dennis Thompson, propose that in deeply divided societies where

---

[1] See Pitts (2006) for a discussion of 19th-century imperial liberalism.
[2] For a discussion of Flavia Agnes' argument, and the strategy of the All India Democratic Women's Association, see Rajan (2003, 158–159).

citizens use incommensurate moral discourses, the exchange of 'reciprocal' reasons—that is, reasons internal to the other's tradition—is necessary to make deliberation 'authentic'. In this framework, it is the deliberation preceding a majority vote—the act of reason-giving and consent-seeking—that is the hallmark of democracy (Rothberg and Thompson 2000, 36). John Rawls, too, deployed the concept of 'internal reasoning' to describe how citizens with different 'comprehensive doctrines of the good' could reach an 'overlapping consensus' on a liberal constitutional order. He argued that the constitutional order would be stable if citizens could find normative reasons 'within' their own doctrines for supporting it (Rawls 1993). Internal reasoning requires an observer to suspend judgement, understand how the lexicon and principles of reasoning in a moral tradition operate, and then communicate with its adherents in their 'moral language', justifying political decisions that require obedience from them in terms that they can understand and accept, from the perspective of their moral tradition.[3]

The All Pakistan Women's Association (APWA) and Women's Action Forum (WAF) made coercive top-down reforms like the Muslim Family Laws Ordinance (MFLO), 1961, a symbol of the women's movement based on the implicit premise that when it came to traditional Islamic scholars, the ends justified the means, as they were irrational, obscurantist and medieval. The *ulama* and Islamists, in turn, condemned them as *maghrib-zadah* (west-stricken) women and these reforms as a western conspiracy against Islam. The polemic deployed by women's rights groups to justify authoritarian reform of religion was reminiscent of the civilizing narrative of imperial liberalism, which according to the legal scholar Makau Mutua persists as the 'savage-victim-saviour' metaphor of human rights discourse (Mutua 2001). The *ulama* responded, as Mutua predicts, with a counter-polemic asserting national pride and portraying campaigners as foreign agents. If, for a moment, we forget the 'outcomes' that the reforms were meant to achieve—the good intentions that were used to justify coercion—and look at the 'process' that preceded them, we will see three tensions at work. First, there is tension between practitioners of 'modern' law and

---

[3] Another way to understand this is through the concept of 'discourse communities'; see Fish (1982).

scholars of the Islamic 'tradition', which is overlaid on a class difference between the modern-educated (and often Westernized) Muslim intelligentsia and madrasa-educated *ulama* who control grassroots institutions. Second, there is a tension between women's rights and religious freedom and, third, between majoritarianism and deliberative democracy. For nearly half of its history, Pakistan has been directly ruled by the military, yet the legacy of constitutional democracy is so strong that every dictator created political parties and parliaments to legitimize himself and the decisions of legal commissions were justified as legitimate because they were the outcome of deliberation and voting, regardless of how 'authentic' the deliberation was.

In raising these questions, I am not saying that parliament should never use a majority to overrule traditional Islamic institutions. In some cases, such as the proposal of the 1949 Taleemat-e-Islami Board that women be excluded from political office, one can only be grateful that constitution-drafters rejected the *ulama*'s suggestions.[4] My question is whether the women's movement in Pakistan should be embroiled in the theological wars between nationalist male elites—one group insistent on 'modernizing' Islam and the other on reviving the Islamic 'tradition'—or whether it should develop an independent position, using the norms of deliberative democracy and religious pluralism. The former approach, which I will trace in this chapter, locks middle-class women's rights groups in a zero-sum battle with the *ulama* and makes it difficult for them to build a mass movement, as the grassroots penetration of traditional Islamic institutions rivals the state.

MODERNITY VERSUS TRADITION IN MUSLIM NATIONALISM

One of the primary conflicts between competing conceptions of Muslim nationalism was whether Islam should be interpreted through 'modern' or 'traditional' methods. On the one hand, Muhammad Iqbal called for the 'reconstruction' of Islamic thought by a parliament of lay Muslims[5]—an idea that was used by elite Muslim men

---

[4] Report can be found as an annex in Binder (1961).
[5] Iqbal's first speech in English (1908) in S. Y. Hashimy (1955). For his views on *sharia*, see Iqbal's 1937 letters to Jinnah, reprinted on pp. 129–133 in Allana (1969).

to argue that it was the duty of 'educated' Muslims, like themselves, to 'uplift' and 'modernize' the nation and release it from the grip of 'parasitical' *ulama*. As Iqbal's speech (and later text) was in English, his argument gained traction among the Muslim elite without them having to consider how the *ulama*, who had a monopoly on grassroots institutions, would react. The largest *ulama* association, the Jamiat-e-Ulama-e-Hind (JUH), supported the Congress, and in 1938, its leader, Mawlana Madni, had a fiery exchange with Iqbal about the meaning of nationalism. He slammed Iqbal's argument that Islam needed a state to 'actualize' itself and stated that territorial nationalism was permissible in *sharia*, since a 'nation' was distinct from a 'community'. So long as Muslims had the right to practice *sharia* in India, they could cooperate with Hindus in the anti-colonial movement and live as one nation; for him, co-habitation in a common territory, rather than religion, was the criterion for nationhood (Salim 1990). Mawdudi, who founded the Jamaat-e-Islami in 1941 and imagined an Islamist utopia in which a vanguard would wrest control of the state to enforce *sharia*, was sceptical for other reasons. He famously said that expecting the Westernized elite of the Muslim League to create an Islamic state was like expecting 'that a lemon tree could at maturity bear mangoes' (Binder 1961, 93). Mawdudi remained aloof from the Muslim League until partition, but in 1945, Muslim League leaders convinced a faction of Deobandi *ulama* to form the Jamiat-e-Ulama Islam in support of Pakistan. They, and sufi leaders, legitimized the Muslim League's demand as 'Islamic' during the Pakistan movement, and within a decade of independence, they had taken on Mawdudi's demand that *sharia* 'sovereignty' be a core constitutional principle—pitting them against the established, westernized elite that dominated the bureaucracy, army and judiciary.[6]

In this chapter, I use the term 'modernist' for the reform movement that began with Sayyid Ahmad Khan, and others, in the 19th century. These thinkers argued that the 'essence' of Islam was located in the ethical teachings of the Quran, while the juristic tradition (*fiqh*) was merely a 'historical accretion' that could be either disregarded or

---

[6] See Ansari (2003) and Gilmartin (1989). Binder (1961) describes in detail the interaction between the *ulama* and Jamaat during Pakistan's early constitutional struggle.

'reconstructed' by modern Muslims. They also insisted that the Quran, too, be (re)interpreted in light of modern society, using touchstones, such as 'reason' (Sayyid Ahmad Khan), modern historiography (Fazlur Rahman) or gender equality (feminist interpreters). However, the Deobandi *ulama* never accepted this distinction between 'essence' and historical 'accretion'; for them, the Islamic tradition could only be understood through the consensus interpretations of early exegetes, *hadith* critics and jurists, which were binding for future generations.[7] There are many ways of contesting arguments made on the basis of the juristic tradition but, for the *ulama*, a refutation is only legitimate if it is based on the scholarly texts considered authoritative in the tradition and within its established conventions of reasoning. The Deobandi *ulama*, too, 'modernized' their institutions in the late 19th century, adopting a standardized curriculum, grades and ceremonies characteristic of a modern colonial school, as well as the latest technologies for fund-raising, communication and outreach (Metcalf 1982). I use the term 'modernist' only to draw a distinction between these thinkers and the madrasa-educated *ulama* who control grassroots Islamic institutions, neither to posit a binary between 'modernity' and 'tradition' nor to invoke the meaning that 'modernism' has in art and literary criticism and other disciplines beyond Islamic studies. My purpose in using these terms is to trace how the prejudices towards tradition, which were embedded in Muslim modernist polemics, influenced Muslim nationalism, as well as the women's rights movement, and led to the formulation of 'modern' as good/progressive and 'tradition' as bad/regressive, eclipsing a far more complex interplay of categories.

As Muslim modernist scholars had no foothold in grassroots Islamic institutions, their isolation inclined them—as well as women's rights campaigners—to collaborate with military rulers to enforce what they saw as an 'enlightened' and 'rational' Islam. Politicians, due to the influence of Islamic institutions, were reluctant to participate in a project to 'modernize' Islam, so such attempts invariably accompanied the suspension of democracy and became a strategy through which military rulers legitimized themselves. Mrinalini Sinha wrote that as

---

[7] See Moaddel and Talattoff (2000) for excerpts of texts written by modernist thinkers and Zaman (2018) for an in-depth history of this conflict.

the debates on the 1929 Child Marriage Restraint Act were framed by nationalist outrage over Katherine Mayo's *Mother India*, it was difficult for women to develop a 'subject position', independent of nationalist discourse (Sarkar and Sarkar 2008, 464). In the case of Pakistan, too, the contours of the intra-nationalist struggle led middle-class women's rights campaigners to side with modernizers, who supported women's participation and rights, but also implicated them in authoritarian reforms of Islam that in the long-term undermined their ability to become a mass movement. Two cases from Pakistan's early history, which were subsequently memorialized by the middle-class women's rights movement as victories for progressivism, will illustrate this. The first case is the 1954 Punjab Disturbances Report (also known as the Munir Report) and second is the 1961 MFLO.

Before I proceed to the cases, I would like to underline two limiting conditions of my study. First, when I urge reasoning 'within' the Islamic tradition, I am referring to reforms in pre-existing state Islamic laws or religious counter-arguments given to traditional Islamic scholars, and am neither endorsing state Islamism, whose pitfalls have been discussed by Hallaq (2013) and Quraishi-Landes (2015), nor condemning secular feminism. In *Faith and Feminism in Pakistan*, Zia (2018) criticized Mahmood (2012), and subsequent scholarship inspired by her framework, for downplaying the experience of secular feminists in Muslim-majority countries. In this chapter, I use Mahmood's methodological premise that we must take non-liberal ways of life on their own terms, instead of distorting their internal meanings through a liberal prism. However, I agree with Zia in an institutional sense. Scholars writing in Mahmood's tradition use the privilege of liberal states and universities to urge recognition of non-liberal ways of life. Women in Muslim-majority countries, such as Pakistan, do not have the right to opt into secular family laws nor do traditional Islamic institutions recognize the 'right of exit' for Muslims (institutionalized through the blasphemy law). It is the denial of this right, which is presupposed by liberal theories of multiculturalism (e.g., Kymlicka 1995), that has put secular Muslim women's rights activists in the quandary that they are forced to deploy a religious idiom to assert their rights, when they may prefer a secular one, and when they use feminist/modernist exegeses, which are more favourable to women and in an idiom they understand, traditional Islamic institutions dismiss them as illegitimate. Second, I explain the perspective of traditional Islamic scholars on women's rights reforms, which is often missing from state Women's Status Commission Reports and non-governmental organization (NGO) publications, not to indict women's rights activists—from a male perspective—but to urge reflection and debate, so that we understand that advocating coercive reforms in state Islamic laws, for modernist reasons, is a violation of religious freedom, and is altogether different from a struggle for secular family laws, which may be a long-term goal worth considering. This chapter is an attempt to look at a longstanding debate from a new angle, so as to open up new lines of debate, and is by no means a definitive analysis of feminism, law and society in Pakistan.

THE MUNIR REPORT

The Munir Report demonstrated that 'modern' legal practitioners looked at *sharia* in an entirely different way than 'traditional' Islamic scholars, due to a process that began in the colonial period. As Bernard Cohn observed, in conquering India, the British conquered an 'epistemological terrain' because the knowledge they generated about Indian society for use in state administration was filtered through the categories and theories that constituted the worldview of an educated Englishman of the late 18th and early 19th centuries (Cohn 1996, 4–5). *Sharia* was just one of the indigenous traditions to be 'lost in translation', to be 'blamed, named, and reframed', in Scott Kugle's words (Kugle 2001). Officials of the East India Company used a few English translations of Hanafi *fiqh* (juristic) commentaries used in Mughal courts, mistaking the juristic 'opinions' as authoritative 'rules', and fixed these 'rules' in place through hierarchical courts and case precedents. Michael Anderson argues that due to their blindness to the oral interpretive practices that mediated the interaction between written text and social context, officials of the East India Company stripped *sharia* of its mechanisms of change, fostering the idea of an 'essentialist, static Islam incapable of change from within' (Khare 1999, 74).

Before it was grafted onto a modern legal system, the juristic tradition was fluid, flexible and varied across time and space. Scholars describe the *ulama*'s authority as a 'fissiparous pluricentrism', which led *sharia* to have 'centrifugal' tendencies, as it was developed by private scholars independent of the state.[8] Not only was *sharia* rendered stagnant, but as East India Company judges were unaware of the conventions of reasoning of the Muslim juristic tradition—the institutions through which conflict on legal opinions was mediated—they attributed juristic disagreement to 'inconsistency' or 'corruption' rather than viewing it as a normal part of moral and legal reasoning (Khare 1999, 73). Legal textbooks and the Indian legal digest standardized this legal knowledge across the breadth of India and created Muhammadan-Anglo Law, the representation of *sharia* inside the colonial state. Muslims trained in colonial law schools learnt of *sharia* through the construct of Muhammadan-Anglo Law and the Muslim legal community was bifurcated into the old and new, the madrasa-educated *ulama* and modern lawyers. Although Muslims used colonial courts for the enforcement of property rights and inheritance laws, they looked to the *ulama* for guidance on rituals and to resolve other disputes (Kozlowski 1985, 131)—leading to a 'dual existence' (Kugle 2001, 34), where their moral tradition no longer had bearing on the state but maintained its roots in society.

The purpose of the 1954 Munir Report was to investigate the causes of anti-Ahmadi riots, but judges used the occasion to condemn the idea of an 'Islamic constitution' as rubbish and evaluated the Muslim juristic tradition through a colonial and Muslim modernist lens, rather than as a 'living tradition' with internal mechanisms of change. Among other things, the Munir Report caricatured the *ulama* as plagued by 'interminable disputation' and 'inconsistency' because they gave different answers to the question, 'Who is a Muslim?' Before the riots erupted, Mawlana Shabbir Ahmad Usmani had written a pamphlet *Ash-Shihab*, in which he argued that the juristic tradition prescribed the death penalty for apostasy. Judges rejected Usmani's argument as 'erroneous' because it was not in the Quran, which in their words 'preaches against compulsion in religious matters', despite the fact that it was drawn from the juristic tradition and continued to be taught in madrasas (Munir Report 1954, 220). The government was compelled

---

[8] Hefner (2004) describes the authority of the *ulama* as a 'fissiparous pluricentrism' and Hallaq (2013) describes *sharia* discourse as 'centrifugal'.

to ban the pamphlet and suppress the riots with martial law precisely because Usmani's view was widely shared among grassroots *ulama*; judges could assert a modernist, progressive reading of the Quran as the 'true' Islam—backed by state force—but they could not get madrasas to accept it because they were not even speaking their religious language.

In Jamaat-e-Islami's rebuttal to the Munir Report, Khurshid Ahmad accused 'high officials' and the 'upper bourgeois classes' of trying to persuade 'ordinary' Muslims to accept an Islam that had been changed to please the international community (Ahmad 1959, 3, 215). He criticized the report for portraying the *ulama* as 'bigoted, illiterate and ignorant fanatics' (Ahmad 1959, 2) and for giving readers the impression that the juristic tradition prescribed death as the 'only' punishment of apostasy. Ahmad pointed out that Caliph Umar believed that death was 'not the only punishment' but 'the highest punishment', while the Hanafi school 'gives immunity to women apostates from death sentence', and the jurist Ibrahim Nakhi argued that an apostate should be allowed an 'unlimited period of time' to 'return to the fold of Islam' (Ahmad 1959, 179). If judges had not viewed conflicting juristic opinions as 'interminable disputation' and 'inconsistency'—as East India Company judges had—they would have realized that juristic disagreements were a source of pluralism and could help them find arguments from 'within' the tradition through which they could challenge Usmani.

THE MUSLIM FAMILY LAWS ORDINANCE

Reformers in Pakistan justified the 1961 MFLO as necessary to counter the 'stagnation' of tradition, much like Indian reformers had justified the 1955 Hindu Code Bill (Chatterjee cited in Bhargava 1998, 357) and in the women's movement literature, it was memorialized, like the Munir Report, as a triumph over religious 'obscurantism'. The controversy began in 1955 when Prime Minister Bogra took a second wife and became the focus of an ongoing anti-polygamy campaign by the APWA (Abbott 1962, 26–32). He appointed a Commission on Marriage and Family Laws with three lay Muslim men, three lay Muslim women and only one *alim*, Mawlana Ihteshamul Haq Thanwi. The president of the committee, Mian Abdul Rashid, was a former chief justice and its secretary was Dr Khalifa Abdul Hakim, who, in

Freeland Abbott's words, advocated 'the rationalistic approach urged a century before by Sir Sayyid Ahmad Khan, the father of Islamic modernism in India and Pakistan' (Abbott 1962, 28). Hakim had been the director of the state-funded Institute of Islamic Culture in Lahore, where he wrote the pamphlet 'Iqbal aur Mullah' to show that the poet laureate himself had regarded the *ulama* as social parasites. The commission used Iqbal's argument about the need to 'reconstruct' Islamic thought to justify interpreting the Quran and *hadith* directly, instead of engaging with what they saw as a 'stagnant' juristic tradition. They suggested state regulation of polygamy, triple talaq, child marriage and inheritance laws and, though Mawlana Thanwi agreed with the need for reforms, he regarded their method of reasoning as un–Islamic and wrote a note of dissent.[9] Due to the outrage this report provoked in religious circles, parliament shelved its proposals.

However, in 1961, Ayub Khan used the cover of martial law to decree the MFLO, using the proposals of this controversial report. According to an APWA newsletter, women celebrated the passage of the MFLO by greeting Ayub with '[h]undreds of garlands, bouquets, loud cheers' and chanted 'Long Live the President'. He, in turn, 'acknowledged their cheers' with a smile, and said: 'Be kind to the men now that you have got your rights. You don't know how frightened they are' (Patel 1979, 91). Of the same event, Mawlana Tonki wrote that 'not even the worst government had the audacity to enforce these black laws', and it was only under martial law, the 'blackest period of this country', that they were imposed by *jabr* (force) 'after putting locks on people's tongues and pens' (Tonki 1963, 230–246). The MFLO was not only forced on Islamic institutions by a military dictator, but in Ayub Khan's parliament, women legislators and Z. A. Bhutto voted against a debate on an MFLO repeal bill. Moreover, a clause was inserted in the 1973 constitution to shield the MFLO from judicial review, which denied conservatives the right to challenge it

---

[9] See 'Report of the Commission on Marriage and Family Laws', *The Gazette of Pakistan (Extraordinary)*, Karachi, 20 June 1956 and 'Note of Dissent of Mawlana Ihteshamul Haq Thanwi', *The Gazette of Pakistan (Extraordinary)*, Karachi, 30 August 1956.

as a violation of freedom of religion.[10] Women's rights activists in one UN-patterned Women's Status Commission after the other suggested more changes in the MFLO—newer, better, faster ways to increase women's status in the Muslim family—but never acknowledged or responded to the *ulama*'s critiques of the law. In the process, they also lost the cooperation of the *ulama* in using moral suasion to discourage polygamy, child marriage and triple talaq, which remained pervasive practices despite the law.

Women's rights campaigners have often been dismissed as 'western-ized' by the *ulama* and Jamaat, but this was a slur originally directed at the Muslim modernist scholars who Ayub Khan had appointed. In a diary entry, Khan asked himself why Mawdudi's followers and the Deobandi *ulama*, in his words 'idiots' and 'rascals', were calling the MFLO anti-Islamic and concluded:

> [O]ne, belonging to a parasitical profession they can only flourish on the ignorance of people.... Secondly, this class of people have been dead against the creation of Pakistan and acted as willing and servile tools in the hands of Congress before partition.... Also, they are the deadliest enemy of the educated Muslim. (Baxter 2007, 5)

After questioning the nationalist credentials of these groups, he said that they were enemies of 'progress' and independent thought and that it was intolerable for them to see 'educated' Muslims leading the country. In his assessment, their religion and philosophy had 'not the slightest affinity to the true spirit of Islam' and out of jealousy, they had declared as *kafir* (infidels) those who struggled for the 'enlightenment' and 'salvation' of the Muslim 'millat': Sir Syed, Jinnah and Iqbal. To propagate this 'enlightened' Islam, Ayub Khan appointed Dr Fazlur Rahman, a McGill-trained scholar of Islam, as the Director of the Islamic Research Institute (IRI) and as a member of the Council of Islamic Ideology (CII) from 1962 to 1968 (CII 1962–1963). Rahman used these state platforms, from which the madrasa-educated *ulama* were excluded, to propose a 'revolutionary' method to 'reconstruct'

---

[10] Begum Khadija G. A. Khan in *National Assembly of Pakistan Debates,* 2 July 1962, p. 887.

Islamic legal interpretation by evaluating *fiqh*, *Sunnah* and the Quran through the methods of modern historiography.[11] Dr Fazlur Rahman's method was based on the premise that many *hadith* reports had been fabricated and that juristic opinions based on them were, therefore, non-binding; he questioned the intellectual integrity of jurists revered by Islamic institutions in Pakistan and described them as being victims of a 'moral pathology' (CII 1962–1963, 12).

In turn, the *ulama* demonized Fazlur Rahman and his colleagues as 'a few putrid crumbs' on the tablecloth of the west (Kandhalwi 1966, 27). Invoking Macaulay's Minute, Mawlana Muhammad Yusuf argued that though Fazlur Rahman was a Pakistani Muslim in terms of blood and colour, yet with respect to his mind and attitude, he was from the 'Orientalist school of thought', because it was the Orientalists who tried to defame Islam by attacking not only its beliefs but by spreading hateful propaganda against the carriers of the tradition (Yusuf 1967, 38). He referred to the state's IRI as the administrative centre of the *fitna* (rebellion) of *tajaddud-pasandi* (modernism) and quoted the poet Ehsan Danish to criticize the western origins of this movement:

You have bought ships of darkness from the West
You have yourself sold the star of the fortune of the homeland
Someone ask the madmen what is this silence
What can be said, the slogan of 'idol-house-destroyer' has been sold.
(Yusuf 1966b, 10)

The *ulama* judged the authenticity of traditions, through criteria internal to it, not by the standards of modern historiography as scholars trained in Western universities did. For them, the tradition was part of religious rituals, not an object of dispassionate study, separate from faith, reverence and obedience. When Fazlur Rahman's project was forced on them by a military dictator, they deeply resented it and viewed it as un-Islamic. This anger was also directed towards women's rights campaigners, who perhaps did not recognize the underlying

---

[11] Rahman gave this description of his research at the IRI at a Princeton University conference of religious representatives from 4–11 May 1966, reported in *Fikr-o-Nazar*, vol. 4, p. 9, and cited in Yusuf (1966a, 30–31).

theological reason for it. When the MFLO was decreed, Mawlana Shafi argued that women wrongly thought that the *ulama* opposed the law because they were enemies of women. He cited the 1939 Dissolution of Muslim Marriages Act as an example of a pro-women reform that was passed after Mawlana Ashraf Ali Thanwi justified the adoption of a Maliki opinion that granted women far greater grounds on which to apply for dissolution, in lieu of the prevailing Hanafi one (Shafi 1963, 10–11). But, by this time, the middle-class women's groups had become enmeshed with modernizing/authoritarian male elites, who were often men from their class and had little interaction or intellectual exchange with the *ulama*.

PORTRAYAL OF MUNIR REPORT AND MFLO IN WOMEN'S MOVEMENT LITERATURE

In order to understand how leaders of middle-class women's rights groups interpreted the Munir Report and the MFLO, we can look at the historical accounts in *Women and Law in Pakistan* (1979) by Rashida Patel, who was a lawyer, APWA member and the founder of WAF, and *Hudood Ordinances: A Divine Sanction* (1990) by sisters Asma Jehangir and Hina Jilani, both lawyers and influential leaders of WAF. Rashida Patel began by citing Iqbal's argument from *Reconstruction of Religious Thought in Islam* that contemporary Muslims had the right to 're-interpret … fundamental legal principles' (Patel 1979, 22). She portrayed the passage of the MFLO as a struggle between the 'enlightened', who wanted reforms, and the 'orthodox', who opposed change:

> …publication of the report on Marriage and Family Laws … brought in its wake serious political controversies between the enlightened and the orthodox …. The orthodox … were not prepared to let anyone but themselves be considered the fountain of all knowledge of Islam and let the power of interpreting … religious laws slip from their hands …. (Patel 1979, 90–91)

Patel did not incorporate the *ulama* or Jamaat's texts in her analysis, neither madrasa journal articles nor the book *Marriage Commission Report X-Rayed* in which they had explained, clause by clause, why the commission report was unacceptable to them (Ahmad 1959). Due to this, she represented the 'orthodox' as a monolith opposed to change. Patel said that by opposing the report, the orthodox had converted a 'social' problem into a 'political' issue. She saw the commission's proposals as the 'true' Islam, which in her view advocated gender equality, but did not see that forcing an interpretation of Islam on the *ulama*, which they did not regard as Islam, was a deeply political, deeply coercive act.

Since this is how women's rights campaigners remembered the origins of the MFLO, they narrated its subsequent history as a desperate struggle for 'survival' against conservative 'attacks' in the assemblies, which were thwarted, Patel (1979, 92) writes, with the support of the President, women's organizations and progressive legislators. A preoccupation with the 'survival' of the Ordinance is due to the fear that if it were repealed, and had to be redrafted through a democratic process, many of the ideal reforms of women's rights activists could be lost. Looking at the MFLO in this way locked women's rights activists in an existential struggle with the *ulama* and Jamaat, who wanted parts of the MFLO to be changed because they violated the integrity of the juristic tradition and could not achieve this through courts because a constitutional clause exempted it from judicial review (only in 2000 did the Federal Shariat Court (FSC) strike down several clauses of the MFLO as un-Islamic). Patel, like other women's rights activists, never claimed that the MFLO was perfect. They wanted changes in it for their own reasons. But whenever the *ulama* and Jamaat challenged the MFLO, they united in its defence, even though they knew that it only went a small way to securing women's rights.

Similarly, Jehangir and Jilani saw themselves pitted against 'fundamentalists' and 'obscurantists', who had 'opposed the creation of Pakistan' and 'strongly criticised the founder of the nation, Muhammad Ali Jinnah' (Asma and Jilani 1990, 17). To support their case, they invoked the Munir Report's caricature that the *ulama* were so intellectually confused that they could not agree on a response to the question, 'Who is a Muslim?' However, they neglected to mention their cross-sect conferences from 1951 onwards, which developed common constitutional demands (with Mawdudi's assistance). Jehangir and Jilani responded to the *ulama*'s demand for *sharia* not with moral theory, or legal arguments, but with the modernist/nationalist dogma of the 1950s. They portrayed conservatives as disloyal to the cause of Pakistan and to the 'founder of the nation', ignoring that the creation of Pakistan was a contingent and unpredictable outcome and that the *zamindar* (landholder) families in Punjab which became dominant in the Muslim League after partition had also opposed it for a long time. The most influential middle-class women's rights groups were led by women with close ties to westernized, modernizing state elites. After General Zia allied with the Deobandi *ulama* and Islamists to decree laws derived from the juristic tradition, prominent women from these groups were compelled to take refuge in western-funded rights NGOs, as they neither had a mass membership nor sustainable indigenous funding. It is important to understand that one reason why their ideas did not gain a mass following was that the theological battle they had involved themselves in—perhaps inadvertently—was deeply unpopular at the grassroots, where there was a mosque staffed by a madrasa-trained preacher in practically every neighbourhood.

BEYOND THE MODERNITY–TRADITION BINARY IN THE SUPREME COURT

The evolution in how the Pakistani Supreme Court has engaged with the juristic tradition demonstrates that there need not be a binary opposition between modernity and tradition or gender equality and religious freedom. There were, of course, judges who shared Ayub Khan's views on tradition. In 1981, Justice Zakaullah Lodhi—who had argued in a law seminar that the juristic tradition was a source of 'stagnation' and what was needed was a 'relaxed, liberal and realistic' interpretation of the Quran—struck down the juristic punishment of *rajm* (stoning to death) as un-Islamic during an appeal to the FSC (All Pakistan Legal Decisions [PLD] 1980, 22–24). His primary reason was that this punishment was not mentioned in the Quran and the *hadith* that jurists had used to derive it were 'contradictory' and 'unreliable' oral accounts—even though the criteria of modern historiography were not used by the country's Islamic institutions to evaluate their tradition (PLD 1982, FSC 158–166, 204–206 and 212). After *ulama* protests,

General Zia gave the FSC the power to review its own judgements and included *ulama* on the bench; this was later seen by women's rights groups as an unwarranted concession to 'obscurantist' groups—like the creation of *shariat* benches in the first place—but it compelled judges to learn how to reason 'within' the tradition. This, in turn, helped them expand both women's rights and civil liberties in the long run, using not only secular but also Islamic arguments that were acceptable to religious institutions.

In the FSC revision judgement on *rajm*, Mufti Taqi Usmani explained to common law judges that just like the principle of *stare decisis* (precedent) was considered mandatory in the interpretation of secular laws, the principle of *ijma-e-ummat* (community consensus) was fundamental in the interpretation of Islamic laws (PLD 1983, FSC 456). Justice Zahoor ul Ikhlaq argued that the *hadith* justifying *rajm* should be accepted as reliable not only because they are *mutawwatir al-maani* (continuous in meaning), a principle of *hadith* criticism, but because they were 'regarded as such' by the Muslim community—because 'they are part of the history of Muslims and even history can provide the basis of a law' (PLD 1983, FSC 311). This question had more theological significance for the *ulama* than it had practical legal impact, as Muslim jurists had required an impossibly high standard of evidence to award *rajm* for adultery (four Muslim men of 'good character' who had witnessed the sexual act). Pakistani sessions court judges who gave this punishment did so without meeting this evidentiary requirement, and their judgements were consistently overturned on appeal, using just the criteria of the tradition itself.[12]

A 1986 judgement of the Shariat Appellate Bench (SAB) of the Supreme Court instructed judges to first attempt to find reasons 'within' the juristic tradition and to depart from consensus interpretations only if there were no way to reconcile juristic opinions with modern circumstances (Shah 1992, 9).[13] This did not mean that the judges were always and forever bound to juristic opinions. On the question of whether

---

[12] See Usmani (2006) for why the Hudood Ordinances led to wrongful convictions.

[13] SAB judgement in *Pakistan vs. Public at Large* (PLD 1986, SC 240) cited in Shah (1992).

human representation in art was permissible in Islam, Justice Nasim Hasan Shah, who wrote the above 1986 SAB judgement, disagreed with early jurists who had declared it un-Islamic because, in his opinion, this prohibition would cause incalculable harm to Muslim culture (PLD 1986, SC 672). The legal methodology of the *shariat* courts could be understood as prescribing a 'good faith' effort at reasoning within the tradition, an attempt to restrain judges from feeling entitled to invoke their individual opinions about the Quran and *Sunnah*—which invariably bled into the project to 'reconstruct' Islam on a modern pattern, contrary to how Islamic institutions saw it.

Karin Yefet argues that gender equality and Islam co-existed in a 'mutually reinforcing' way as Pakistani judges were required to co-read constitutional guarantees of 'non-discrimination on the basis of sex' and *sharia* compliance (Yefet 2011, 565, 591). For instance, in 1959, courts had ruled that *khula* (dissolution of marriage) could be awarded by a court without the husband's consent. This went against the prevailing consensus in the Hanafi juristic tradition on this question but the FSC, with a leading Deobandi *alim* on the bench, maintained the interpretation by 'giving it an Islamic garb', arguing that a wife merely needed to show the court that the couple could no longer live 'within limits of Islam' to obtain a dissolution (Yefet 2011, 587–589). Moreover, in 2005, when the Muttahida Majlis-e-Amal (MMA), a coalition of the Jamaat and *ulama* parties, passed the Hasba Bill, in order to create a 'moral police' that would regulate 'un-Islamic' conduct in public spaces, the Supreme Court struck down several provisions as a violation of fundamental rights, justifying its action with both secular reasons and reasons from within the religious texts used by MMA itself—rather than relying on the reconstruction narrative (Khan 2005, 413–464).[14]

From the two reports I have discussed between 1954 and 1955 to countless articles and books written till the present day, Muslim liberals, including women's rights campaigners, have cited Iqbal's *Reconstruction* to give nationalist legitimacy to the project of forcibly 'modernizing' Islam. However, in a 2010 FSC judgement, Justice Afzal re-interpreted Iqbal's argument. He argued that Iqbal believed that parliament had the

---

[14] For a discussion of how Islamic principles have been used to expand civil liberties, see Lau (2006) and Lombardi (2010).

right to reform Islamic laws but needed 'technical assistance' on how to 'correctly interpret *sharia*'—a task that was performed in Pakistan by the CII (to which elected governments invariably appointed the most influential *ulama*, rather than modernist scholars) and the FSC (which included *ulama* judges). For him, Iqbal was not a messiah of state-enforced 'modernity' but a pragmatist who believed in reconciling the 'tradition' with 'modernity' through the cooperation of traditional Islamic scholars and representatives elected through modern democratic institutions. Justice Afzal added that in formulating its judgement, the FSC had to balance three elements: 'legislative competence; the touch-stone of fundamental rights, and the yardstick of Islamic injunctions' (PLD 2010, FSC 148–149). The judiciary's evolution bore the imprint of 60 years of struggle between two diametrically opposed nationalist elites—modernist and Islamist—to control the state. During this strug-gle, each managed to insert constitutional and legal protections for their views—secular fundamental rights, on the one hand, and Islamic judicial review and *ulama* judges on the other—which required the Supreme Court to accommodate and balance both.

PERSISTENCE OF CIVILIZING NARRATIVE IN PUBLIC DEBATES ON RELIGIOUS LAWS

Unfortunately, the judiciary's evolution beyond the modernity–tradi-tion binary did not spill over into the women's rights movement, as activists continued to call the *ulama* 'obscurantist mullahs' and the *ulama* continued to dismiss them as *maghrib-zadah* (west-stricken) women. Flavia Agnes explores a similar disjuncture between legal interpreta-tion and public discourse during the controversy over the 1985 Shah Bano judgement in India. The law that reversed this judgement was interpreted by women's rights groups and the media as a concession to 'communalism', and by the Hindu right as 'pandering' to Muslims, because it denied a divorced Muslim woman maintenance after her *iddat* period had ended. However, on closer inspection, Agnes found that courts had used the law to give women far more substantial one-time divorce settlements as *mehar*, by invoking Islamic principles, than they would have received as monthly maintenance (Needham and Rajan 2007, 294–315).

Similarly, in Pakistan, whenever reforms of Islamic laws are contemplated, the narrative of 'enlightened' Muslims civilizing 'obscurantist mullahs' obscures legal nuances. The 2006 Protection of Women Act, which removed the crime of rape from the Zia-decreed Hudood Ordinances to the secular Pakistan Penal Code, was presented by liberals from the centre-left Pakistan's People's Party and women's rights groups, such as WAF and Aurat Foundation, as a great victory for women. However, the theological justification for the law followed the same pattern as Ayub Khan's MFLO and left women with far fewer protections than they could have negotiated had they not allied with yet another 'modernizing' Muslim dictator.

Like Ayub Khan, General Musharraf excluded the *ulama* from the CII and appointed scholars of Islam trained in modern universities in their place—calling his ruling philosophy 'Enlightened Moderation'. At a 2005 speech to the CII, he referred to Muslim jurists as 'fossilized interpreters' from whose 'clutches' *sharia* had to be 'rescued' for it to be able to respond to the needs of modern society (CII 2004–2005, 299–300, 302). Mawlana Aziz-ur-Rahman, in turn, mocked Musharraf as a puppet of America, who was defacing Islam just to show Americans that he could make Pakistan 'modern' (Rahman 2003, 4–6). Women's rights groups, and allies, echoed Musharraf's polemic from Pakistan's leading English newspaper calling the *ulama* 'literalist' and 'unreasonable' (*Daily Times* 2006), their amendments 'barbaric' (*Daily Times* 2006) and their motives 'obscurantist' (*Dawn* 2006)—and urged Musharraf to ignore their protests.

Given how much time Pakistani English newspapers and the international media devoted to criticizing *sharia*, it would seem that the only cause of rights abuse was the Islamic doctrine that influential *ulama* considered unchangeable: the *hadd* punishments of stoning to death and 100 lashes for adultery, fornication and rape prescribed by the juristic tradition. However, in practice, the law led to rights abuse due to a complex of factors. First, trial courts were awarding the *tazir* (state-discretionary) punishment of imprisonment to couples who lacked marriage/divorce licences because they were co-reading the law with the MFLO (*sharia* did not require registration). Second, the offence was made non-bailable, which led to years in prison awaiting trial. Third, the corruption endemic to the *thana-katcheri* culture led the law to be weaponized against the marginalized, like other laws. Rights groups insisted on removing the *hadd* punishment for rape because they felt that its evidentiary requirement of '4 male Muslim eyewitnesses of good character' discriminated on the basis of gender. This provision did not practically affect rape convictions (unless judges were misinterpreting the tradition) and was the reason why these corporal punishments were not given in practice. It was also a theological ground for the *ulama* to reject the law as un-Islamic and to resist removing the *tazir* section, which caused the *most* abuse and which *ulama* regarded as the state's discretion to change. At the same time, they ignored the suggestion of a Jamaat-e-Islami women's group that the government should create women-staffed medico-legal boards because a key hindrance to rape convictions was the lack of government personnel to gather evidence in a timely manner (*Daily Times* 2003)—a point that Justice Dorab Patel had also made in the preface to *Hudood Ordinances: A Divine Sanction*.

Contrary to media discourse on the issue, 'modernity' and 'tradition' were not irreconcilable binaries. Rights abuses could often be traced to the way that religious 'tradition' had been incorporated in the 'modern' legal system and there were strategies, either from within tradition or proposed by groups advocating for a revival of tradition, to improve 'modern' law.

REFERENCES

Abbott, Freeland. 1962. 'Pakistan's New Marriage Law: A Reflection of Quranic Interpretation'. *Asian Survey* 1 (11): 26–32.

Ahmad, Khurshid, ed. 1959. *Marriage Commission Report X-Rayed: A Study of the Family Law of Islam and a Critical Appraisal of the Modernist Attempts to 'Reform' It*. Karachi: Chiragh-e-Rah Publications.

Allana, G. 1969. *Pakistan Movement Historical Documents*. Karachi: Department of International Relations, University of Karachi.

Ansari, Sarah. 2003. *Sufi Saints and State Power: The Pirs of Sind, 1843–1947*. Cambridge, Delhi: Cambridge University Press.

Baxter, Craig, ed. 2007. *Diaries of Field Marshal Mohammad Ayub Khan, 1966–1972*. Karachi: Oxford University Press Pakistan.

Bhargava, Rajeev, ed. 1998. *Secularism and Its Critics*. Delhi: Oxford University Press.

Binder, Leonard. 1961. *Religion and Politics in Pakistan*. Los Angeles, CA: University of California Press.

'CII Amendments to Hudood Must Be Legalized'. *Daily Times* (editorial), 8 July 2006.

Cohn, Bernard S., and Milton Singer, eds. 1968. *Structure and Change in Indian Society*. Chicago, IL: Aldine.

Cohn, Bernard. 1996. *Colonialism and Its Forms of Knowledge: The British in India*. Princeton, NJ: Princeton University Press.

Council of Islamic Ideology Annual Report 1962–1963, Islamabad.

Council of Islamic Ideology Annual Report 2004–2005, Islamabad.

Devji, Faisal. 2013. *Muslim Zion*. Cambridge, MA: Harvard University Press.

Fish, Stanley. 1982. 'Interpretation and the Pluralist Vision'. *Texas Law Review* 60: 495–505.

Gilmartin, David. 1989. *Empire and Islam: Punjab and the Making of Pakistan*. Oxford: Oxford University Press.

Hakim, Khalifa Abdul. 1952. *Iqbal aur Mullah*. [In Urdu]. http://apnaorg.com/books/urdu/iqbal-aur-mullah/book.php?fldr=book

Hallaq, Wael B. 2009. *Shari'a: Theory, Practice, Transformations*. Cambridge, UK; New York, NY: Cambridge University Press.

———. 2013. *The Impossible State: Islam, Politics, and Modernity's Moral Predicament*. New York, NY: Columbia University Press.

Hashimy, S. Y., ed. 1955. *Islam as an Ethical and a Political Ideal: Iqbal's Maiden English Lecture*. Lahore: Orientalia.

Hefner, Robert. 2004. *Remaking Muslim Politics: Pluralism, Contestation, Democratization*. Princeton, NJ: Princeton University Press.

Iqbal, Muhammad. 1930. *Reconstruction of Religious Thought in Islam*. http://www.allamaiqbal.com/works/prose/english/reconstruction/index.htm.

Jehangir, Asma, and Hina Jilani. 1990. *The Hudood Ordinances: A Divine Sanction?* Lahore: Rohtas Books.

'JI for New Body to Deal with Crimes against Women'. *Daily Times*, 24 October 2003.

Kandhalwi, Mawlana Muhammad Malik. 24–27 July 1966. 'Dr. Fazlur Rahman kay Deeni Tahreefat' [Dr. Fazlur Rahman's distortions of religion]. *Al-Haqq*, Jild 1, Shumarah 10.

Khan, Makhdoom Ali. 2004–2005. 'Pakistan: Legality of a Hasba Bill to Introduce an Islamic Ombudsman in the North-West-frontier Province'. *Yearbook of Islamic and Middle Eastern Law* (Vol. 11), 413–464. Leiden, The Netherlands: Brill Publishers.

Khare, R. S., ed. 1999. *Perspectives on Islamic Law, Justice, and Society*. Lanham and Oxford: Rowman and Littlefield.

Kozlowski, Gregory C. 1985. *Muslim Endowments in British India*. Cambridge, MA; New York, NY: Cambridge University Press.

Kugle, Scott Alan. 2001. 'Framed, Blamed and Renamed: The Recasting of Islamic Jurisprudence in Colonial South Asia'. *Modern Asian Studies* 35 (2): 257–313.

Kymlicka, William. 1995. *Multicultural Citizenship: A Liberal Theory of Minority Rights*. Oxford: Oxford University Press.

Lau, Martin. 2006. *The Role of Islam in the Legal System of Pakistan*. Boston, MA; Leiden, The Netherlands: M. Nijhoff Publishers.

Lodhi, Zakaullah. 1979. 'Ijtihad in the process of Islamization of laws'. Address at seminar on 'Application of *Shariah*' organized by the Ministry of Law and Parliamentary Affairs in Islamabad, 9–11 October, PLD 1980, pp. 22–24.

Lombardi, Clark B. 2010. 'Can Islamizing A Legal System Ever Help Promote Liberal Democracy?: A View from Pakistan'. *University of St. Thomas Law Journal* 7 (3): 649–691.

Mahmood, Saba. 2012. *Politics of Piety: The Islamic Revival and the Feminist Subject*. Princeton, NJ: Princeton University Press.

Metcalf, Barbara D. 1982. *Islamic Revival in British India: Deoband, 1860–1900*. Princeton, NJ: Princeton University Press.

Moaddel, Mansoor, and Kamran Talattof, eds. 2000. *Modernist and Fundamentalist Debates in Islam: A Reader*. New York, NY: Palgrave Macmillan.

Mutua, Makau. 2001. 'Savages, Victims, and Saviors: The Metaphor of Human Rights'. *Harvard International Law Journal* 42 (1): 201–245.

National Assembly of Pakistan Debates, 2 July 1962.

Needham, Anuradha D., and Rajeswari Sunder Rajan, eds. 2007. *The Crisis of Secularism in India*. Durham and London: Duke University Press.

'Note of Dissent of Mawlana Ihteshamul Haq Thanwi'. *The Gazette of Pakistan (Extraordinary)*, Karachi, 30 August 1956.

Patel, Rashida. 1979. *Women and Law in Pakistan*. Karachi: Faiza Publishers (Urdu edition published by All Pakistan Women's Association in 1981).

Pitts, Jennifer. 2006. *A Turn to Empire: The Rise of Imperial Liberalism in Britain and France*. Princeton, NJ: Princeton University Press.

Quraishi-Landes, Asifa. 2015. 'Islamic Constitutionalism: Not Secular. Not Theocratic. Not Impossible'. *Rutgers Journal of Law and Religion* 16: 553–579.

Rahman, Mawlana Aziz-ur. 2003. 'Roshan khyal aur pasmandah Islam? [Enlightened and backward Islam]' *Al-Balagh*, July, 3–8.

Rajan, Rajeswari Sunder. 2003, *The Scandal of the State: Women, Law, and Citizenship in Postcolonial India*. Durham and London: Duke University Press.

Rawls, John. 1993. *Political Liberalism*. New York, NY: Columbia University Press.

'Repealing Hudood laws'. *Dawn* (editorial), 4 July 2006.

'Report of the Commission on Marriage and Family Laws'. *The Gazette of Pakistan (Extraordinary)*, Karachi, 20 June 1956.

'Report of the Court of Inquiry Constituted under Punjab Act II of 1954 to Enquire into the Punjab Disturbances of 1953'. Lahore: Punjab Govt., 1954.

Rothberg, Robert I., and Dennis Thompson, eds. 2000. *Truth v. Justice: The Morality of Truth Commissions*. Princeton, NJ; Oxford: Princeton University Press.

Salim, Ahmad, ed. 1990. *Khutbat-iMadni*. Lahore: Nigarishat.

Sarkar, Sumit and Tanika Sarkar, eds. 2008. *Women and Social Reform in Modern India: A Reader*. Bloomington, IN: Indiana University Press.

Shafi, Mawlana Muhammad. 1963. 'Aa'ili Qanoon par mukhtasir tabsarah' [A brief comment on the family law]. *Bayyinat* April.

Shah, Justice Dr Nasim Hasan. 1992. *Islamization of Law in Pakistan*. Islamabad: Shariah Academy, International Islamic University.

Tonki, Mawlana. 1963. 'Aa'ili Qawaneen Shari'at ki Roshni' [Family laws in the light of Shariat]', Part 7. *Bayyinat*, September.

Usmani, Mawlana Taqi. 2006. 'The Islamization of Laws in Pakistan: The Case of Hudud Ordinances'. *The Muslim World* 96 (2): 287.

———. 1978. 'General Zia kay Aylanat'. *Al-Balagh*, March, 3–9.

'WAF "Outraged" at Govt–MMA "Machinations"'. *Daily Times*, 13 September 2006.

Yefet, Karin Carmit. 2011. 'The Constitution and Female-initiated Divorce in Pakistan: Western Liberalism in Islamic Garb'. *Harvard Journal of Law and Gender* 34: 565, 591.

Yusuf, Mawlana. 1966a. 'Princeton University Amreeka mai'n Dr. Fazlur Rahman ki Islam kay khilaf zehar afshani [Dr. Fazlur Rahman's poisonous remarks against Islam in Princeton University, America]'. *Al-Haqq*, 23–40, Jild 2, Shumarah 2, 30–31 November.

Yusuf, Mawlana Muhammad. 1966b. 'Idara-e-Tahqiqat-e-Islami ka Modern Islam: Ek Nazar Main' [Islamic Research Institute's modern Islam: At a glance]. *Al-Haqq*, 9–16, Jild 2, Shumarah 3, December .

———. 1967. 'Idara-e-Tahqiqat-e-Islami ka Modern Islam: 4' [Islamic Research Institute's modern Islam: 4]. *Al-Haqq*, , 30–41, Jild 2, Shumarah 6, March.

Zaman, M. Qasim. 2018. *Islam in Pakistan: A History*. Princeton, NJ: Princeton University Press.

Zia, Afiya S. 2018. *Faith and Feminism in Pakistan: Religious Agency or Secular Autonomy?* Brighton: Sussex Academic Press.

Chapter 3

Journeying in the Vernacular
Pilgrimage, Tourism and Nationalism in Hindi Travelogues

Shobna Nijhawan

INTRODUCTION

With the expansion of the railway network from the mid-19th century onwards and other public infrastructure enabling new forms of population mobility, new conceptions of travel in colonial India melded with older ones and impacted the lives and (imagined) travels of the vernacular-reading public. Alongside, one specific literary (and ethnographic) print genre, that is, travel writing or the travelogue, emerged in Hindi and other South Asian vernacular languages, such as Bengali, Marathi, Gujarati and Tamil, in the second half of the 19th century (Das 1991, 177–178). First introduced in Hindi periodicals by the writer and editor Bharatendu Harishchandra (1850–1885), a writing traveller and pilgrim who also published travel letters of his contemporaries (Dalmia 1997, 322–328), the Hindi travelogue developed into a distinct genre over the decades.[1] By the 20th century, it had become

---

[1] See also Das (1995, 251–254), Kumkum Chatterjee (1999, 192–227), Sandeep Banerjee and Subho Basu (2015, 609–649). Apart from the travelogue, new conceptions of travel also manifested in other literary genres, such as fictional

a regular feature in Hindi literary periodicals. Under the auspices of prominent Hindi periodical editors, such as Mahavir Prasad Dwivedi (1864–1938, editor of *Sarasvatī*), Dularelal Bhargava (1895–1975, editor of *Mādhurī* and *Sudhā*) and Ramrakh Singh Sahgal (1896–1952, editor of *Chāṁd*), amongst many others, the travelogue was popularized as a literary genre with a specific nationalist purpose of promoting modern literature in the standardized Khari Boli Hindi language while also creating a national sense of travel in the vernacular. A look at the travel destinations of approximately 20 travel writers published in one single periodical, *Sudhā* (lit. nectar, ambrosia 1927–1941), reveals that the nation as a subcontinent and as Hindu was indeed being mapped by Hindi writers.

Since the 1990s, when scholarship on travel literature emerged in North American academia, travelogues have been subcategorized as travel memoirs, travel diaries, travel essays, travel guides and more recently travel blogs, amongst others. The travelogues discussed in this chapter may well be grouped into such categories. It needs to be remembered, though, that such boundaries are constructed and not always accurate. I, therefore, use the terms travelogue and travel narrative interchangeably, while referring to travel memoir and travel manual whenever it seems accurate to do so. My purpose is to examine travel literature from the perspective of the service (*sevā*) that authors sought to render to Hindi literature (*sāhitya sevā*) and to the emergent nation in the early 20th century. Together with essays that covered themes concerning archaeology, anthropology, science, the arts (dance, drama and music), economics, politics, history, languages and literature, travel writings in Hindi periodicals aspired to educate the modern middle-class reader in Hindi and turn him/her into a deserving member of the nascent nation.

Hindu pilgrimage sites (*tīrth sthān*) all over British India, as well as Hindu, Jain and Buddhist historical sites, feature as prominent destinations in Hindi travelogues. Supposedly secular travel destinations were for the most part located in the British Indian hill stations Shimla, Solan

prose and poetry. There existed a subcategory of Hindi novels 'related to travel' (*yātrāsambandhī*).

Hills, Mussoorie, Srinagar, Dehradun and the immensely popular travel destination Nainital.[2] Sites of imperial and nationalist interest were New Delhi (Raisina), which formed the seat of the colonial government, and Wardha/Sevagram where Gandhi had set up his ashram.[3] While travel destinations in north India dominated the travel accounts published in Hindi periodicals, places in central India and the Deccan were also included regularly.[4] What may today be distinguished as pilgrimage and tourism was not a clear-cut distinction for the travel writers to whom temples became tourist attractions, ashrams turned into lodges, holy waters offered opportunities for a pleasant swim and historical and archaeological sites were projected as important markers of the Hindu-Indian nation and its national and religious heritage. Buddhist and Jain sites of history and worship (most notably Sarnath, Rajgriha, Nalanda and Ayodhya/Saket) were appropriated into this Hindu nationalist narrative. One of the travel writers discussed in this chapter, Lakshminarayan Tandan 'Premi'—a self-proclaimed modern Hindi writer and traveller and a proponent of Hindutva ideology—is an example of a writer who travelled 'sacred', 'secular' and 'nationalist' locations in the early 1940s.

Travel writing found in periodicals predates the 'official' history of the Hindi travelogue, which is often linked to prominent writers, such as Sachchidananda Hirananda Vatsyayan 'Agyeya' (1911–1987) and Rahul Sankrityayan (1893–1963), who is said to have established

---

[2] See for example, Dhaniram 'Premi' (*Sudhā* December 1929), Shivnarayan Tandan 'Premi' (*Sudhā* May 1928), Gurunarayan Sukul (*Sudhā* June 1932), Prithvipal Sinha (*Sudhā* August 1929), Dharmadev Shastri (*Sudhā* August 1940), Lakshminarayan Tandan 'Premi' (*Sudhā* November 1940, December 1940) and Beohar Rajendra Sinha (*Sudhā* August 1939).

[3] See Kaushalya Devi 'Gorovala' (*Sudhā* September 1928) and Lakshminarayan Tandan 'Premi' (*Sudhā* August 1941, 43–54).

[4] While I have not encountered a travel account of the supposedly holiest city for Hindus Benares/Kashi, I am hesitant to draw conclusions regarding this absence, as it is not entirely clear to me whether the city was kept outside the fold of the modern Indian traveling gaze or whether such accounts were present, but not available in the periodical issues that I have been able to consult.

travel writing as a literary genre (Machwe 1998).[5] Located in a time-line between the earliest (Harishchandra) and the supposedly most developed travelogues (Sankrityayan) in modern Hindi, this chapter is an inquiry into the form and content of travelogues of the late 1920s to the early 1940s. I contend that this is a period in which travel writing about places of interest within British India was conceptualized in the light of nation-building and religious-spiritual identity formation. The travel writers took on distinctly 'religious' and 'secular' nationalist identities depending on what place they were describing. Furthermore, travel writing developed through the interplay of travel writers, publishers and an emerging Hindi-reading and travelling public who sought information in the vernacular not only on where and how to travel, but also on how to imagine the nation(-to-be). At the same time, travel writing was conceptualized as a distinct literary genre that offered the possibility for literary expression in standardized Khari Boli Hindi for the education and entertainment of the Hindi reader, thus, also furthering the linguistic and literary project of creating a standardized national language and canon. Examples of this genre of literary writing are found in travel accounts to the Himalayan mountain range, a particularly popular North Indian travel destination. This chapter explores the articulations of literary, national(ist) and Hindu imaginings by examining the style, form and content of several travelogues published in the well-known Hindi periodical *Sudhā* in the first-half of the 20th century. It also focuses on the travel writing of one specific author, Lakshminarayan Das Tandan 'Premi', to track the Hindu nationalist project of nation creation.

(IM)PRINTING THE NATION: TRAVELOGUES, TOURISM, PILGRIMAGE

By the 1930s, the tourism infrastructure in British India—set up at first with Anglo-Indian travellers and colonial government employees in mind—had become accessible to upper middle-class vernacular travellers and writers. To promote their travels and communicate

---

[5] Two national awards on Hindi travel writing conferred by the Government of India are named after Rahul Sankrityayan.

their experiences amongst the middle-class reading public, travel writers used the vernacular print medium. Hindi literary periodicals of the early 20th century such as *Sarasvatī*, *Mādhurī*, *Chāṁd* and *Sudhā*, published travel writing on a regular basis. Such writings, primarily authored by Hindu travellers and devotees, provided the Hindi reader—a potential traveller—information in a 'useful' (*upayogi*), that is, entertaining and purposeful, manner. Grouped in publishers' catalogues under the heading *bhramaṇ* or *yātrā-sambandhī*, they offered 'factual' travel-related information and shared personal experiences. 'Factual' information (geographic, climatic, geologic, botanic, demographic and so on) was gathered through multi-lingual sources that included travel guidebooks and pilgrimage manuals in Hindi, English and other vernacular languages, essays, colonial surveys and other publication formats, often prepared under the colonial government by Orientalist scholars in collaboration with native scholars of the 19th and early 20th centuries.

Apart from nationalist discourse, and yet imbibed in it, English-language railway guidebooks on Indian travel destinations influenced travel writing. Written from the 'imperial gaze' for Anglo-Indian travellers, they also became guides for the vernacular writer and traveller (Mukhopadhyay 2014). Travel writers in Hindi occasionally refer to travel guides, such as the *Kashmir guide* of the Indian Railways, as particularly useful for planning a journey.[6] Historical and mythological information on places, sites and their genealogies was also couched in the language of 'facts' useful for the traveller, pilgrim and periodical reader. It was commonly drawn from oral and written sources, including religious scripture and renderings thereof, found in the immensely popular pilgrimage manuals of the time. Smaller and larger presses and publishing houses, often conveniently located in pilgrimage towns, had recognized their commercial potential and began producing and distributing them at low cost through various networks in bazars, at railway stations and at pilgrimage sites. To what extent the travel writers discussed in this chapter relied on pilgrim guides that commonly

---

[6] See for example Dube (1940, 391). Such travel guides are, however, not promoted in these periodicals' advertisement sections, which may be due to the fact that they were English-language publications.

spread word of the 'glory' of pilgrimage sites (*tīrth sthān*) and appealed to pilgrims to visit such places cannot be determined. Stark (2008) has laid out this history of the commercialization of print and the circulation of Hindi literature from the city of Lucknow by the Naval Kishore Press (est. 1858) in the second half of the 19th century. Such entrepreneurship continued well into the 20th century.[7] Travelogues in the Hindi periodical of the late 1920s and 1930s, however, were a conscious effort to offer readers highbrow literature on the topic of travel and pilgrimage that distinguished itself from Hindi pilgrimage manuals.

The most important characteristic of travelogues was the auto-biographical voice of the travel writer that accounted simultaneously for bias and authority gained through the first-hand experience of travelling to a certain place. Descriptions of the logistics of arrival (most commonly by train) detail the arrival to a place and how to navigate its sites of interest, the (dis-)advantages of lodging at a certain hotel or ashram, places where clean food could be obtained and dangers and beauty to look out for on a hike. Photographs of people, places, sites and the author himself accompanied the text.[8] Analysing travelogues of the second half of the 19th century, Dalmia comments:

---

[7] A comparison of pilgrimage manuals and travelogues is yet to be undertaken. Unfortunately, I did not have access to the pilgrimage manuals, which were also promoted in *Sudhā*'s advertisement section. As the advertisement held, it was important to carry these books as guides not only for information, but also for budgeting purposes during the pilgrimage (*Sudhā*, April 1934).

[8] I use the male gender as the writings consulted for this essay are almost exclusively written by men. Amongst the few female Hindi travel writers, Rameshwari Nehru's travels to Burma in the late 1910s published in the women's periodicals *Stri Darpaṇ* have been previously written about (Nijhawan 2012). Kumari Kaushalyadevi Gorovala, who was a regular contributor to *Sudhā* wrote an account of Raisina (New Delhi), which she got to visit upon returning from Shimla. Her writing style follows the common pattern of travelogues written in Khari Boli Hindi. Her account was featured in the special literature issue of *Sudhā*. In comparison, Prabhavati Devi's account of the Pashupatinath Temple in Kathmandu was rather dry (*Sudhā*, March 1940, 119–122).

The journey meant, then, a mapping of the country in that the traveller took experiential and cultural possession of it. It meant a new awareness of cultural identity, in togetherness and separateness. In writing of it, the traveller shared this experience with his readers. (Dalmia 1997, 322)

In the early 20th century, the sense of 'togetherness and separateness' as well as the urgency to share the experience of a travel still featured centrally. The author of a travelogue claimed full authority over the writing of his travel experiences as well as of providing an honest and accurate account of the conditions of a certain place and its people. Unlike in earlier accounts, hassles at railway stations or racism on the train were no longer addressed by travel writers in the way they were in the travel accounts of travellers discussed by Dalmia (1997, 323) and—in the case of gender discrimination—Prasad (2012). The sense of 'writing the nation' had certainly developed by the 1930s and if critique was voiced, it happened out of a sense of 'imagined community' and social reformist concern with the subject citizens of an emerging Indian nation, and not from the perspective of the victimized subject.

Travel narratives may simultaneously be read as reflections on the impact of colonial modernity on travellers' lives and personal tastes, as well as on places and lives written about. In their claim to be factual, 'true' and honest about their observations, travel writers also critically assessed colonial society. They did not shy away from voicing personal and class-conscious dismay over the social condition of people (most commonly the labourer) or over the dirtiness of a certain quarter and crowdedness of a bazar. In such cases, their tone was colloquial, sometimes polemic, exaggerated and full of pity for the plight of people and places. It was their 'inside-out and outside-in' status of the visitor of their own country, away from home while simultaneously at home in the nation that made travel writers contemplate national places, spaces and boundaries as mediated by categories of caste, class, ethnicity and religion, amongst others. Travel writers expressed their happiness upon meeting people from their own caste during their travels and voiced concern for people of lower classes. They were fully aware of their own privilege of being informed travellers as well as of their upper middle-class, high-caste Hindu identity. This manifests even more intensely when self-proclaimed Hindu travel writers incorporated and occasionally appropriated Buddhist, Jain and Muslim sacred places into their narratives (see the writings of Lakshminarayan Tandan 'Premi' below).[9] As for gender, the travelogues I have consulted were written by and for the male reader, the assumption being that he would facilitate travels for the entire family.[10] Arguably, travelogues in Hindi periodicals were not solely published to promote travel and tourism; they were as much meant to be recollections of a writer and intersected with other literary genres of the essay, fiction and autobiography that all featured centrally in Hindi literary periodicals of the time.[11]

While travel was not a new phenomenon of the 20th century, disseminating travelogues through the by then well-established Hindi print networks became a popular way for writers and readers to imagine the geography and territory of the nation. Maps, however, were not included in the accounts, which is curious as they would have been an added visual dimension useful for fostering 'territorial attachments [that] infuse iconic significance, tinged with feelings of security, belonging, enclosure, entitlement, and exclusion' (Ludden 2003, 1057). Instead, all travelogues were accompanied by a visual narrative provided by the travel writer through photographs. In vernacular periodicals, where travelogues were commonly serialized, they were grouped under the essay section, which also introduced readers to related themes, such as literary criticism, (auto-)biography and life history, the arts and sciences, history, archaeology, economics, trade and politics. In their entirety, periodicals were essential to nation formation through literature in a variety of genres and covering a diversity of themes (Nijhawan 2018).

---

[9] While no specific Islamic pilgrimage site is addressed in the writings that I have consulted, mosques and Islamic heritage sites often became geographical markers in travelogues.

[10] There was no scarcity of women travellers on the British Indian railways, which even led to public debates on their accommodation in women-reserved zenana carriers. See Prasad (2012) for an account of these debates.

[11] Some travelogues were primarily memoirs whereas others could even be read as anti-travel writing. See Siyaramsharan Gupta's account in which he deplores that he did not get to leave his hotel room in Nainital due to the bad weather and consequently never got to see a glimpse of the Himalaya (*Sudhā* 1939, 349–355).

All essays were carefully edited and written in Khari Boli Hindi prose—the standardized, but by no means inflexible, language of prose writing promoted in literary periodicals of the time. The choice of lexis depended on individual authors, who chose a more or less Sanskritized Khari Boli Hindi variation with a low to moderate number of Urdu words. The same holds true for questions of style and aesthetics when it came to descriptions of natural scenery, architecture, religious experience and personal emotions. Professional and lay travel writers had a relatively clear sense of the Hindi reader: he was a sophisticated Hindu and for all intents and purposes likely to embark on a travel with the travel report of the writer at hand.[12] Hence, details of a place were provided in order to enable the readers to navigate streets and paths of the travel destination. We do not know whether readers accepted such advice or began travelling to a certain destination after reading travelogues. Whereas travel writers frequently mention how they had consulted travel guidebooks prior to their travels, their writing is equally embedded in the thriving field of Hindi literary writing in periodicals of the time.

Before I introduce travelogues from the early 20th century, two disclaimers are required. (a) Travel was not restricted to (British) Indian destinations. Travel to European cities in England, Scotland, France, Italy and Switzerland (London, Edinburgh, Paris, Rome, Genoa, Naples, Geneva, Lugano and Zürich) resulted in publications in literary, women's and children's periodicals and travel monographs.[13] Likewise, women, political activists, religious authorities and students traveled to destinations in North America and Asia (Japan, Persia and Russia). Such writings offer an 'Eastern' gaze on to the West and warrant a study of their own. (b) Conceptions of travel had also not emerged out

---

[12] It needs to be clarified that travelogues or travel essays were not guidebooks, which were a separate genre not discussed in this essay. While it is likely that subscribers consulted back issues of periodicals prior to their travels, they would have also had easy access to travel guides.

[13] See, for example, Krishna Nehru (*Sudhā* December 1928), Kripanath Mishra (*Sudhā* February 1929, September 1929, June 1930), Dhirendra Varma (*Sudhā* November 1936, March 1937, August 1938), Surya Narayan Vyas (*Sudhā* August 1938, June 1940) and Dhaniram 'Prem' (*Sudhā* February 1930). Shukdev Bihari Mishra wrote a travel report covering his trip to Europe, serialized in *Sudhā* in 1931.

of a vacuum, as pilgrimage travel, such as the (*tīrth-*)*yātra* for Hindus, the *hajj* and visits to Sufi shrines for Muslims, trade-related travel and travel due to long-distance marriage arrangements had been established as pre-colonial modes of travel.

The travel accounts discussed in this essay testify to new conceptions of travel: Objectives for travelling into the Inner Himalayan region, as listed by Rameshvardayal Dube (*Sudhā* October 1940, 391), were to escape the heat, to get medical treatment, to visit religious sites or, in his case, 'just for travelling—nothing else' (*ghūmne, keval ghūmne ke liye*). This is not to suggest that travel had become a secular touristic activity exclusively. Sacred sites were popularly promoted as the supposedly secular hill stations (which had a sacred history in and of themselves). (Hindu) nationalism and spirituality combined in curious ways in the travelogues to turn the modern 'secular' traveller into a modern Hindu traveller who performed *darśan* (viewing and being viewed) at a Hindu temple or at Gandhi's ashram while seeing (*dekhnā*) or strolling (*ghumnā*) Buddhist and Jain places of worship and revelling in the beauties of nature.

PILGRIMAGE AND TOURISM BETWEEN THE SACRED AND SECULAR

Hindi travel writings of the first half of the 20th century reflect the changing notions of pilgrimage and tourism to urban and rural destinations of British India in the context of rising nationalist awareness and the anti-colonial struggle. The vernacular accounts of travel serialized in the Hindi literary and sociopolitical periodical *Sudhā* (1927–1941) reflect the intersections of 'sacred/divine', 'secular', 'national', 'social' and 'natural' spaces, and literature, which increasingly became the medium to express a Hindu nationalist discourse on travel. Travel writing was not a profession for most of the authors whose texts I have consulted but came as a by-product to other professional and leisurely engagements that required travel to certain places. In their observations and descriptions of people and places, linguistic and ethnic diversity featured centrally, as did conscious and unconscious engagements with questions of class, caste and privilege. Travel narratives of the late 1920s to the early 1940s could contain anything that travel writers literally saw on their travels (mostly out of trains and while on foot) and at the travel destinations with the railway station receiving a special mention as a variantly modern site. The constant modernization of the British Indian railway system prompted writers to frequently comment on coaches, engines, tracks, speed and infrastructure.[14] This was particularly true for travel to the hill stations, which was challenging and not always comfortable.[15]

Travelogues offered plenty of factual information that also broached the utilitarian–nationalist importance of (re)-discovering and claiming supposed heritage sites on the subcontinent. This process had begun in Hindi under the travel writing of Bharatendu Harishchandra (Dalmia 1997) and continued well into the 1920s to the 1940s even though the concept of travel had changed by that time. Improved infrastructure made remote places accessible to the financially secure middle classes and aided such 'rediscovery'. In the process, selected 'sacred' places with historical significance were marked as sites of importance to what came to be projected as 'secular' Indian nationalist history in text and image of travelogues.

Through a focus on Bengali travelogues on the Himalayan region between the late 19th and early 20th centuries, Banerjee and Basu (2015) argue that there was a secularization of the sacred and new imaginings of nation-spaces in the period. While writers such as Devendranath Tagore had identified the Himalayas as a Hindu-religious site towards the end of the 19th century, a new generation of travel writers of the early 20th century infused 'the sacred Himalayan

---

[14] Part of the UNESCO World Heritage Sites are the two railway sites in India, that is, Kalka–Shimla Railway (completed 1903) and the Darjeeling Himalaya Railway (completed 1881).

[15] See Vishveshvarnath Reu (*Sudhā* August 1939), Lakshminarayan Tandan 'Premi' (*Sudhā* November 1940, December 1940, January 1941, March 1941, May 1941, June 1941, July 1941, August 1941), Siyaramsharan Gupta (*Sudhā* November 1939).

geography with a secular politics' by embedding it in nationalist discourse without necessarily discarding the Hindu identities of the writers (Banerjee and Basu 2015, 610).

Nandini Chandra (2007) and Charu Gupta (2017) have analysed travel writings in children's periodicals and of Swami Satyadev 'Parivrajak' (1879–1961) respectively to comment on the unique nationalist 'pedagogic imperative' that sought to create an awareness of citizenship and 'imagined communities' by defining cultural history, geography and ethnicity, and the cultural creation of 'the biological bodies of nations' where a colonized nation attempted to reclaim a space of freedom through the carving of 'perfect masculinist bodies' (Chandra 2007, 293–325; Charu Gupta 2017). Elsewhere, I have analysed how Rameshwari Nehru (1886–1966) urged for the political mobilization of Indian women in her account of travels to Burma (Nijhawan 2012). Here, I wish to examine the content and form of the texts to underline the criss-crossing frontiers of the national-political and the religious-secular.

HIKING THE HIMALAYAS

Rameshwardayal Dube's (1940) travel narrative of an extended family vacation in the Himalayas precedes what Mustonen (2006, 160) terms as 'backpacking tourism' or 'trekking'. Dube himself describes it in the Hindi idiom of (worldly) strolling (*keval ghūmne ke liye*). A well-recognized Hindi writer and literature graduate, Dube had prepared for the 24-day stay in and around Srinagar, Kashmir, based on different guidebooks. He was travelling with a group of people 'aged between eight and eighty' that included female travellers, whom he praised for their hiking abilities and endurance (391). Rather than booking a hotel or ashram in the conventional manner of the time, his group had hauled a lorry and was travelling with 'tents, mats, tables and chairs, leather socks, woollen clothes, some medicine and own food' (392). Dube spends the first evening in awe:

> Upon lying down, it occurred to me how far away I was from home in this corner of the Kashmir Valley, lying somehow on the veranda

of this post office. What a big country, so many high mountains, how far away and I (a man) how small and insignificant.[16]

Dube's reflections would continue throughout the trip and intermingle with many 'spiritual' experiences triggered by the natural scenery, projecting the Himalayas as metonymous of the nation. While heavy rain made the hike especially arduous on the second day, the beauty of the lush valley encouraged the group to continue with fervour. At the same time, Dube directs his attention to the carriers of his luggage, oscillating between pity and esteem. Ill-paid and exploited, with torn clothes and emaciated bodies, the carriers were essential for a successful vacation on account of their special skills in navigating muddy mountain paths with heavy loads on their backs. They knew how to pass dangerous slopes and were experienced in forecasting hazardous weather conditions. This notwithstanding, they remained the subaltern 'other' in ethnic, linguistic and economic terms and Dube's comments remain token statements—well observed—but delivered from a privileged and secure place.

Dube represents a style of writing that Banerjee and Basu (2015, 614) have specifically attributed to an upper middle-class awareness that focuses on the spiritual and the secular rather than the sacred religious. Dube's emotive style is accompanied by his urban, middle-class identity markers, in which the account ends with a 'return to civilization' marked by the shaving of the beard by Dube and his friend at the end of the hike. A photograph of this moment concludes the travelogue.

SHACKLED MOUNTAINS? 'SHIMLA'S STAIN'

Despite being one of the most popular travel destinations, the hill station Shimla reveals its 'dark' side in the travel narrative by Beohar Rajendra Sinha (1939). Entitled 'Shimla's Stain/Disgrace', it begins in typical travelogue fashion with a description of the journey to

---

[16] '*Leṭne par khayāl āyā, ghar se dūr, kitnī dūr, kaśmīr-ghāṭī ke is kone meṁ, is coṭe-se ḍāk-bāṅgle ke barāmade meṁ, kahaṁ leṭā huā hūṁ. Kitnā baṛā deś, kitne ūṁce pahāḍ, kitnī dūr aur maiṁ (ek manuṣya) kitnā laghu, kitnā kṣudra.*' (Dube 1940, 392).

Shimla. Rajendra Sinha, an employee with the Imperial Council of Agricultural Research, had been summoned to a board meeting in Shimla and decided to extend his stay there for one week before continuing his travels to Kashmir for his summer vacation.[17] He briefly lays out the travel route from Hardwar via Rishikesh to Kalka, from where he embarked on to the small and adventurous Kalka–Shimla Railway, in a third-class carriage of the train, as he says, to gain experience.[18] He describes the scenery as it passed: fields and mountains, mountain-dwellers and tourists and the change in temperature as the train reached higher altitudes. Rajendra Sinha then introduces the reader to the hill station with some shocking facts: as the increase in population from 60,000–70,000 to 80,000–90,000 inhabitants in the summer months was leading to congestion, the lack of proper canalization was causing sanitary problems and mosquito-borne disease. He criticizes the local politicians for not investing in Shimla's infrastructure and for not improving the condition of the economically deprived and exploited classes. The climax of Rajendra Sinha's critical account concerns the deplorable condition of temporary migrant workers (*kulī*), whose miserable living and working conditions severely constrained Rajendra Sinha's pleasure in Shimla's stunning nature and scenery:

> All the days that I stayed in Shimla, this load kept occupying my mind and this is why I could not cherish Shimla's natural beauty…. The figure of the *kulī* [labourer] is attached on to the heavenly beauty of Shimla like a stain and painted on to it like a chronic disease.[19]

---

[17] No biographical information on the author could be retrieved.

[18] According to colonial records found in the statistical abstracts related to British India, about 460 of the 520 million travellers on Indian railways, travelled in third-class carriers. The decision to travel third class may thus not be overrated. For statistical abstracts of the early 20th century, see http://dsal.uchicago.edu/statistics/1910_excel/index.html

[19] '*Jitne dinoṁ śimle meṁ rahā, yahī bhar citt ko dabāe rahā, aur isī kāraṇ śimle ke prākṛtik saundarya kā pūrā ānand nahīṁ uṭhā sakā. […] Yah kulī-mūrtī śimle ke svargīya saundarya-pat par kalaṅk kī tarah dṛḍh tathā sthir rogoṁ meṁ citrit hai*' (Rajendra Sinha 1939, 68).

He emphatically admonishes a fundraising event organized by the Young Women's Christian Association in support of Jewish refugees, wondering whether 'those women' will ever 'direct their attention towards functional ways for reforming the condition of the inhabitants of their own Bharat' (Rajendra Sinha 1939, 68).

The remainder of Rajendra Sinha's essay is ethnographic in nature and provides detailed information on to the labourers' ethnic, religious, linguistic and cultural background, their working and living conditions, food consumption and clothing, offering a compassionate narrative of their poverty and exploitation.

AT THE INTERSECTION OF RELIGION, NATURE AND NATIONALISM: THE TRAVEL WRITINGS OF 'PREMI'

One prolific and yet understudied Hindi travel writer whose accounts simultaneously fall into the categories of the 'secular', 'sacred' and Hindu nationalist is Lakshminarayan Tandan 'Premi'.[20] His travelogues were serialized in the 1940s and 1941s in the Hindi literary periodical *Sudhā*. The MA graduate covered his North Indian travels to Nainital, Mussoorie, Dehradun, Sarnath, Nalanda, Rajgriha, Hardwar, Vindhyachal and Tanda falls, amongst other places, as well as a travel to Maharashtra (Aurangabad) to visit the Ellora caves. Couched into the genre of the travelogue was also a travel to Wardah and Sevagram, where he interviewed Mohandas Karamchand Gandhi, provided a detailed description of Sevagram Ashram and visited places of economic and nationalist interest in Wardha. Writing in Sanskritized Khari Boli Hindi, 'Premi's' travelogues straddle tourism and pilgrimage, as they make their way through places marked as national(ist), historical and/or religious sites. 'Premi' sometimes travelled alone, at

---

[20] Not much is known about this writer except the information provided in the Hindi periodical *Sudhā*, where he is praised as a literary gem (*sāhityaratna*). Lakshminarayan Tandan 'Premi' is not to be confused with the Hindi writers Harikrishna 'Premi' and Jagdishchandra Solanki 'Premi'.

other times with Rashtriya Swayamsevak Sangh (RSS) compatriots, and also with family and friends (including children, seniors and women). In all cases, the travelogue proved suitable to reflect on his experiences of his nation and to give his readers advice shall they be planning their own travels.

'Premi's travel accounts pair factual information with his very own personal experiences. He inserts himself into the places he visits and the texts he writes and complements his text with photographs. In 'Merī Nainitāl-Yātra', he dwells at length on a hike to China Peak, the beauty of the flora and fauna of which caused him to exclaim: 'man forgets all about his domestic duties (*ghar–grhasthī*) and worldly troubles, his eyes directed at the beauty of the nature, his soul satisfied, he forgets about his own vanity' ('Premi' 1940, 492). At the same time, the beauty of nature is enhanced by the presence of Nainidevi temple. 'Premi' expresses his joy at the sight of every local temple as it made his heart pound by awakening his Hindutva (Hinduness).[21] The account furthermore enlists 33 places worth visiting, including missionary schools and colleges, government buildings, a cinema hall and a skating rink.

Descriptions of the mansions of Nainital and their beauty at night when they are lit and the commanding Secretariat Bhavan rival those of the beauty of the mountains and lakes. Unlike Rajendra Sinha, 'Premi' is not moved by the condition of the labourers. He admonishes the poverty, exploitation and dirt in the inner town of Nainital, a congested and overpopulated space that caters to the need of the government, mentions the aversion of a fine local gentleman to the village of Tallital, a low-income and dense area, a Hindustani (*sic*) basti, and concludes that he enjoyed Mussoorie much more than overpopulated Nainital with its contaminated drinking water, stressed government employees and the lack of infrastructure. He highlights the importance of protecting pristine nature with its water and vegetation, but does not directly refer to the colonial government.

---

[21] '*Hindutva kā bhāv ek bār hṛday meṁ hiloreṁ mārne lagtā hai*' (Tandan 1940, 490).

'Premi's account of Hardwar (now in Uttarakhand and in the United Provinces in colonial times) provides an account of pilgrimage tourism undertaken by the modern Indian (Hindu) traveller of the early 20th century who delights in religious experience, good food and comfortable travelling. Also known as Gangadwara, Hardwar (in Shaivaite terminology) or Haridwar (in Vaishnavite terminology) is considered to be one of the seven most sacred and mythologically significant places for Hindus to visit. 'My Travels to Hardwar' begins with a description of the author's arrival by train, his check-in at the *dharamshala* and his first dip in the holy, albeit freezing cold, waters of the river Ganges (addressed as Gangaji). 'Premi' takes the reader along as he strolls the riverbanks (*ghāṭ*) and bazars, visits numerous temples, undertakes spiritually rewarding hikes in the mountains, and takes an air trip over Hardwar and its surroundings. Only at the end of his narrative does he speak of Hardwar as the holiest city of Hindus, explain the origin of its name and describe features of the Kumbh Mela.

Apart from being a Hindu pilgrim and tourist, 'Premi' is also an ethnographer who observes saints, tourists, other pilgrims and women. He feels the presence of the 'nation' in this intersection of the worldly and the spiritual: an arduous mountain hike receives spiritual reward upon either reaching a temple (for *darśan*) or experiencing breathtaking scenery. 'Premi' does not only visit the religious sites, but also the educational institutions for which Hardwar was known. He and his friends stroll the riverbank before reaching Aminabad bazar that embodies the diversity of bustling Hardwar:

> There were speeches, there was storytelling, there was a bell ringing, there was a religious service, there was a crowd of saints and devotees as well as worldly women and men [*strī–puruṣ*]' ... This place offers so much happiness, peace and satisfaction to the soul that man deviates from the imaginary world. ... It's an uncommon sight—thousands of men and women [*nar–nārī*] are bathing, thousands are looking at the beauty of Gangaji, thousands are praying. (Tandan 1941a, 428)

If 'Premi' was bothered by the 'Hindustanis' in Nainital, the 'Punjabis' in the main bazar and the ghats of Hardwar arouse his indignation. 'He disapproves of the customary naked bathing of Punjabi women and condemns the dirty food stores and restaurants run by the Punjabis in the bazar. It is only after the author and his co-travellers' chance upon a 'pandey from Mathura', a pilgrim guide, that they enjoy a clean and tasty meal. 'Premi' is aware that some Brahman guides try to exploit pilgrims, but he credits most of them as being trustworthy and of good service to the travellers.

In 'Sārnāth kī Madhur Smṛti', 'Premi' takes on the persona of the educated 'citizen-traveller' interested in the country's religious and ethnic diversity. His accounts of travels to Buddhist and Jain places of worship in Bihar such as Nalanda, Bihar Sharif and Rajgriha are short, prosaic and less interspersed with personal accounts and emotional and spiritual exuberance than his visits to Hindu sites of interest. They offer historical and archaeological information in text and image on significant places.[22] They are interspersed with comments for the Hindu traveller: 'Nalanda is not the *tīrth* of Hindus, but there is another site not far away in a village for Hindus to visit' (142). 'Premi' reminds readers that they will not be able to stay in Rajgriha's Buddhist ashram meant only for Buddhists. At the most, they can find shelter at the Jain ashram, where Buddhists and Hindus are accepted.[23] He mentions 'a mosque next to a bridge', and a Japanese temple not accessible to non-Japanese people (145), and visits Burmese and Jain temples just to see (*dekhnā*) and not to worship (*darśan karnā*). As in other narratives, he recounts his experience of an adventurous hike, an almost essential part of all his travels.

The author's travel to Sarnath, 'four miles north of Kashi' is inscribed as sweet reminiscences: '*Sārnāth kī Madhur Smṛti*' (Tandan 1941b, 677).[24] Even if the title does not immediately make it appear as

---

[22] Linguistically, authors distinguish the level of certainty of a statement they are making by using the subjunctive and presumptive moods in their writing. 'Premi' often uses the these two moods. He, for example, gives an estimate of a lake's dimensions (and uses the subjunctive mood '*hogā*' rather than the more definitive '*hai*').

[23] During his travel in Wardha, 'Premi' notes that Hindus *and Muslims* are entitled to stay in the Sevagram Dharamshala.

[24] *Smṛti* also designates Hindu scriptures, which are 'remembered' rather than 'heard' (*Śruti*). A reader of the time will have associated the word with the Hindu

such, a close look at the text reveals the author's dilemma in visiting a major pilgrimage site for Buddhists. Even while he is party to the larger movements of the archaeological rediscovery and religious revival of Buddhism (including Dalit (neo-)Buddhism and Tibetan Buddhism) and Buddhist sites of pilgrimage,[25] he is well aware that he cannot claim these spaces as sacred for himself. 'Premi' and his group visit the museum, Buddhist temples and stupas, and take photographs. They find Sarnath to be a peaceful and extraordinarily clean place. At the same time, what takes centre-stage in 'Premi's' narrative is the village and a 14-year-old girl he met there while searching for drinking water. 'Premi' is deeply impressed by her health, beauty and simplicity. The girl, in turn, is also curious about visitors from the city. The girl and her father become emblematic of 'true Indianness' (*bhāratīyatā*) that, the author notes, can still be seen in 'our villages'.[26] This is the moment when 'Premi' turns Sarnath from a major Buddhist pilgrimage site into a symbol of the nation and its essence. Secular joy evokes the vision of an amorphous yet emergent nation. Such a nationalist perception of travel also manifests in 'Premi's' description of his trip to Wardah.

After an event of the RSS in Nagpur, 'Premi' travelled to Wardha by train, and then took a horse carriage to Sevagram to visit the ashram in which the then widely revered nationalist leader Mahatma Gandhi (1869–1948) resided. He describes other places of interest that he finds on the way. He chats with a Punjabi from Sialkot and other 'pilgrims' who have come to pay visit to the Mahatma. 'Sevagram is a model for simplicity, economy, love, a self-sufficient, simple life, high thoughts and dutiful devotion', he holds.[27] In making Wardha and Sevagram a part of his travelogue series, he chooses a decidedly Indian nationalist location with the iconic leader Gandhi at its centre. All the information on Gandhi, his daily routine and life in the ashram, it bears mention, is obtained through an interview with Gandhi and his secretary. The

---

epics, the Vedanga or Shastra literature. Also note that 'Premi' did not use the word yād (memory), which was a commonly used term in Hindi and Urdu.

[25] For an insightful discussion, see Singh (2010, 193–217) and T. Guha-Takurta (2013, 77–109).

[26] '*Hamāre gāṃvoṃ meṃ ab bhī saccī bhāratīyatā ke darśan ho sakte haiṃ*', (Tandan 1941b, 677).

[27] '*Sevāgrām sādagi, mitavyay, prem, advyavhār, svāvalamban saral jīvan aur ucc vicār evam kartavya-parāyaṇta ādi kā ādarś hai*' (Tandan 1941d, 43).

secretary reminds the author that 'There should not be any errors and misconceptions printed' and that he be careful to not 'mislead the public.'[28] 'Premi' is fully aware of his responsibility as a writer and inserts a disclaimer for the reader into his text.

Even though 'Premi' retains the main elements of a travel narrative and avoids using the word *yātrā* (religious travel) in the title, his focus on the 'few hours' spent at Sevagram Ashram and his meeting with Gandhi are expressed in terms of a sacred pilgrimage. The meeting with Gandhi is described as *darśan*, the accompanying images of Gandhi deify him as (a) 'Sevagram's saint', (b) reverential *bāpū* (*pūjya bāpū*), (c) *bāpū* spinning cotton and (d) the travelling Mahatma Gandhi. This writing turns the Sevagram Ashram and Wardha into Hindu national-ist sites and Mohandas Karamchand Gandhi into an icon of the Hindu nationalist struggle.[29]

CONCLUSION

Since the early 20th century, the travelogue or travel writing has been an established and distinct, albeit porous, genre and scholars dealing with vernacular travel literature can draw from a sizeable corpus of texts of colonial travel writing. Through a close examination of a variety of travelogues, this chapter has probed and questioned the clear distinctions between tourism and pilgrimage and religious and secular travel. The travel writers discussed here show the imbrications of the religious and the secular, as well as nationalist and Hindu nationalist in the imaginings of the nation-to-be.

Differences in the conception of travel characterized travel writ-ers, such as Rameshwardayal Dube, Beohar Rajendra Sinha and Lakshminarayan Tandan 'Premi', in a period marked by heightened anti-colonial resistance, nationalist thought and the discovery and con-struction of sites of archaeological, religious and nationalist significance. What emerged through their literary imaginings of the nation were

---

[28] '*Kahāṁ koī galat bāt dhoke se nā chap jāy, iskā dhyān rakhiegā jisme pablik ko galatfahmī nā ho jāy*', (Tandan 1941d, 49).

[29] Paola Bacchetta (2010, 551–572) has posed such a question with regard to RSS activities in Ahmedabad.

distinct vernacular writings that drew on the travellers very own literary and cultural idioms. Given that the travel writings discussed in this chapter were not travel guides published as monographs, but part of the essay section in a Hindi periodical, they fulfilled more purposes than that of the travel guide: they were also exercises in literary writing of the nation and of religion.[30] The triangulation of Hindu, traveller, and Indian enables a certain kind of heuristics to emerge in which different categories—often products of the (post-)colonial episteme—speak to one another. Apart from the travel writers discussed here, Hindi travel writers like 'Agyeya' and Rahul Sankrityayan also grappled with these categories when articulating their (travel) narratives. 'Premi', for example, writes about Nalanda, the mosque, the Japanese temple, the Buddhist ashram and the Jain ashram and while there is a nuancing of the Hindu gaze at play, he also foregrounds his 'modern-secular Indian' identity with a certain ethnographic gaze that draws on the systems of taxonomy pervasive within the colonial episteme. Further work will be required to compare this 'gaze' from that deployed by Indian travellers of the time period travelling outside India.

REFERENCES

Bachetta, Paola. 2010. 'The (Failed) Production of Hindu Nationalized Space in Ahmedabad, Gujarat'. *Gender, Place and Culture: A Journal of Feminist Geography* 17 (5): 551–572.

Banerjee, Sandeep and Subho Basu. 2015. 'Secularizing the Sacred, Imagining the Nation-Space: The Himalaya in Bengali Travelogues, 1856–1901'. *Modern Asian Studies* 49 (3): 609–649.

Chandra, N. 2007. 'The Pedagogic Imperative of Travel Writing in the Hindi World: Children's Periodicals (1920–1950)'. *South Asia: Journal of South Asian Studies* 30 (2): 293–325.

Chatterjee, Kumkum. 1999. 'Discovering India: Travel, History and Identity in Late 19th Century and Early 20th Century India'. In *Invoking the Past: The Uses of History in South Asia,* edited by D. Ali, 192–227. Delhi: Oxford University Press.

Dalmia, Vasudha. 1997. *The Nationalization of Hindu Traditions: Bhāratendu Hariśchandra and Nineteenth-century Banaras.* Delhi: Oxford University Press.

---

[30] Nationalist writing not only occupied travel writing, but also other types of essays in literary periodicals, such as those on the sciences, music and the arts (see Nijhawan 2018).

Das, Sisir Kumar. 1991. *A History of Indian Literature 1800–1910. Western Impact: Indian Response*. New Delhi: Sahitya Academy.

———. 1995. *A History of Indian Literature 1911–1956. Struggle for Freedom: Triumph and Tragedy*. New Delhi: Sahitya Academy.

Devi, Prabhavati. 1940. 'Paśupathināth kā Mandir' [The Pashupathinath Temple]. *Sudhā*, March, 119–122.

Dube, Rameshwardayal. 1940. '*Himālay ke antarāl mein*' [Inside the Himalayas]. *Sudhā*, October, 391–398.

Guha-Takurta, T. 2013. 'The Production and Reproduction of a Monument: The Many Lives of the Sanchi Stupa'. *South Asian Studies* 29 (1): 77–109.

Gupta, Charu. 'Masculine Vernacular Histories of Travel in Colonial India: The Writings of Satyadev Parivrajak'. Unpublished paper presented at Northwestern University, Evanston, IL, October 2017.

Gupta, Siyaramsharan. 1939. '*Himālay kī jhalak*' [A glimpse of the Himalaya]. *Sudhā*, November, 349–355.

Ludden, David. 2003. 'Presidential Address: Maps in the Mind and the Mobility of Asia'. *The Journal of Asian Studies* 62 (4): 1057–1078.

Machwe, Prabhakar. 1998. *Rahul Sankrityayan*. New Delhi: Sahitya Academy.

Mukhopadhyay, Aparajita. 2014. 'Colonised Gaze? Guidebooks and Journeying in Colonial India'. *South Asia: Journal of South Asian Studies* 37 (4): 656–669.

Mustonen, Pekka. 2006. 'Volunteer Tourism: Postmodern Pilgrimage?'. *Journal of Tourism and Cultural Change* 3 (3): 160–177.

Nijhawan, Shobna. 2012. 'At the Margins of Empire: Feminist Configurations of Burmese Society in the Hindi Public (1917–1920)'. *The Journal of Asian Studies* 71 (4): 1013–1033.

———. 2018. *Hindi Publishing in Colonial Lucknow. Gender, Genre and Visuality in the Making of a Literary Canon*. New Delhi: Oxford University Press.

Prasad, Ritika. 2012. 'Smoke and Mirrors: Railway Travel and Women in Colonial India'. *South Asian History and Culture* 3 (1): 26–46.

Rajendra Sinha, Beohar. 1939. '*Śimlā kī Kalaṅk*', *Sudhā*. August, 67–71.

Singh, Upinder. 2010. 'Exile and Return: The Reinvention of Buddhism and Buddhist Sites in Modern India'. *South Asian Studies* 26 (2): 193–217.

Stark, Ulrike. 2008. *An Empire of Books. The Naval Kishore Press and the Diffusion of the Printed Word in Colonial India*. New Delhi: Permanent Black.

Tandan, Lakshminarayan. 1940. 'Merī Nainitāl-Yātra' [My travels to Nainital]. *Sudhā*, November, 468–496.

———. 1941a. 'Merī Hardvār-Yātra' [My travels to Haridwar]. *Sudhā*, June, 427–436.

———. 1941b. 'Sārnāth kī Madhur Smṛti' [My sweet reminiscences of Sarnath], *Sudhā*, January, 677–680.

———. 1941c. 'Merī Rājgṛh-Yātrā' [My travels to Rajgirh]. *Sudhā*, March, 141–146.

———. 1941d. 'Sevāgram meṁ kuch Ghaṇṭe' [Few hours in Sevagram]. *Sudhā*, August, 43–54.

Chapter 4

Race, Religion and the Politics of Counting
Historicizing Hindu Nationalism

Sayori Ghoshal

The Mahomedans have a future and they believe in it—we Hindus have no conception of it. Time is with them—time is against us. At the end of the year they count their gains, we calculate our losses.' The Mahomedans are 'growing in number, growing in strength, growing in wealth, growing in solidarity, we are crumbling to pieces. They look forward to a united Mahomedan world—we are waiting for our extinction. (Mukerji 1909, 97)

Upendra Nath Mukerji was not unique in his time for penning communally divisive arguments, nor was he a fanatic, espousing 'irrational' religious sentiments. In fact, Mukerji, a doctor trained in Edinburgh and with the Indian Medical Services since 1884, derived his theories and conclusions primarily from the national census data. He claimed that the Muslim race, which was 'in a minority of 4 lakhs' 30 years back, 'had not only made up the deficiency, but were nearly 25 lakhs more numerous than the Hindus' (1909, 1). Referring to the Hindus, the title of Mukerji's work circulated like an apocalyptic prediction—*A Dying Race*. His work influenced Swami Shraddhananda, founder of the Punjab Arya Samaj, when the two met in Calcutta in 1912. Mukerji impressed on Shraddhananda the thesis of the 'dying race' and the argument that 'within the next 420 years the Indo-Aryan race would be wiped off the face of the earth unless steps were taken to save it' (Shraddhananda 1926, 14).

While in the 1870–1880s, 'Muslim' and 'Hindu' became increasingly consolidated and mutually exclusive categories, by the early 20th century, Hindu and Muslim nationalisms turned into organizing principles for public politics. Multiple factors went into the consolidation of pan-India Hindu and Muslim identities. For instance, in the case of Muslims, religious revival movements in the 1880s played a major role (Ahmed 1981), and the data collection initiated with the censuses contributed to the rise of Hindu nationalism (Cohn 1987; Datta 1999). Even the colonial mode of documenting inter-community conflicts among the various Indian groups led to the construction of Hindu–Muslim 'communalism' (Pandey 1990). However, what remains under-theorized is how, besides religious reforms and the census, Hindu and Muslim identities were also constituted by notions of biological difference and enumerative reasoning in general.

HINDU NATIONALISM AS 'RELIGIOUS' NATIONALISM

In most theories of nationalism, religious nationalism is considered an aberration. The modern nation-state is construed to be either equidistant from all religious faiths or as relegating religious practices to the private and personal (Anderson 1991, Gellner 2006 and Hobsbawm 1990). Other scholars argue that religious nationalism is not opposed to or the precursor of modern nationalism since secularism is not integral to the definition of nationalism. The predominant thrust of the latter approach is that religious nationalism is neither an outright oxymoron nor a pre-modern carry-over into modern nationalism. Desirable or not, religious nationalism in this framework is considered just as modern as secularism (Friedland 2002). Several scholars working on India conceive religious nationalism as a modern, specifically colonial, construct. Partha Chatterjee (1993) has demonstrated how the beginning of national history was also the beginning of the Hindu fundamentalist rhetoric in India. Peter van der Veer (1994), following Gyanendra Pandey (1990), argues that just as secular nationalism was an import through European imperialism, communalism or religious nationalism too was formed via the orientalist worldview of the colony as essentially pre-modern, religious and irrational. Going against academic and public advocates of secularism, van der Veer in fact emphasizes how the political will and colonial/enlightenment origin of both secular nationalism and communalism are similar. Ashutosh Varshney (1993, 232) argues that the 'ideological trend' of Hindu nationalism can be traced back to the anti-colonial desire to 'resurrect India's cultural pride'. If secular nationalism is based on territory and culture, Hindu or religious nationalism is based on territory and religion (235).

In this regard, most scholars seek to examine the relation between secularism and religious nationalism through the specific case of Hindu nationalism; Hindu nationalism is thus studied as religious nationalism and in contrast to secularism. Although from the 19th century onwards, 'nationalism in India has fed upon religious identifications' (Veer 1994, 2), how did Hindu (and Muslim) nationalism come to be seamlessly translated into *religious* nationalism?[1] What other aspects, ideas and practices went into the production of such nationalisms, other than religious or theological differences and what thereby remains unexamined in such an equation? For instance, how would an argument like Mukerji's—which is framed through elaborate statistical calculations, which imagines the Hindus and Muslims as 'races', and which concludes that Hindus were endangered and might actually become 'extinct'—contribute to the conceptual history of Hindu nationalism? Within the public discussions on the questions of Hindu identity, the Hindu's weakening condition and perceived threat from other communities, the racial-qua-biological was as much a part of the vocabulary,

---

[1] Religious nationalism does not preclude cultural nationalism; even when culture refers to 'aesthetics', 'civilizational heritage' and 'classical traditions'. In the Indian context, this often excludes non-Hindu and non-Brahminical lineages. On the overlap between culture and religion in the discourse of Indian nationalism, see Ahmed (2000). I am grateful to the reviewer for highlighting the need to acknowledge this.

rhetoric and contentions as were questions of faith and religiosity. To understand the history of Hindu nationalism in this early formative phase, it becomes crucial to examine how notions of race and religion 'co-constituted' this history, as well as how sustenance for these conflicts were drawn from practices of science (physical anthropology and statistics), just as from governmental administrative technologies (e.g., census and ethnographic surveys).

There have been attempts to read race into Hindu communalism; but in such accounts the understanding of race has been rhetorical (Baber 2004)—tracing the evocation of the term itself by Hindu nationalists without accounting for the specificity of race—that is, the principle of biological determinism which precedes and trumps possibilities of discrimination (Chakrabarty 1995). Meanwhile, Jaffrelot (1995) argues that although Hindu nationalists drew from the European science of racism, they could not reconcile the politics of *exclusion* with the traditional Indian politics of *domination*, that is, the caste system. However, although the European racism of extermination was replaced by domination in the Indian context, biological racism continued to be operative and was formative of the Hindu nationalist discourse.

Hindus and Muslims were relevant identities in the pre-colonial world but were always striated by conjoined identities of caste, linguistic communities and class. The national censuses and the reformist movements which aimed at people across class boundaries produced the Hindu or the Muslim identity in terms of the 'imagined community', where the close-knit boundary of the neighbourhood was transcended to enable identities across regions, class, caste and languages (Anderson 1991). But in this transformation, it was not just religious faith that served as the basis of the imagined homogeneity of Hindu (or Muslim or Christian) community. The possibility—even if not a definite affirmation—of racial homogeneity within these communities increasingly earned a central place among advocates of Hindu nationalism (Viswanathan 1998). Thus the 'Hindu', as it came to refer increasingly to a religious and faith-based community (i.e. across class, caste and languages) in the early 20th century simultaneously came to signal a racial or biological congruity.

RACE IN 'RELIGIOUS' DIFFERENCE

Unlike religion, which is unequivocally understood as a 'social' product and where the focus is on the question of whether it can be considered a historical or a modern construct,[2] the contention regarding race has to do with the question of its 'natural' basis or a (purported) reality in nature.[3] Although scholarship on modern race and racism locates its origin in the late 18th–early 19th centuries, the assumption remains, even if implicit, that there is some correspondence of the broad categories of racial types (which remain actually quite consistent through the 19th century from Johann Friedrich Blumenbach to Paul Topinard in France and Herbert Risley in India), with those in 'nature'. Thus, despite the decline of popularity of race science from the 1920s (Barkan 2003; Stepan 1982), the biologism of race continued to remain unchallenged in several quarters—for instance, in physical anthropology which continued to flourish in postcolonial India (Mukharji 2015).

In the 1920s colonial India, race had a significant presence not just among the colonial administrators with regard to their surveys and policies for the colonized, but also, even if with varying connotations and implications, among the different communities in India. In such public perception, the racial connotation—in contrast to religiosity—was the aspect of both biological origin and physical prowess as an inherent character of a community. There certainly were techniques and knowledge of difference between the self and other in the pre-modern world (some of which might even have used the term 'race'), but the modern notion of race was novel due to the 'fact that 'science', the body of knowledge rationally derived from empirical observation, then supported the proposition that race was one of the principal determinants of attitudes, endowments, capabilities and inherent tendencies among human beings' (Curtin 1965, 29). The understanding of race in terms of racial difference and racial affinity in these public debates on sectarian

---

[2] As one of the initial proponents of this debate, see Smith (1978).

[3] Here 'race' refers to 'a new context for the study of man' that emerged within 'the modern, biological and human sciences' in the early 19th century (Stepan 1982, x).

rivalry, comparison and conflict drew on the knowledge produced in the anthropological and biological sciences (Bates 1995). Regardless of the veracity quotient of these 'sciences', what is significant is the recurrence of such an understanding of race in these sectarian debates; and this comes through when a seemingly faith-based community (e.g., 'Muslims') is essentialized through certain 'inherent' and 'hereditary' physical and physiological characteristics. This imperative of race, along with ideas of religiosity and the politics of enumeration, constituted Hindu nationalism in India. Therefore, despite the consensus on discarding race and race science, we still need to account for the remnants of such an understanding of race—because it continued to be used and deployed to understand the 'other'; critiquing the colonial project of racializing Indians cannot imply we ignore how such understandings became popular among—at the least—the Hindu upper castes.

In the Indian subcontinent, scholars have understood 'race' to be the *modus operandi* for 'the rule of colonial difference' (Chatterjee 1993). Produced within scientific theories, the notion of racial difference was deployed as a political trope for the colonizers to govern the subject population—through medical science, biological science, sanitation measures—as well as to regulate the boundaries of their own imperial privilege (Sinha 1995; Stoler 2002). The only attention 'racial difference' receives as a principle of hierarchy 'within' the colonized population is in the discourse of caste; especially, with regard to how the imperial administration restructured it from 'fuzzy' to a more rigid, enumerated structure (Dirks 2001; Kaviraj 1992). Caste and religion became the 'sociological keys to the understanding of Indian people' (Cohn 1987, 242) and the essentialized principle through which all knowledge and practices of Indians were thereafter distilled and comprehended (Dirks 2001). Herbert Risley (1891), who was the most important advocate of anthropometry and race science in India and conducted the ethnographic survey of Bengal, suggested that race was the organizing basis of caste hierarchy. He applied the European science of anthropometry for the first time in the subcontinent to classify the Indian population (1908). Although some of the other administrators challenged Risley's racial theory of caste, 'it should not therefore be forgotten that the [colonial discourse on castes and tribes] was situated in a political order in which concepts of race were habitually used quite instrumentally' (Bates 1995, 30). In fact, for many of the colonial ethnographers, 'the new, progressive and scientifically verifiable insights of race theory outweighed or at least sharply modified notions of 'caste' as a fundamental fact of Indian history or Indian social organisation' (Bayly 1995, 170). Colonial epistemology and governance thus rigidified caste hierarchies along the lines of racial hierarchy (Bandyopadhyay 1985) where race served as a lens through which the imperial regime could comprehend, classify and govern the subject population (Fuller 2017). But how did race and the implications of racial difference figure in the discourses generated by Indians themselves? How was race used as a parameter to understand a community's predicament vis-à-vis not only the colonizer but other communities that ranked closer to one's own and yet had to be perceived as an unassimilable other? The public debates on Hindu nationalism, as we see in Upendra Nath Mukerji and Jatindra Mohan Datta's work, was one such discursive site where race featured as a constitutive factor.

In the late 19th century, the formulation of the dichotomy of the 'manly Englishman' and the 'effeminate Bengali' was in order to maintain the colonizers' racial privileges (Sinha 1995). The same 'scientific' reasoning from European and Anglo-Indian race science structured the Hindu ideas of racial difference from the Muslims; however, it was not a simple reversal of the hierarchical structure, where Hindu nationalists would claim their racial superiority over Muslims. Instead, knowledge about race as a biological and hereditary feature was used to construct a discourse on why the Hindus were on the decline physically and physiologically, why their population was dwindling and thus why they were degrading 'in their own land' whereas the Muslim as a racial, religious outsider was flourishing (Mukerji 1909).[4] The charge of effeminacy served a double purpose for the Hindu; owing to the Muslim's sexuality, virility and physical strength, this other became at once a model for emulation and an object of contempt. Thus, the attempt to understand the declining condition and 'religious-mindedness' of the Hindu was necessarily embroiled with the question of the

---

[4] Such a reading of the Hindu nationalist discourse also serves the purpose of moving beyond, as Banerjee-Dube suggests, 'a clear separation between the 'colonizer' and the 'colonized' (2015: 141).

community's biological and physiological condition (Datta 1946a). Although the Indian writers, statisticians and anthropologists hardly advocated racism per se, the preoccupation with the racial origin of the non-Hindu communities or the Hindu's degenerating reproductive and mortality rate over the decades, foregrounded the racial-qua-biological basis of Hindu nationalism.

THE DYING HINDU RACE

The colonial practice of decennial census was a major source of ideas about Hindu identity as distinct from and threatened by the non-Hindu (Bandyopadhyay 1992; Datta 1999; Jones 1981). The published censuses reported the statistical data as well as provided descriptions of the 'caste system, the religions of India, fertility and morbidity, domestic organization, and the economic structure of India' (Cohn 1996, 8). Based on the 'slower growth rates of Hindus', the Census Commissioner, C. J. O'Donnell calculated 'the number of years for Hindus to disappear altogether' (Datta 1999, 24). This thesis—which became the basis for Mukerji's book—continued to be harped on and circulated in the public domain. Herbert Risley evoked this idea again around the 1901 census operation (Datta 1999). The next major public discourse about comparative demographics between Hindus and Muslims erupted with the partition of Bengal in 1905. The dominant population in the new province of Eastern Bengal and Assam turned out to be the Muslims, much to the Bengali Hindus' despair and anxiety (Bandyopadhyay 2015). Mukerji's thesis of the Hindus as a 'dying race' and the discussions it generated can be read against this background; it was conditioned by anxiety around demographics and its socio-political implications for the communities. However, only a preoccupation with demographics originating in the colonial census certainly cannot explain the racialization of 'religious' differences. Race was not used in these debates as merely a rhetorical device—which could be interchangeable with religion or community or nation—or as an additive factor to simply entrench the 'already' given differences between Hindus and Muslims. Rather, notions of racial and religious differences equally constituted the discourse of Hindu nationalism. And, when the purpose of enumerative reasoning shifted radically with the rise in representational politics, the obsession with racial difference altered but did not dissipate.

Mukerji's *A Dying Race* contains articles that were initially published in the newspaper *The Bengalee* (founded in 1862, Calcutta) indicating a wider circulation than a single monograph might accrue.[5] His treatise comprises numerical figures, percentages and demographics, accompanied by passionate and anxious laments over—what he conceives as—the 'dramatically' increasing numbers of 'Mahomedans' and the rapidly declining numbers of Hindus. After several citations from the decennial censuses between 1872 and 1901, he remarks: 'The question that strikes one is, why two communities, living side by side, practically under the same conditions, should show such disparity in their respective rates of growth' (1909, 2). He recalls that various groups across the world 'have dwindled and finally disappeared from their own country' and concludes that a similar thing was happening to the Bengali Hindus 'in their own land' (1909, 2). Given these historical instances, he finds that Bengali Hindus 'are also a decaying race' and that, 'Year after year they [Bengali Hindus] are being pushed back, the land once occupied by them is taken up by the Mahomedans and their relative proportion to the population of the country is getting smaller and smaller' (1909, 4–5).

When Mukerji delves further into his sources (census reports, district reports, popular publications and ethnographic observations) for the major causes of increase in the Muslim population, he comes across a reality over-determined by poverty and caste hierarchies for most Hindus. In several cases, lower caste Hindu widows are found to

---

[5] Moving the discussion away from figures like V. D. Savarkar and M. S. Golwalkar to U. N. Mukerji and Jatindra Mohan Datta challenges the exclusive focus on the *institutional* historiography (from RSS and Hindu Mahasabha to the contemporary Bharatiya Janata Party) of Hindu nationalism. The ideas that would engender and sustain Hindu nationalism were not restricted to the political institutions and discourses but significantly shaped the 'secular' popular as well.

'desire' Muslim men. This idea can be traced back to the 19th-century Hindu reformers who advocated widow remarriage on the grounds of 'untrammeled sexuality' of Hindu widows (Datta 1999, 30). As Pradip K. Datta points out, Mukerji differs from the agenda of these reformist projects in so far as he relocates the object of reform from Hindu women to Hindu men (1999). Mukerji observes that Hindu widows remarry and convert to the Islamic faith to escape poverty and caste oppressions: 'She has no other alternative but to marry a Mahomedan, who is generally better off than a Hindu of the cultivating class, unless she takes to an immoral life' (1909, 7). After this discussion of caste restrictions and polygamy,[6] matters which could be said to relate directly to questions of faith and religious practices, he moves on to discuss the 'superior physique of the Mahomedans as compared with that of the Hindus'. He claims that, 'Very few Bengali Hindus work as porters. Their poor physique stands in the way. One can get a fair idea of the physique of the two communities by looking at the Mahomedan porter and the Hindu sweetmeat-seller on the Railway platform' (1909, 8).

Mukerji (1909, 11) explains this by turning an 'anthropological' eye towards his neighbours: 'a colony of Mahomedan duftries', who place higher value on health as their 'only asset', spend more on food than their Hindu counterparts; this, in turn, is possible only because land in Bengal now 'practically belongs to' the Muslim. Mukerji analyses the absence of Hindus in certain professions. Discussing in detail the history of one profession—carpentry—he remarks that most of the men working in this trade are Muslims. He notes that only Hindus from a certain caste take up carpentry. Although lower castes like Namasudras and Bagdis could enter the trade, as a matter of fact they tend not to. Moreover, the Muslims work for a lower wage than the Hindus. The latter—to their disadvantage—believe that they were better workers than their Muslim competitors and consequently demand higher wages. According to Mukerji, the Hindu assumption was not completely baseless, but he cautions that '[h]ereditary dexterity, if not an entire myth, has been greatly exaggerated' (1909, 19).

---

[6] Going against the stereotype, Mukerji in fact claims that polygamy is largely absent among Muslims in Bengal (1909: 8).

Describing the Hindu carpenters' quarters and their habits as almost inverse, Mukerji also comments on how deeply religious the Muslims are. 'Early in the morning and in the evening when they come back from their work, one can hear them reading their sacred books from almost every hut' (Mukerji 1909, 21). The Hindus have no religiosity, are regular drinkers and are illiterate. Besides, as a doctor, Mukerji also claims the advantage of seeing and being able to compare Hindu and Muslim physiologies who he treats as outpatients in a dispensary. By the time they are 30, Hindus seem to become 'a physical wreck', clearly owing to their illiteracy, and eating and drinking habits. Here, Mukerji connects the physiological to the religious. He attributes the systematic physiological degradation of the Hindus to their addiction to drugs and drinking. This habit, in turn, is seen to sprout and spread among Hindus, given their lack of religious rigor. In contrast, Muslims, irrespective of their social class, are members of religious congregations where religious and moral teachings are regularly imparted, resulting in their thriving physical health (Mukerji 1909, 70). For Mukerji 'the chauvinistic anxiety produced by a declining proportion of Bengalis, is relocated in the Muslim' (Datta 1999, 31), through the use of religious and biological parameters.

It is the notion of the 'body' where the religious and the racial is arguably intertwined. As Sinha has demonstrated, 'enfeebling diet' of the (Hindu) Bengali was often cited in colonial discourses about the effeminacy of the Bengali men. Although she does not bring the racial aspect of 'religious' communities to bear on this discourse of diet, effeminacy and 'degeneration of contemporary Indians' (Sinha 1995, 20–21), it can be suggested, building on this argument, that this concept of effeminacy was to some extent not only internalized by the Hindus vis-à-vis the colonizer, but also to a large extent mapped on to the discourse of racial difference vis-à-vis the Muslims. Physical habits of working, eating or drinking—stemming from religious prescriptions—were considered to have direct effect on the physiological and biological constitution of the individuals of a community. The biology of the individuals of a community, in turn, was mapped on to an imagined—in the sense of calculated—body of a ('religious') collective. The condition of this collective biological body could then be referred to in terms of demographics and reproductive rates, birth rates and mortality rates. These terms of measurement pervade the nationalism debates in the 1920–1930s. The focus on diet and physiology transforms the simplistic politics of numbers into a question of racial difference. Whereas the calculation of representational politics based on the numbers in a community is about the present, the relation between rates (of reproduction, mortality and so on) and the assumptions of physiological health and physical prowess is based on heredity and biology. Here, the concern is not just with the current demographics of Hindus (and Muslims) but—significantly—with the reproductive (and other) 'rate' of the community. Measures of rate within a population group indicates 'phenomena that occur over a period of time, which have to be studied over a certain period of time; they are serial phenomena. The phenomena addressed by biopolitics are, essentially, aleatory events that occur within a population that exists over a period of time' (Foucault 2003, 246). 'Rate' then, given its very specific career in modern politics, exceeds the here-and-now concerns of representational politics and enters the domain of heredity and racial lineage. Inculcating 'good' eating habits, cultivating physical strength and physiological health of a community presumes a notion of a community that is biologically hereditary and not based strictly on questions of religious faith, which theoretically is subject to changes through conversion or renunciation.

Kishori Lal Sarkar published a monograph in response to Mukerji's thesis. Overall, Sarkar tends to agree with Mukherji on the question of the dying race but foregrounds malaria and poverty as the primary causes, implying a lack of nutrition which affected the physiology of the communities. More specifically, by readjusting certain enumerative moves and assumptions, Sarkar (1911, 2) demonstrates the 'decline of *both* the races' (emphasis added). But more significantly, Sarkar questions Mukerji's use of 'dying race' as a phrase itself—what does it mean for a race to be dying and therefore for a race to be living?

One is deeply disappointed in going through the essays of Lt Col Mukherjee, written with so much energy and earnestness, to find that amidst the long dissertations on Bagdis, Haris, coolies and agricultural labourers, there is hardly one word as regards the rapid decrease of the intellectual middle classes of both the Hindu and the Mahomedan communities … If the Hindu and Mahomedan middle class gentry disappear (the uppermost class is admitted to be disappearing) and only the *coolie* population and the agricultural labourers remain, will it be proper then to say that the race is existing? (Sarkar 1911, 11–12)

Instead of moving away from a racial imagination, this is a further entrenchment of the intertwinement of the biological basis of racial thinking with cultural and religious nationalism; Sarkar demonstrates a concern with not only the demographics of a 'race', but its intellectual and cultural quality that recalls for us the eugenic understanding of race—where breeding of desirable qualities/sections of the population group is emphasized over others—in the name of the enhancement of the race.[7]

THE CHANGING RACIAL IMPERATIVE

As mentioned above, Mukerji was a voice that stood out not for being exclusive but for being representative of the public political common sense[8] which drew simultaneously from racial theories of contemporary race science, enumerative practices like the census, and notions of religiosity to measure and compare communities. These derivations then became the grounds on which Hindu nationalism came to be formulated during the first half of the 20th century. A sense of continuity of the preoccupation with race is conveyed by Jatindra Mohan Datta—a Hindu Mahasabha member as well as a statistician and fellow at the Royal Statistical Society in London, who published extensively in the 1930s and 1940s in both English and Bangla. He wrote quite regularly for particularly the *Modern Review*—a widely circulating Calcutta periodical—founded in 1907 by Ramananda Chatterjee and popular among the English-educated Bengali-reading public. By the time Datta engaged with the question of Hindus, Muslims and their respective nationalisms, the political terrain had altered in at least one

---

[7] This is an illustration of Ahmed's (2000, 19) argument: "'Hindu culture" can only be the culture of caste Hindus'.

[8] Kishori Lal Sarkar (1911) and Sakharam Ganesh Deuskar (n.d.) published monographs in response to Mukerji's thesis. Several others also responded in the journal *Modern Review* (1911).

major way. The Morley–Minto Reforms had begun the process of granting separate electorates and seats in the legislative assembly for Muslims in 1909. The Government of India Act of 1919 and 1935 further strengthened 'communal' representation in governing bodies. British Prime Minister Ramsay Macdonald's Communal Award of 1932 offered proportionate representation to communities and further extended the provision of separate electorates to communities, besides the Muslims. This was replaced by the Poona Pact the same year (agreed to by B. R. Ambedkar and M. K. Gandhi) which removed the provision of separate electorates and retained reservation of seats for 'lower' castes in the electoral system. In this move towards self-government and the rise of representational politics, the significance of numbers for communities continued; although, unlike in the earlier decades, it was now crucial to establish the numerical strength of Hindus rather than their weakening or declining condition, in order for that to be translated into political leverage. 'Race' continued to be a primary factor for producing the Self and the Other in Hindu nationalism; but now it was more important to foreground the racial sameness of Indian Muslims rather than their 'alien-ness'. Thus, the renewed attempt in the public sectarian debates was to establish that Indian Muslims were Hindu converts and—assuming that religious conversion failed to affect racial change—the point was to consider Muslims as Hindus in so far as that made Muslims ineligible for separate political and legislative representation. Despite the extreme contrast in the way the role of demographics and enumeration altered, the preoccupation with the racial origin of Bengali Muslims persisted.

Datta (1931b) argued that 'an overwhelmingly large number' of contemporary Muslims were descendants of Hindu converts and that the 'foreign element in them is exceedingly small, and whatever foreign element there may be, it is diluted by repeated intermarriages with the native element in course of centuries'. Elsewhere, Datta construed Bengali Muslims as distinctly different from the Hindus in terms of 'public spirit', 'religious-mindedness', heroism, language, and on 'where their loyalties truly lie'; in this essay, in order to invalidate all political claims by the Muslims in India, especially Bengal, Datta chose to demonstrate that the

Bengali Muhammadan is not essentially different from the Bengali Hindus, either by race or by language. His claim to a separate recognition is untenable...His religion is but skin-deep; he has got no past and his past is not glorious. He tries to shine in the reflected glory of the Pathan or the Mughal conquerors, forgetting that it was his ancestors who were conquered; that it was his father who was oppressed and, perhaps, forcibly converted. His attempt belongs to the same plane of absurdity if the Santal Christian convert were to claim that his ancestors came with Clive and conquered Bengal on the glorious field of Plassey in 1757. (Datta 1931b)

Besides dismissing conversion in an off-hand gesture as unsubstantial, Datta rejects any biological basis of difference between the Muslims and the Hindus of Bengal. However, in doing that and in bringing together the Santal Christian and the Bengali low-caste Muslim, he unwittingly demonstrates the inevitability of the question (and the possibility) of racial difference of other communities vis-à-vis the dominant Hindus. In fact, the almost sudden introduction of Santal Christians to establish the 'absurdity' (besides perhaps underlining that Bengali Muslims shining 'in the reflected glory of the Pathan or the Mughals' is not so absurd by itself) of Bengali Muslims clearly states the greater value of racial over religious affiliation. Datta plays to his readers' sensibilities by making this unwarranted comparison; it is not difficult to surmise that he meant to invoke the stereotype figure of the 'tribal' Santals and the white European (the 'true' Christians) to drive home the absurdity of imagining that the two share the same lineage. In rendering the Other's religion as 'skin-deep', he implies that race—which is often mapped on to the skin—is deeper than that, in one's blood and physiology. Thus, religious conversion cannot override one's racial history. Keeping aside the fact that Datta did not think in these terms about Hinduism as a religion (it was definitely not just skin-deep), the question of race here is not important for what it reveals about the exact racial origin of the 'religious' community, but for what it foregrounds: an obsession with trying to ascertain origins and the consequent conclusions about a community's claims on religiosity and the nation.

A STYLE OF REASONING

A focus on the prevalent use of numbers in these public sectarian debates reveal how enumeration was not only a 'modality' (Cohn 1996) for colonial administrative purposes but was also a 'style of reasoning' (Hacking 1985), of deriving conclusions and constructing claims, within the arena of public politics. The prevalence of an enumerative form of public reasoning has been related to the rise of representational politics and the popularity of the colonial census (Appadurai 1993; Cohn 1987; Dirks 2001; Kaviraj 1992). Despite generating insightful arguments about how the colonial practice of census was more 'productive' of identities and not merely documenting what was already on the ground, what is missed is how Hindu nationalists came to mobilize enumerative evidence, so abundantly and credibly, in the service of political arguments, such as racial and religious difference.[9] Although the census was undoubtedly a major source of data for these public intellectuals, the enumerative common sense was not contained by it. In fact, this public form of reasoning was, at least partly, also informed by the simultaneously emerging discipline of statistics. These early-decade (Hindu) nationalist statisticians were invested in questions of racial and religious difference of communities.[10] Using statistical methods and anthropometric data, they attempted to establish measurable differences—in terms of racial origin, racial mix and purity, and degree of religiosity—between various non-Hindu communities. This rise in a statistical way of thinking to argue for political motives, produced a vocabulary of enumerable categories within the sectarian discourse.

Rates of reproduction, percentages of demographic change, numerical figures in public organizations, public welfare and education made up major portions of these debates. Therefore, absolute numbers of the various populations were less significant in these discussions, than the

---

[9] Appadurai (1993) demonstrates how numbers, not just the census, became an integral part of the colonial imagination; but he does not refer to the nationalists.

[10] A significant example is Prasanta Chandra Mahalanobis (1893–1972) who is considered the 'father' of Indian statistics. His work on anthropometry continued into the late 1940s and was published in a well-reputed academic journal *Sankhya* contrary to scholarly view. (Mukharji 2015)

logic of numerical thinking, which enabled these intellectuals to calculate qualitative group features, such as national loyalty and religiosity. For instance, Ramesh Chandra Banerjee (1934) argues that since the Muslims were demanding a share in Bengal's administrative structure, it was only justified that one compares the contribution of Hindus versus Muslims in various branches of public work. Banerjee compares endowments given to Calcutta University for disbursal to students in the form of scholarships, stipends and prizes. He notes that there are 266 endowments by Hindus and that 'some...are of very substantial value' (Banerjee 1934, 312), omitting to mention the exact amount. The Muslim endowments are five in number; he carefully differentiates that four of them total to a meagre ₹6,000 and merely footnotes that the other one alone amounts to ₹5,000. The numerical endeavour continues. In terms of the proportion of students who benefit from these endowments, he remarks that of the five Muslim endowments, three are 'such that Muslim students have the best chance of securing their advantages'—and stops short of qualifying it any further. For the Hindus, he states clearly that, out of the 266 endowments, 259 are open to all students, irrespective of caste and creed. Additionally, non-governmental schools opened by Christians are 30, by Muslims are 37 and by Hindus are 1,006. Since 'a community's claim to superior Govermental [sic] powers can only be justified by its superiority in the field of public service', Banerjee concludes that the Hindus have a greater numerical percentage of 'public spirit' than the Muslims, thus, debunking the Muslim demand for a greater role in the administration (Banerjee 1934).

Jatindra Mohan Datta writes about religious favouritism in Bengal administration. He states, 'In the Bengal Legislative Council, out of a total of 140 seats, thirty-nine are occupied by members returned by the Muhammadans on a communal basis' (Datta 1931a). To refute the legitimacy of the Muslim demand for reservation of legislative seats, Datta decides to bring to light the already existing Muslim-bias, not just in the main administrative bodies, but in the 'by-ways of administration'. He turns to the estates in Bengal that are managed by the Court of Wards. He claims that in the case of the five Dacca Nawab family estates (which are understood to be Muslim-owned), the government charges 1.25 per cent of the gross income for its supervision. For the

Bhawal estate, which is Hindu, the rate charged is 1.75 per cent of the gross income (Datta 1931a). Datta also compares the proportion of Hindus and Muslims who had received the Victoria Cross, awarded to Indian soldiers by the British empire for bravery. Comparing these figures against the total population of each community respectively, he concluded that 'the Hindus are *twice* more ready to defend India; they are *twice* more courageous and brave than the Muhammadans … the higher the level of heroism the lesser becomes the number of Muhammadans' (Datta 1946b).

Measurements of blood dilution and admixture of Muslim 'foreign' ancestry feature as part of several statistical and anthropological works. The question of Muslim racial origin—whether Indian Muslims were converts from the local Hindu population or were 'descendants of those who originally came from Arab lands'—had provoked specula- tion among the British and evoked responses from some Muslims since the first national censuses (Viswanathan 1998, 156). The British soon settled this question in favour of conversion; as Viswanathan remarks, this definitely helped the British dismiss separatist claims of Muslims. However, there is a resurgence of the question of Muslim racial origin in significantly different terms, in the 1920s–1930s. No longer restricted to the domain of colonial administration, the questions of racial origin of Indian Muslims and the degree to which their blood had mixed and been diluted with 'local' Hindu lineage, are taken up by Indian anthropologists and statisticians. For renowned anthropologist Dhirendra Nath Majumdar (1947), the furthest extent to which racial admixture can take place is best represented through the serological data for the Indian Muslim population. Conversion would yield, according to the discipline's premise, same anthropometric measurements as the communities they live amongst or marry within. Admixture, mean- while, would yield serological and anthropometric results that exhibit lineages of the various races mixed. Communities with demonstrated admixture would not be able to claim racial purity or any biological distinction from other adjacent communities, but nor would they be considered part of the dominant race with which the admixture took place. The theory of racial fusion thus keeps at bay the danger of racial purity turning into the logic of racial superiority, but, at the same time, it makes it possible through the science of anthropometry and serology (and genetics later on) to trace the varied lineages and to 'reveal' foreign elements in such races.

Enumeration became central to the Hindu nationalism discourse, and going beyond the framework of comparative demographics, produced a normative vocabulary that could rationalize and mobilize the Hindu anxiety of decline as statistical and scientific. The enumerative mode of operating was certainly not exclusive to the discourse of Hindu nationalism; however, in discussions of religiosity and racial difference—which constituted the discourse of Hindu nationalism—the logic of numerical reasoning lent objectivity and organization.[11] Further, instead of using data directly from existing administrative records, these public figures were inventive in their use and analysis of numerical figures—and even went so far as to rewrite familiar categories as numerical, comparable and therefore 'objective'. The statistical language, in the form of proportions and rates were applied to a wide range of 'objects': from the degree of blood admixture to 'religious-mindedness' and 'public-spirit'. For the first time perhaps, heroism, religiosity and loyalty became numerically measurable and comparable categories used to hierarchize communities. Moreover, this practice of perceiving the social through the statistical made religious difference and racial difference interchangeable registers of identification. By racializing religious difference, it became possible to statistically construct the 'Other' as incompatible with the hegemonic (Hindu) community.

CONCLUSION

In the context of the 20th-century public debates among Hindu nationalists, one could say then that religious distinctions 'hide the most persistent remnants of a history of racism' (Anidjar 2008, 20). The attempt here has been to re-examine the relation of religion and race, in the specific context of Hindu nationalism. By focusing on how

---

[11] In European historiography, the simultaneous rise of race science and statistics has been extensively explored; for example, see Hacking (1990) and Desrosières (1998). In the Indian context, this conjunction has not been adequately engaged with; as exception, see Mukharji (2015).

general claims and notions from race science—in terms of biological categories and physiological conditions of communities—permeated communal politics, I have suggested that the history of Hindu nationalism is constituted as much by ideas of racial as by religious differences. Although scholars have studied race as used by religious nationalists, the relation between race and religion has remained historically and conceptually separated. In most instances, the claim has been that religious propagandists have 'used' race to further their religious nationalist agendas. Instead, religious identity and racial difference, far from being operative on separate registers, were in fact produced in conjunction, such that the implications of being Hindu and Muslim were as much about faith and ritual, as about biology and heredity. Although passion and anxiety informed the public tone of these debates, more important was the scientific and statistical basis on which the claims of religiosity and racial difference were forged. Numbers were not mere embellishments on an otherwise ready argument; but through the very technique of calculating percentages, statistical correlation and derivations, the argument about differences of race and religiosity came to be constructed as 'objective'. Drawing from the logic and content of race science and enumerative technique from statistics, Hindu nationalists did not merely construct a Hindu version of racism; they reconfigured Hindu nationalism itself through the triangulation of race, religion and enumeration. In this triangulation, we can read not only what historical specificities constituted the so-called 'religious nationalism', but also what the concept of *religious* nationalism entailed, foregrounded and at the same time obfuscated.

REFERENCES

Ahmed, Aijaz. 2000. *Nationalism and Globalization.* Occasional Paper Series 4, Department of Sociology, Pune.

Ahmed, Rafiuddin. 1981. *The Bengal Muslims, 1871–1906: A Quest for Identity.* New York, NY: Oxford University Press.

Anderson, Benedict R. (1983) 1991. *Imagined Communities: Reflections on the Origin and Spread of Nationalism.* London: Verso.

Anidjar, Gil. 2008. *Semites: Race, Religion, Literature.* Palo Alto, CA: Stanford University Press.

Appadurai, Arjun. 1993. 'Number in the Colonial Imagination'. In *Orientalism and the Postcolonial Predicament*, edited by Carol Breckenridge and Peter Veer, 314–340. Philadelphia, PA: University of Pennsylvania.

Baber, Zaheer. 2004. "'Race', Religion and Riots: The 'Racialization' of Communal Identity and Conflict in India'. *Sociology* 38 (4): 701–718.

Bandyopadhyay, Sekhar. 1985. 'The Raj, Risley and the Tribes and Castes of Bengal'. *India Past and Present* 2 (1): 41–52.

———. 1992. 'Construction of Social Categories: The Role of Colonial Census'. In *Ethnicity, Caste and People*, edited by K. S. Singh, 26–36. Delhi: Manohar.

———. 2015. *From Plassey to Partition and After: A History of Modern India*. New Delhi: Orient Blackswan.

Banerjee, Ramesh Chandra. 1934. 'Hindu and Muslim Public Spirit in Bengal'. *Modern Review* 55 (1–6): 312–316.

Banerjee-Dube, Ishita. 2015. *A History of Modern India*. Delhi: Cambridge University Press.

Barkan, Elazar. 2003. 'Race and The Social Sciences'. In *The Cambridge History of Science*, edited by Theodore Porter and Dorothy Ross, 693–707. Cambridge, UK: Cambridge University Press.

Bates, Crispin. 1995. 'Race, Caste and Tribe in Central India: The Early Origins of Indian Anthropometry.' In *The Concept of Race in South Asia*, edited by P. Robb, 219–259. Delhi: Oxford University Press.

Bayly, Susan. 1995. 'Caste and 'Race' in the Colonial Ethnography of India.' In *The Concept of Race in South Asia*, edited by Peter Robb, 165–218. Delhi: Oxford University Press.

Chakrabarty, Dipesh. 1995. 'Modernity and Ethnicity in India: A History for the Present'. *Economic and Political Weekly* 30 (52): 3373–3380.

Chatterjee, Partha. 1993. *The Nation and Its Fragments: Colonial and Postcolonial Histories*. Princeton, NJ: Princeton University Press.

Cohn, Bernard, ed. 1987. 'The Census, Social Structure and Objectification'. In *An Anthropologist among the Historians and Other Essays*, 224–254. Delhi: Oxford University Press.

———. 1996. *Colonialism and Its Forms of Knowledge: The British in India*. Princeton, NJ: Princeton University Press.

Curtin, Philip D. 1965. *The Image of Africa: British Ideas and Action, 1780–1850*. London: Macmillan.

Datta, Jatindra Mohan. 1931a. 'Communalism in the Bengal Administration'. *Modern Review* 49 (1): 45–49.

———. 1931b. 'Who the Bengali Mohammedans Are?' *Modern Review* 49 (3): 303–309.

———. 1946a. 'An Analysis of the 'Religious-Mindedness' among the Hindus'. *Modern Review* 79 (1–6): 365–367.

———. 1946b. 'Relative Heroism of the Hindus and the Muhammadans of India'. *Modern Review* 79 (1–6): 463–464.

Datta, Pradip K. 1999. *Carving Blocs: Communal Ideology in Early Twentieth-century Bengal.* New York, NY: Oxford University Press.

Desrosières, Alain. 1998. *The Politics of Large Numbers: A History of Statistical Reasoning.* Massachusetts: Harvard University Press.

Dirks, Nicholas B. 2001. *Castes of Mind: Colonialism and Making of Modern India.* Princeton, NJ: Princeton University Press.

Foucault, Michel. 2003. *Society Must Be Defended: Lectures at the Collège de France, 1975–1976.* New York, NY: Picador.

Friedland, Roger. 2002. 'Money, Sex, and God: The Erotic Logic of Religious Nationalism'. *Sociological Theory* 20 (3): 381–425.

Fuller, C. J. 2017. 'Ethnographic Inquiry in Colonial India: Herbert Risley, William Crooke, and the Study of Tribes and Castes'. *Journal of the Royal Anthropological Institute* 23 (3): 603–621.

Gellner, Ernest. 2006. *Nations and Nationalism.* Malden, MA: Blackwell Pub.

Hacking, Ian. 1985. 'Styles of Reasoning'. In *Postanalytic Philosophy,* edited by J. Rajchman and C. West, 145–164. New York, NY: Columbia University Press.

———. 1990. *The Taming of Chance.* New York, NY: Cambridge University Press.

Hobsbawm, E. J. 1990. *Nations and Nationalism Since 1780: Programme, Myth, Reality.* New York, NY: Cambridge University Press.

Jaffrelot, C. 1995. 'The Ideas of the Hindu Race in the Writings of Hindu Nationalist Ideologues in the 1920s and 1930s'. In *The Concept of Race in South Asia,* edited by Peter Robb, 327–354. Delhi: Oxford University Press.

Jones, Kenneth W. 1981. 'Religious Identity and the Indian Census'. In *The Census in British India: New Perspectives,* edited by G. Barrier, 73–102. Delhi: Manohar.

Kaviraj, Sudipta. 1992. 'The Imaginary Institution of India'. In *Subaltern Studies: Writings on South Asian History and Society VII,* edited by Partha Chatterjee and Gyanendra Pandey. Delhi; New York, NY: Oxford University Press.

Majumdar, Dhirendra N. 1947. *Racial Problems in Asia.* New Delhi: Indian Council of World Affairs.

Mukerji, Upendra Nath. 1909. *A Dying Race.* Calcutta: Mukerjee and Sons.

Mukharji, Projit. 2015. 'Profiling the Profiloscope: Facialization of Race Technologies and the Rise of Biometric Nationalism in Inter-war British India'. *History and Technology* 31 (4): 376–396.

Pandey, Gyanendra. 1990. *The Construction of Communalism in Colonial North India.* New York, NY: Oxford University Press.

Risley, Herbert H. 1891. *The Tribes and Castes of Bengal.* Calcutta: Government Press.

———. 1908. *The Peoples of India.* London: W. Thacker & Co.

Sarkar, Kishori Lal. 1911. '*A Dying Race' How Dying?* Calcutta: Lakshmi Printing Works.

Shraddhananda, Sanyasi. 1926. *Hindu Sangathan: Saviour of the Dying Race.* Delhi: Arjun Press.

Sinha, Mrinalini. 1995. *Colonial Masculinity: The 'Manly Englishman' and the 'Effeminate Bengali' in the Late Nineteenth Century*. Manchester and New York, NY: Manchester University Press.

Smith, Wilfred Cantwell. 1978. *The Meaning and End of Religion*. New York, NY: Harper & Row.

Stepan, Nancy. 1982. *The Idea of Race in Science: Great Britain, 1800–1960*. Hamden, CT: Archon Books.

Stoler, Ann. 2002. *Carnal Knowledge and Imperial Power: Race and the Intimate in Colonial Rule*. Berkeley, CA: University of California Press.

Varshney, Ashutosh. 1993. 'Contested Meanings: India's National Identity, Hindu Nationalism, and the Politics of Anxiety'. *Daedalus* 122 (3): 227–261.

Veer, Peter van der. 1994. *Religious Nationalism: Hindus and Muslims in India*. Berkeley, CA: University of California.

Viswanathan, Gauri. 1998. *Outside the Fold: Conversion, Modernity, and Belief*. Princeton, NJ: Princeton University Press.

Chapter 5

Temple Construction and the Coming of a Nation
The Birla Mandir in Delhi

Anne Hartig

A few months into India's independence/partition, Ghanshyam Das Birla (1894–1983), a driving force and financial backbone of the Indian nationalist movement, agreed to give an interview to Margaret Bourke-White (1904–1971).[1] The American photojournalist, who covered this significant period of modern history for the *Life* magazine, was clearly thrilled to speak to one of India's most affluent and influential business-men. Ghanshyam Das (also known as GD) and his family not only had strong ties with Mohandas Karamchand Gandhi (1869–1948) and other leading figures but also were involved in a large and varied number of enterprises and philanthropic endeavours.[2] The most visible was (and

---

[1] Much has been written about Ghanshyam Das Birla and his family. For a general overview, see Kudaisya (2006). The interview between GD and the American journalist can be found in Bourke-White's *Halfway to Freedom* (1950).

[2] The family promoted the development of education. For instance, they supported the foundation of the Benares Hindu University and, on Gandhi's request, Aligarh Muslim University. They also established institutions, such as planetariums, museums and hospitals, in different parts of India, and were involved with mass media, such as newspapers (*Hindustan Times*) and publishing (Gita Press).

continues to be) the patronage of impressive temples dedicated to different deities throughout the country.[3] Among other things, such as his friendship with Gandhi, GD also briefly spoke with Bourke-White about the family's patronage of temples, emphasizing: 'Frankly speaking ... we build temples but we don't believe in temples' (quoted in Bourke-White 1950, 71). He explained that the temples were built 'to spread a kind of religious mentality' (quoted in Bourke-White 1950, 71). How can we understand the patronage of temples if not in terms of piety? What does 'religious mentality' serve as a proxy for? In this chapter, I argue, that the temple building project undertaken by the Birla family was contributing to the political project of nation building. Being the first massive temple patronized by the family, my focus is on the Lakshminarayan/Birla Mandir in Delhi. Inaugurated in 1939, it is not only the first of many impressive Birla temples but also an important example of the (Hindu) temple in the modern period. Addressing modern desires, it outlines the departure of the temple from historical temple architecture. I intend to annotate the contours of this temple-building project in the course of this chapter, arguing that the temple stood as a crucial site for the articulation of a discourse on national identity that was bound with religious identity.

The 19th-century concept of the nation-state, according to which the people of the nation are conscious of and share a common identity and culture (ethnicity and language), became a defining political and social force leading to the foundation of various modern states in Europe and elsewhere.[4] This idea also found cache among some sections of the Indian populace. Primarily upper caste (Hindu) elites and political leaders perceived the fragmentation and diversity of the Indian people as a central problem—if *united* they would have the power to reclaim 'their' land and establish an independent modern Indian state,

---

[3] Birla temples share the same fate as most other modern temples, attracting a lot of popular but little scholarly attention.

[4] Important publications on the development of nationalism in India include Jaffrelot (1999), Bapu (2013), Bhatt (2001), Chatterjee (1999), Gould (2004), Hansen (1999), Rajagopal (2001) and Markovits (1985). Jones (2006), Van der Veer (1994) and Zavos (2000) focus particularly on the role of religion and religious organizations within this context.

not unlike the European model (Bapu 2013; Jaffrelot 1999; Markovits 1985). However, due to the ethnic, racial and linguistic diversity, they struggled to identify a common bond that could encompass this diversity, or, in other words, generate a sense of community among the people. It is against this backdrop that religious belief and affiliation were established as a distinctive and central marker of belonging (Jaffrelot 1999; Van der Veer 1994; Zavos 2000). Concomitantly, the very idea or definition of religious adherence was expanded. For instance, marginalized groups, such as the Untouchables (Dalits), were gradually absorbed into the larger Hindu fold; other religious beliefs of the continent, such as those of Buddhists, Sikhs and Jains were also enfolded in this new definition.[5] If religious identity and its functions were changing, religious architecture had to reflect these new movements. In this vein, this chapter focuses on the Lakshminarayan/ Birla Mandir, pointing to its central role in this shift.[6] It outlines the circumstances leading to the temple's construction, charting the rise of the (Hindu) nationalist movement, which (re)defined 'Hindu' and coupled it to 'India'. Accordingly, it reads the Lakshminarayan/Birla Mandir in this context of the coming of a new nation, as well as the reconfiguration of a capital city.

In 1911, the colonial government decided to shift the imperial capital to Delhi, trying to escape violent demonstrations of nationalist sentiments in Calcutta, giving new importance to Delhi.[7] However, in Delhi too emotions were running high (Gupta 1981; Hosagrahar 2005; Jones 1986). According to Jones, the increase of religious controversy and communal riots prompted organizations, such as the Bharat Dharam Mahamandal, the Sanatan Dharm Sabha and the Hindu

---

[5] For instance, in reaction to the Khilafat movement, Vinayak Damodar Savarkar established a framework closely associated with that of the (ethnic/racial) nation. He claimed that Sikhs, Jains, Buddhists and other 'Indic' groups share the same racial and cultural roots and must thus be considered one nation (Savarkar 1969).

[6] For more details, see Hartig (2017).

[7] The making of New Delhi has constantly attracted scholarly attention. Nilsson (1973), Irving (1981) and Metcalf (1989) are foundational publications in this regard. Later, important studies include Hosagrahar (2005), Legg (2007) and Guerrieri (2018).

Mahasabha, to set up quarters in the city (Jones 1986). Delhi's population was nearly equally divided between the Hindus and Muslims, the former exceeding slightly (Blake 2002; Gupta 1981). The significance of building a temple in Delhi has to be understood in this complex constellation. For the agents of Hindu nationalism, who claimed that the Indian subcontinent is essentially marked by Hindu culture and history, Delhi was a sore point—although commonly associated with Yudhishthira's splendid capital Indraprastha—described in the Mahabharata, Delhi played no particularly important role in Hindu imagination and sacred geography, which reflected also in its lack of a major *tirtha* (sacred place, site, temple and so on; Jones 1986; Rajagopalan 2010; Talbot 2016; Taneja 2008). This absence stood out in great relief against the abundance of Islamic architecture. On the eve of the construction of the new imperial capital, the Archaeological Survey of India prepared the *List of Muhammadan and Hindu Monuments* (Sanderson 1916–1922).[8] This document listed around 200 mosques only within the walled city against a total of less than 100 temples in and around Delhi. These pre-modern temples were seldom situated on main roads and had altogether low visibility in the urban-scape.[9] Further, their design blended with that of the surrounding buildings, having greater resemblance with Mughal buildings than with historical temples. Some temples, such as the Ladliji Mandir and the Chitragupta Mandir (Figure 5.1), closely resembled the *diwan-i aam* of Mughal emperors. Also, the Shivalayas (Figure 5.2), scattered over the city, featured architectural elements and designs, such as slender-tapered columns, lobed arches and a bulbous dome, which immediately recalled the small pavilions of Mughal palaces and gardens. Delhi's Muslim-dominated architecture-scape contrasted the Hindu nationalists' narrative of India as Hindu Rashtra (Hindu nation). If the construction of temples generally takes place at religiously significant sites, the construction of a massive Hindu temple in Delhi

---

[8] The report was particularly critical as it was meant to be used to plan the construction of New Delhi and to avoid the demolition of any structure of historical or religious value.

[9] This section draws from Asher (2000, 2003), as well as from my own research.

Figure 5.1 *View of the Chitragupta Mandir in Paharganj, Delhi*
Source: Author.

Figure 5.2 *A Small Shivalaya in Katra Neel, Old Delhi*
Source: Author.

was clearly politically motivated, intended to transform Delhi into a Hindu capital (Jones 1986; Rajagopalan 2010; Talbot 2016; Taneja 2008). Supplanting this material and living past the Lakshminarayan/ Birla Mandir draws upon a mythical origin—installed at the gate of the temple's park is a plaque showing Yudhishthira laying the foundation of Delhi.

But the extant Islamic architecture was nonetheless instructive for Hindu nationalists. They scrutinized Islam and Christianity for means of generating and fostering a sense of community and noted the pivotal role played by mosques and churches (Davis 2015). Balakrishna Shivram Moonje (1872–1948), a Brahmin from Nagpur, who later became the president of the Hindu Mahasabha and founding member of the Hindu nationalist, organization Rashtriya Swayamsevak Sangh, for instance, identified the mosque as a place where Muslims could strengthen their sense of community (Jaffrelot 1999). Moonje was not the only one at the time imagining the Hindu temple doing the same for Hindus. In his influential book *Hindu Sangathan: Saviour of the Dying Race* (1926), the leading Arya Samajist Swami Shraddhananda (1856–1926) argued on similar lines (Jaffrelot 1999). According to Shraddhananda, the reluctance among Hindus to 'unite' derived from the lack of a common meeting place. Like Moonje, he compared the situation of the Hindus to that of the Muslims and their places of worship—specifically the 17th-century Jama Masjid (which was said to be the largest mosque in Asia at the time of its construction) and the Fatehpuri Masjid, both in Delhi, stressing that these mosques were built to accommodate several thousands of Muslims. Delhi's temples, however, could accommodate but a fraction of these numbers. As the photograph, taken inside the Yogmaya Mandir (Figure 5.3), exemplifies, there was space for just around a dozen devotees in the city's historic temples. It is in this complex context that several agents of Hindu nationalism reviewed the possibilities of constructing a massive Hindu temple and large congregational space in the imperial capital city.

Finally, the Benares Hindu University's founder and member of the Imperial Legislative Council, the nationalist, Madan Mohan Malaviya (1861–1946) persuaded the British government to permit the

Figure 5.3 *Aarti inside the Small Garbhagraha (Sanctum) of the Pre-modern Yogmaya Mandir in Mehrauli, Delhi*
Source: Author.

construction of the Lakshminarayan/Birla Mandir (Chaturvedi 1982).[10] However, the land allotted by the government had its drawbacks. It was situated at the fringes of New Delhi, not in its centre, reflecting the colonial administration's hierarchies.[11] In the past, only royal/elite figures would have had the resources to carry out such an ambitious project. In the 19th and 20th centuries, increasingly, temple construction costs were borne by those who had gained from colonialism—indigenous trading and banking communities.[12] In the case of the Lakshminarayan/Birla Mandir (Figure 5.4), it was the affluent Birla family who almost single-handedly sponsored the construction of this pet project of Hindu nationalists.

---

[10] On 26 March 1933, Malaviya and Maharaja of Dholpur, Udaybhanu Singh, laid the temple's foundation stone.

[11] New Delhi was organized according to the then existing sociopolitical hierarchy, with the Viceroy's House raised on the top of a hill in its centre.

[12] For more details on temple patronage in the 19th century, see Bayly (1973), Hardy (2007) and Michell (2015).

Figure 5.4 *View of Delhi's Lakshminarayan/Birla Mandir, from Mandir Marg (Earlier Reading Road)*
Source: Author.

Considering what was at stake with the construction of this temple, its patrons must have pondered extensively how to present themselves in stone. Eventually, they commissioned Sris Chandra Chatterjee (1873–1966), a forward-looking architect and urban planner responsive to nationalist ideology.[13] While some of his contemporaries tried to induce a sense of community among India's diverse population through religion and language, Chatterjee identified architecture as central means in this direction. The Calcutta-based architect, who was also a devoted follower of Gandhi and supporter of the Congress Party, was keen to create a new unique/national architectural idiom and identity for an independent and modern India. The Lakshminarayan/ Birla Mandir and other buildings, such as the Arya Dharm Sangha Dharamshala (1935) in Sarnath and the headquarters of the Hindu Mahasabha (1939), a stone's throw from the temple in Delhi, were part of a much larger vision—he hoped that his designs would eventually

---

[13] To date, the most comprehensive study on the architect is Gupta (1991).

be followed across the Indian subcontinent as a part of a vision of 'Indian national architecture', but this never materialized (Chatterjee 1942, 1949).

In keeping with the nationalist spirit of his time, Chatterjee took great pride in the art and culture of ancient India, understanding it as an essential part of Indian identity. Consequently, the vast vocabulary of pre-modern Indian art and architecture served as his inspiration. Chatterjee mentioned for instance that he intended the Lakshminarayan/Birla Mandir to feature a figure of Surya driving seven horses, sun-windows and four large carved wheels like those at the 13th-century Sun Temple at Konark.[14] Aiming for an 'All-India Hindu style of architecture', Chatterjee did not echo the style of a particular previous architectural era but attempted to combine, as he said, 'all Classical styles of ancient Indian architecture' (Chatterjee 1942, 84). He extracted forms and motifs, such as the *chaitya* arch/window, from their original context and synthesized them to what he refers to as 'neo-Indian style' (Chatterjee 1942, 84). In his effort to create an architecture suitable for modern India, Chatterjee not only experimented with design but also with different materials and techniques. Instead of building the Lakshminarayan/Birla Mandir of stone, as his forbearers would have done, Chatterjee utilized a large variety of materials, including, for instance, concrete, plaster, manufactured stone, marble and glass. The colouring was also distinctly painted in yellow and dark red, colours considered auspicious in Hinduism.

The Lakshminarayan/Birla Mandir was laid out as per the historical *pancayatana* (quincunx) layout, followed, for instance, by the 6th-century Dashavatar Mandir in Deogarh and the 11th-century Kandariya Mahadeva Mandir in Khajuraho. However, the popular historical layout was adapted to the times. For instance, aiming to create a temple where Hindus from across sectarian boundaries would meet, shrines dedicated to Shiva and Devi, were added on either side of the temple's

---

[14] However, these important motifs were eventually 'omitted in the course of construction without any knowledge or consent of the architect' (Chatterjee 1942, 83).

central shrine, dedicated to Lakshmi and Narayan. This arrangement entailed an unusually spacious *mahamandapa* (pillared hall in front of the sanctum). A gallery, running overhead around the hall (Figure 5.5) provided additional space for large congregations—exactly what the agents of Hindu nationalism, such as Moonje and Shraddhananda, had been aiming for. That the creation of congregational space was a decisive concern in designing the temple is also illustrated in the

Figure 5.5 *Photograph of a Large Gathering, during the 1930s, at the Lakshminarayan/Birla Mandir*

Source: All India Arya (Hindu) Dharma Seva Sangha (n.d.)

Figure 5.6 *Stage and Lawn at the Temple's Adjoining Park, Named 'Indraprastha Dharma Vatika'*
Source: Author.

adjoining park.[15] In addition to an artificial mountainous landscape, which is dotted with colourful cement-animals, addressing modern desires of leisure and entertainment, this park has extensive lawns and a stage (Figure 5.6) that, to date, accommodate large gatherings numbering in thousands. Additionally, the temple's 'Gita Bhavan' was built to accommodate smaller regular gatherings. It is likely that the idea to build this hall, which houses a larger-than-life *murti* (icon) of Krishna, was inspired by Shraddhananda (Davis 2015). The influential Arya Samajist, who aspired to unify the Hindu nation promoting the Bhagavad Gita as their bible/national text, urged the construction of temples that could hold large congregations, and an additional hall where the scriptures could be daily recited (Davis 2015).

---

[15] The park has been discussed in great detail in Jain (2017b). As leisure became a more integral part in modern life, it has become a necessity for temples to provide some form of leisure and entertainment. Compare with Srinivas (2006).

Gatherings, large or small, may be powerful means to generate a sense of community, but they are temporary, that is, their effect is short-lived. To ensure something permanent, the ideological framework on which the temple was built found expression in diverse didactic plaques, marking a critical departure from the pre-modern temple.[16] There are images of various deities (Figure 5.7) with elongated faces

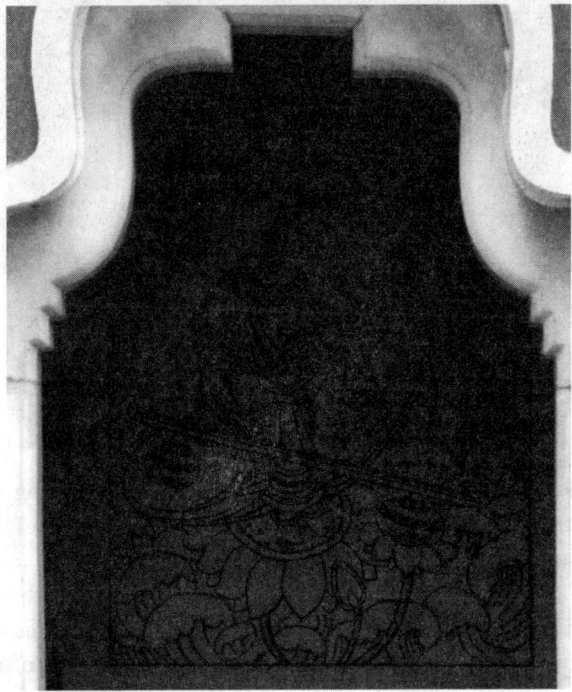

Figure 5.7 *Image of Goddess Saraswati inside the Lakshminarayan/ Birla Mandir*

Source: Author.

---

[16] A detailed study of these images would be incredibly helpful for an in-depth understanding of the role and meaning of the Lakshminarayan/Birla Mandir, as well as other modern (Birla) temples. Aggravating the situation is that the authorities do not permit photography inside the temple. Additionally, is the temple's gallery no longer accessible for the public, making it impossible to undertake a comprehensive study of the programme.

Figure 5.8 *A Plaque at the Lakshminarayan/Birla Mandir, New Delhi, Showing the Maharastrian Poet Tukaram*
Source: Author.

and limbs, demonstrating an affinity with the Bengal School.[17] There are also plaques with images of artistically lower quality of popular (Hindu) men and women, for instance, the 17th-century poet Tukaram (Figure 5.8) and Shabari, a devoted female follower of Ram.[18] Born out of Hindu ideals and morality, these images were meant to encourage

[17] The Bengal School was an artistic movement countering the academic style promoted by the British. In search for forms of expression of a national identity, artists turned to the frescoes at Ajanta and Bagh and miniature paintings. Fascinated by the idea of Pan-Asia and Pan-Asianism, also East Asian painting techniques and styles became important sources of inspiration.

[18] Generally, these images were accompanied by short explanatory excerpts in Sanskrit, Hindi and/or English. Tulsidas's *Ramayana* describes Shabari—an old tribal woman—living in an ashram as an act of atonement (Rajagopalan 2010).

Figure 5.9 *A Plaque from the Lakshminarayan/Birla Mandir in Bhopal Similar to the One at the Lakshminarayan/Birla Mandir in Delhi, Showing the Bhagavad Gita as Boat*

Source: Author.

onlookers to emulate the pious path. However, there are also more complex compositions, conveying the Hindu nationalist agenda. At the entrance to the Gita Bhavan, for instance, is a plaque (Figure 5.9) that attested the significance of the Bhagavad Gita.[19] Here, the Bhagavad Gita is shown as a boat navigating its Gita-abiding passengers, including

---

[19] On the role and significance of the Bhagavad Gita as crucial in the thinking and discourse of the time, see Davis (2015).

leading figures of the nationalist movement, such as Madan Mohan Malaviya, Bal Gangadhar Tilak (1856–1920) and Gandhi, through a crocodile-infested stormy sea that, according to the accompanying inscription, represents 'the painful ocean of worldly life which is full of the crocodiles of lust, anger, greed and infatuation'. Nationalist Hindu leaders are borne by the power of the Holy Scripture, cementing the idea of a unitary and pan-Indian 'Hinduism' guided, like the Abrahamic religions, by a religion of the book.[20] Further, there are painted images of Chandragupta, Ashoka, Shivaji, Guru Nanak and other historical figures, several of which are kept, like masterpieces in a museum, behind glass and framed with heavy wooden frames.[21] This exhibition of historical figures extends into the park. It evokes India's long Hindu heritage by establishing a line of achievements of 'Arya (Hindu)' heroes. Conspicuous by their absence are Islamic and Christian figures. Instead of inserting Mughal emperors, such as Akbar and Shah Jahan, the Rajasthani ruler Suraj Mal, the Mewari king Pratap Singh I and even Prithviraj Chauhan have been included in this chronology of brave men, which narrates the nation, while also acknowledging the patron's roots in the Mewar region.[22] As such the exhibition seems inspired by resistance against Muslim and British invasion, implying what Vinayak Damodar Savarkar (1883–1966) proclaimed in the instrumental treatise *Hindutva: Who Is a Hindu?*, that is, 'Hindu' and India are synonymous. Moreover, there are a few images visualizing other popular themes of the Hindu nationalist framework, such as the notion of 'Greater India' (Akhand Bharat: Undivided India).[23] For instance, one of the door jambs at the park's gates has been enhanced with an image showing an ancient Chandi Mandir, built by Maharaj Kirtivarma in Java (Figure 5.10). Other door jambs are decorated showing temples in China and Myanmar. Further, the temple's park contains a model of an 'Old

---

[20] Compare with Davis (2015). Furthermore, the temple features a 'Ved Mandir'. Instead of housing a *murti*, this small north-facing shrine contains a copy of the Vedas wrapped in cloth, attesting the primacy of scriptures.

[21] I will discuss the influence of the museum on the modern temple elsewhere.

[22] Prithviraj Chauhan occupies a precarious position in this heroic assembly. After all, it was his defeat that gave way to Muhammad Ghori and other outsiders occupying large parts of India (Talbot 2016).

[23] For more details on this concept, see Bayly (2004).

Figure 5.10 *Carved Door Jamb at the Lakshminarayan/Birla Mandir, Showing an Ancient Temple That, According to an Inscription, Was Built by Maharaj Kirtivarma in Java*

Source: Author.

Hindu Temple' built in Java by the same king. These references clearly signal Hindu/India as a religion/culture/nation dominating over South and Southeast Asia.

Apart from these images, there are numerous plaques inscribed with slokas, maxims and quotes from the scriptures. The Sanskrit quotes from scriptures are often followed by translation in Hindi, and, sometimes, in English, making the scriptures accessible to literates. One of the issues addressed in these plaques is that of entry. Several of the plaques, especially those near an entrance, stress that 'Harijans' (a patronizing term coined and popularized by Gandhi for Untouchables) are allowed to enter. Having been introduced to the idea of putting an end to untouchability by Lajpat Rai (1865–1928), a leading Arya Samajist and, like Gandhi, beneficiary of the Birla family, Ghanshyam Das publicly rejected untouchability and supported Gandhi and his campaigns.[24] Thus, entry to Untouchables became a leitmotif of all Birla temples.[25] This inclusivity and liberality, however, came with reservations, prejudice and policing (Jain 2017a). A plaque near the temple's entrance, for instance, emphasizes that the temple is open to 'all' Hindus (including Harijans), on the condition of 'cleanliness'. Further, it insists that sick people and beggars are not allowed to enter, or even approach the temple. Other plaques champion the idea of a Hindu *community*, affirming 'Sanatanists, Aryasamajists, Buddhists, Jains, Sikhs, etc.' as 'Aryadharami Hindus' (Figure 5.11). That this idea too leans on Savarkar's Hindutva is substantiated in another plaque that mentions that with 'exception of all foreigners … and distinguished and famous Indian gentlemen, no local Muslim and Christian Gentlemen should enter the temple Gardens … without the permission of temple

---

[24] As a representative of Gandhi's All India Harijan Sevak Sangh, GD even campaigned in Kerala for the Temple Entry movement in 1936 (Kudaisya 2006).

[25] Birla Mandirs are celebrated for being open to all people. See, for instance, Hutchinson (1947). However, many of those actually affected were rather critical. They regard the impressive temples as political gesture that does not address the root causes of poverty. The workers at the Birla mills, for instance, threw doubt on why the Birla family does not have the same resources to improve their deplorable living and working conditions (Bourke-White 1950).

Figure 5.11 *Plaque at the Lakshminarayan/Birla Mandir Evoking the concept of 'Hindu'*[a]

Source: Author.
[a] An identical plaque can be found at the Hindu Mahasabha's headquarter.

authorities.'[26] Apart from addressing once again the issue of Muslim and Christian presence, this inscription hints at the founder's desire to demonstrate the presence and rising power of Hindus not only to the Indian subcontinent but to the world at large. Old photographs capture well how in its early days the Lakshminarayan/Birla Mandir, with its three towering *shikharas* (superstructure built over the sanctum), was

---

[26] The temple authorities assured Jain that this regulation has never been enforced (Jain 2017a). That Muslims and Christians are not welcome becomes clear from another inscription, which states that during fairs and festivals only Hindus were permitted to do business.

Figure 5.12 *View of the Lakshminarayan/Birla Mandir and the Adjoining Park, Shortly after Its Inauguration in 1939*

Source: All India Arya (Hindu) Dharma Seva Sangha (n.d.)

all the more visible, with the barren landscape now working towards accentuating the temple's imposing profile, symbolizing a powerful Hindu presence in India's modern capital (Figure 5.12). That the massive temple on Reading Road (today Mandir Marg) aroused great public interest was obvious since its inauguration, during which, according to *The Times of India* (1939), nearly 50,000 people gathered.[27]

---

[27] The temple was inaugurated by Gandhi on 18 March 1939.

The construction of the Lakshminarayan/Birla Mandir was positioned as a step towards (re)claiming Delhi and Hindu India, as witnessed by publications of the period. The English weekly *The Hindu Outlook*, a mouthpiece of the Hindu Mahasabha, anticipated the temple writing: 'It is said that such a big and beautiful Temple was never built at Delhi since the days of the last Hindu Emperor—Prithvi Raj Chauhan' (quoted in Jones 1986, 346). If 19th- and early 20th-century colonial narratives of Delhi sketched Delhi as a city of mosques, tombs and forts, Krishna Gopal's guidebook *Delhi in Two Days*, published in the late 1930s, portrayed Delhi as a Hindu city, built on the ruins of Yudhishthara's Indraprastha.[28] For Gopal, the Lakshminarayan/Birla Mandir added 'an unrivalled jem (*sic*) to the glories of the Imperial Capital, which no discriminating visitor can afford to ignore' (Gopal ca. 1939, 70). Thus, the cover of his publication includes an illustration of the city's landmarks that shows the Lakshminarayan/Birla Mandir towering over the silhouette of the Jama Masjid and the Council Chamber (Parliament House), as if to indicate Hindu/Indian supremacy over the Muslim and British structures.

Being an impressive temple, the Lakshminarayan/Birla Mandir has been attracting several hundred people daily, including national and international tourists. Accordingly, the temple must be understood as a medium that, like, for instance, pictures and other visual media, has considerable impact on the discourse of religion, identity, history and nation. The analysis of the Lakshminarayan/Birla Mandir's architectural and visual programme revealed how its 'religious message' mixed with Hindu nationalist ideology. Further, it suggests that the temple was planned to serve as a unifying matrix that not only brings together Hindus/Indians but also defines and propagates Hindu/Indian history, Hindu/Indian culture, Hindu/Indian art and Hindu/Indian architecture, thereby imbuing national identity with a certain *sacredness*. In other words, the construction of the temple and its message seem to be more political than GD led us to believe. As outlined in this chapter, it is in the context of the colonial period that upper caste (Hindu) elites and political leaders identified religious belief as a means to generate

---

[28] Yet another idea that finds reference at the Lakshminarayan/Birla Mandir.

feelings of social cohesion, essential to take collective political decisions forward. Further, they understood that this required a substantial amount of homogeneity, which was yet to be ensured. Rooted within the wide matrix of social interests, the temple turned into a major political playground, including references to the framework of nationalist ideologies. Its politics of entry make it very clear who 'belongs' to the nation and who does not. It does so even as it opens its doors to groups who were refused entry to temples.

REFERENCES

All India Arya (Hindu) Dharma Seva Sangha. n.d. *A Glimpse of the Lakshminarayan Temple, New Delhi.* Delhi: Imperial Fine Art Press.

Asher, C. 2000. 'Mapping Hindu–Muslim Identities through the Architecture of Shahjahanabad and Jaipur'. In *Beyond Turk and Hindu: Rethinking Religious Identities in Islamicate South Asia,* edited by D. Gilmartin and B. Lawrence, 121–148. Gainesville, FL: University Press of Florida.

———. 2003. 'Hidden Gold: Jain Temples of Delhi and Jaipur and Their Urban Context'. In *Jainism and Early Buddhism: Essays in Honor of Padmanabh S. Jaini,* edited by Olle Qvarnström, 359–377. Fermont, CA: Asian Humanities Press.

Bapu, P. 2013. *Hindu Mahasabha in Colonial North India, 1915–1930: Constructing Nation and History.* London: Routledge.

Bayly, C. 1973. 'Patrons and Politics in Northern India'. *Modern Asian Studies* 7 (3): 349–388.

Bayly, S. 2004. '"Greater India": French and Indian Visions of Colonialism in the Indic Mode'. *Modern Asian Studies* 38 (3): 703–744.

Bhatt, C. 2001. *Hindu Nationalism: Origins, Ideologies and Modern Myths.* Oxford: Berg.

Blake, S. P. 2002. *Shahjahanabad: The Sovereign City in Mughal India, 1639–1739.* Cambridge: Cambridge University Press.

Bourke-White, M. 1950. *Halfway to Freedom: In the Words and Pictures of Margret Bourke-White.* Bombay: Asia Publishing House.

Chatterjee, P., ed. 1999. *The Partha Chatterjee Omnibus: Comprising Nationalist Thought and the Colonial World, the Nation and Its Fragments, and a Possible India.* New Delhi: Oxford University Press.

Chatterjee, S. C. 1942. *Magadha: Architecture and Culture.* Calcutta: University of Calcutta.

———. 1949. *India and New Order: An Essay on Human Planning.* Calcutta: Calcutta University Press.

Chaturvedi, S. 1982. *Nāgar Śailī ke Naye Hindu Mandir.* Delhi: Prabhat Prakashan.

Davis, R. 2015. *The Bhagavad Gita: A Biography*. Princeton, NJ: Princeton University Press.

Gopal, K. ca. 1939. *Delhi in Two Days: A Complete, Up-to-date and Illustrated Guide, of Old and New Delhi with History and Map*. Delhi: Model Press.

Gould, W. 2004. *Hindu Nationalism and the Language of Politics in Late Colonial India*. Cambridge: Cambridge University Press.

Guerrieri, P. 2018. *Negotiating Cultures: Delhi's Architecture and Planning from 1912 to 1962*. Oxford: Oxford University Press.

Gupta, N. 1981. *Delhi between Two Empires 1803–1931: Society, Government and Urban Growth*. Delhi: Oxford University Press.

Gupta, S. 1991. 'Sris Chandra Chatterjee: The Quest for a National Architecture'. *The Indian Economic and Social History Review* 28 (2): 187–201.

Hansen, T. H. 1999. *The Saffron Wave: Democracy and Hindu Nationalism in Modern India*. Princeton, NJ: Princeton University Press.

Hardy, A. 2007. *The Temple Architecture of India*. Chichester: Wiley.

Hartig, A. 2017. *Shifting Sites of the 'Sacred': Contestations around the Regional, the National and the Global in Contemporary Hindu Temple Architecture in Delhi* (Unpublished PhD Thesis). School of Arts and Aesthetics, Jawaharlal Nehru University, New Delhi.

Hosagrahar, J. 2005. *Indigenous Modernities: Negotiating Architecture and Urbanism*. London: Routledge.

Hutchinson, P. 1947. 'Religion around the World'. *Life* 22 (10): 106–118.

Irving, R. 1981. *Indian Summer: Lutyens, Baker and Imperial Delhi*. New Haven, CT: Yale University Press.

Jaffrelot, C. 1999. *The Hindu Nationalist Movement and Indian Politics, 1925 to the 1990s: Strategies of Identity-Building, Implantation and Mobilisation*. New Delhi: Penguin Books.

———., ed. 2007. *Hindu Nationalism: A Reader*. Princeton, NJ: Princeton University Press.

Jain, K. 2017a. 'Gods in the Time of Automobility'. *Current Anthropology* 58 (S15): S13–S26.

———. 2017b. 'Tales from the Concrete Cave: Delhi's Birla Temple and the Genealogies of Urban Nature in India'. In *Places of Nature in Ecologies of Urbanism*, edited by Anne Rademacher and K. Sivaramakrishnan, 108–136. Hong Kong: Hong Kong University Press.

Jones, K. 1986. 'Organized Hinduism in Delhi and New Delhi'. In *Delhi through the Ages: Essays in Urban History, Culture and Society*, edited by R. E. Frykenberg, 332–350. Delhi: Oxford University Press.

———. 2006. *Socio-religious Reform Movements in British India*. Cambridge, UK: Cambridge University Press.

Kudaisya, M. 2006. *The Life and Times of G. D. Birla*. New Delhi: Oxford University Press.

Legg, S. 2007. *Spaces of Colonialism: Delhi's Urban Governmentalities*. Oxford: Blackwell.

Markovits, C. 1985. *Indian Business and Nationalists Politics 1931–39: The Indigenous Capitalist Class and the Rise of the Congress Party*. Cambridge: Cambridge University Press.

Metcalf, T. 1989. *An Imperial Vision: Indian Architecture and Britain's Raj*. London: Faber and Faber.

Michell, G. 2015. *Late Temple Architecture of India 15th to 19th Centuries: Continuities, Revivals, Appropriations, and Innovations*. New Delhi: Oxford University Press.

Nilsson, S. 1973. *The New Capitals of India, Pakistan and Bangladesh*. Lund: Studentlitteratur.

Rajagopal, A. 2001. *Politics after Television: Hindu Nationalism and the Reshaping of the Public India*. Cambridge: Cambridge University Press.

Rajagopalan, M. 2010. 'Postsecular Urbanism: Situating Delhi within the Rhetorical Landscape of Hindutva'. In *The Fundamentalist City? Religiosity and the Remaking of Urban Space*, edited by N. AlSayyad and M. Massoumi, 257–282. London: Routledge.

Sanderson, G. 1916–1922. *List of Muhammadan and Hindu Monuments*. Calcutta: Superintendent Government Printing.

Savarkar, V. 1969. *Hindutva: Who Is a Hindu?* Bombay: Veer Savarkar Prakashan.

Shraddhananda, S. 1926. *Hindu Sangathan: Saviour of the Dying Race*. Delhi: Shraddhananda.

Srinivas, T. 2006. 'Divine Enterprise: Hindu Priests and Ritual Change in Neighbourhood Hindu Temples in Bangalore'. *South Asia: Journal of South Asian Studies* 29 (3): 321–343.

Talbot, C. 2016. *The Last Hindu Emperor: Prithviraj Chauhan and the Indian Past, 1200–2000*. Cambridge: Cambridge University Press.

Taneja, A. 2008. 'History and Heritage Woven in the New Urban Fabric: The Changing Landscapes of Delhi's 'First City': Or, Who Can Tell the Histories of Lado Sarai?'. In *Patterns of Middle Class Consumption in India and China*, edited by Christopher Jaffrelot and Peter van der Veer, 157–169. New Delhi: SAGE Publications.

The Times of India. 1939. 'Mr. Gandhi Opens Temple'. Delhi, 21 March.

Van der Veer, P. 1994. *Religious Nationalism: Hindus and Muslims in India*. Berkeley, CA: University of California Press.

Zavos, J. 2000. *The Emergence of Hindu Nationalism in India*. New Delhi: Oxford University Press.

Chapter 6

Guru-led Faith Movements
The Case of The Art of Living Foundation

Himani Kapoor

One of the important transformations to emerge on the global scene of religion, especially Hinduism, over the last few decades has been the rise of devotionalist organizations led by gurus. Many of these movements cut across national and cultural boundaries, predominantly promoting meditation and particular forms of yoga. Since yoga is often considered to be easily adaptable to different cultures, many guru-led groups take pride in increasing their geographical footprint, and adding different ethnicities, races and social groups to their organization. Does it mean that such organizations are potential avenues to proliferate a certain kind of cosmopolitanism in religion that cuts across all borders and boundaries while still being sustained by faith? Studies on faith movements and guru-led groups do not affirm this position positively. This chapter studies one such guru-led organization, by the name of The Art of Living Foundation (AOLF), in its potential for promoting religious cosmopolitanism. The idea of religious cosmopolitanism here refers to the set of ethos by which 'cultural and religious differences are neither hierarchically organised nor dissolved, but accepted for what they are and indeed positively affirmed' (Beck 2010).

The reasons for this choice are, first, that The AOLF along with its leader Sri Sri Ravi Shankar has attracted wide public attention and media coverage, and is therefore well known, and, second, and more importantly, that the organization proposes the motto of *Vasudhaeva Kutumbhakam* or 'one world family' as its ideal. Apart from having a living guru, the organization takes pride in resolving issues related to peacekeeping and conflict resolution. For these reasons, other yoga gurus and their groups having a significant following in India and abroad do not fit neatly into this study. While it may be possible to comment on the idea of cultural nationalism and guru–led organizations, for which gurus like Swami Ramdev and Chinmayananda Saraswati are apt examples, Ravi Shankar is distinct for his intermittent engagement with secular ideals as well as identity politics. This chapter looks into the different ways in which The AOLF negotiates the cosmopolitan ideals of 'one world family' with cultural nationalism in India.

Before setting up The AOLF in 1981, its founder leader was earlier associated with another widely known faith-based organization by the name of Transcendental Meditation (TM). As a part of TM, Ravi Shankar had travelled extensively around the world as a teacher. In terms of its international footprint, The AOLF has had a significant following after the establishment of its international centres in 1989, in the United States and Germany. Today, the organization is known to have a huge number of followers, and according to the official webpage of AOLF, the organization has now spread to about 350 million people worldwide with followers in 155 countries.

Irrespective of the transnational outreach, and its constant insistence upon its own cosmopolitan outlook, it has often been termed as a Hindu religious organization at heart. For instance, Alexis Avdeeff in, 'Internationalisation of a contemporary Hindu Movement' (2010), associates it with 'internationalized Hinduism'. On the other hand, Stephen Jacobs, in his perceptive study of the movement, *The Art of Living Foundation: Spirituality and Wellbeing in the Global Context* (2015), has called it both secular and religious at the same time. Rather than categorizing The AOLF as a New Religious Movement (NRM), or a Hindu-Inspired Meditation Movement (HIMM),[1] Jacobs categorizes

---

[1] The term 'HIMM' or 'Hindu-Inspired Meditation Movements' has been suggested by Lola Williamson in her work *Transcendent in America: Hindu-Inspired*

The AOLF as a Hindu-Derived Meditation Network, which capital-izes upon the modern-day preoccupation with well-being and health. The first section of this chapter briefly discusses the history of The AOLF in the national and international contexts. Thereafter, it con-trasts the promotional material published by the organization in the form of pamphlets and videos, in India and abroad, to throw light on the differences in its outlook at both these sites. The final section takes into consideration the articles published in the monthly magazine *Rishimukh*, in the context of its deployment of Hindu nationalism and archaic primordialism.

WHAT IS THE ART OF LIVING FOUNDATION?

The AOLF represents itself as 'a non-governmental organization, involved in humanitarian projects with a special focus on stress elimina-tion'. Although there are a number of areas that the organization works with, for instance as an NGO and also having a retail outlet for con-sumer goods and health-related products, primarily, the organization is engaged in teaching yoga and breathing rhythms, by way of offering short-term courses, which can be taken in lieu of a certain fee. Here, trained volunteers demonstrate and teach a variety of yogic exercises, meditation and the yogic techniques that are unique to The AOLF, like the *Sudarshan Kriya* (a form of rhythmic breathing exercise). Depending upon the age, interest and ability of the participant, a variety of courses are offered, which may include different individual as well as group activities on offer, mostly directed at physical and mental well-being.

Most of the promotional material and advertisements published for promoting The AOLF courses, by and large, highlight the various national and international social service initiatives under its wing. In the monthly magazine *Rishimukh*, two sections are routinely dedicated to the various social work tasks taken up by the organization. Some of these include peacekeeping missions in places like Kashmir, Sri Lanka, Iraq, Costa Rica and Kosovo, among others. Other humanitarian

---

Meditation Movements as New Religion (2010) where she studies three popular guru-led faith Movements established in United States; TM, The Self-realization Fellowship and Siddha Yoga.

projects include disaster relief, rural development, prisoner rehabilitation and charitable schools.

In India, the organization was set up initially with a rural school by the name of 'Ved Vignan Maha Vidya Peeth' in 1981. By the next decade, the organization had significantly grown to have international centres in various countries with a growing network of followers from different parts of the world. Interestingly, the same decade also marked the emergence of a new middle class following the liberalization of the Indian economy in 1991. This class had a higher disposable income in addition to being more upwardly mobile. Much of the AOL's following in India belongs to this upwardly mobile middle class (Jacobs 2015: 157).

Having been awarded the Padma Vibhushan by the government of India in 2016 (the second highest civilian award conferred by the Indian State), Ravi Shankar is also a well-known public figure, who frequently travels to various places in India and abroad, for spreading AOLF's teachings and other humanitarian efforts. The initiatives taken by the organization towards peacekeeping in certain conflict-stricken parts of the world have been emphasized in its various publications. Ravi Shankar's biography indicates that his peacekeeping negotiations have also been instrumental in spreading the Gandhian values of nonviolence around the world. It also states that as a child Ravi Shankar had questioned caste-based discrimination, purposely flouting the norms of purity by going on a bicycle ride with the caretaker of his family's paddy field, who was considered untouchable (Narasimhan 2018). For his followers, Ravi Shankar is the epitome of joy and love.

COSMOPOLITAN VERSUS RELIGIOUS COMMUNITY ORIENTATION: A LOOK AT THE AOLF'S PROMOTIONAL PAMPHLET AND VIDEOS

In one of the promotional pamphlets published by The AOLF research centre in Germany, the scientific research associated with yogic breathing and *Sudarshan Kriya* is shared. The chief health aspects emphasized upon in the document are reduced stress levels, better immunity, brain function and so on. Curiously enough, the philosophy behind this practice of disciplining the breath, also known as *pranayama,* is not shared in these promotional pieces. The *pranayama* is simply described as a 'science of health promotion', a sort of time-tested practice of exercise and 'restoring optimal health'. These practices also taught by The AOLF, the pamphlet says, 'continue to be independently investigated by modern medical science'.

The short description of The AOLF at the end of the pamphlet also declares that the Foundation's International Research and Health Promotion Center (IRHPC) welcomes 'scholarly research' on its programmes from all 'interested parties'.[2]

The front page of this pamphlet shows two people doing *pranayama* on one side and the depiction of a chemical experiment on the other. The bar and pie diagrams are essentially eye catchy and interestingly do not say anything about the philosophical idea of the *Self,* or for that matter the principles associated with yoga. While Vedic primordialism does play a part in the validation of the health benefits associated with the *Sudarshan Kriya,* it is, however, the supposed verifiability of the research that is strongly emphasized. Added to this is the openness to be 'independently investigated by modern medical science at universities, hospitals and other research institutions'. This adds to the credibility that its potential audiences may associate with the organization. In this context, Joanne Punzo Waghorne (2014), in 'Engineering an Artful Practice: On Jaggi Vasudev's Isha Yoga and Sri Sri Ravi Shankar's Art of Living', offers the observation that a 'new kind of proof texting' is at play, wherein instead of isolated quotations from sacred texts, data from the emergent fields of neurosciences and cognitive studies are invoked, which appeals to the legitimacy of science interestingly mirrored by the rise of serious interest in cognitive science within the academic study of religion. The brand of yoga, therefore, which gets promoted, is curiously divested of its traditional trappings. The reference to Vedic testimony here garners further authenticity. In the same

---

[2] See 'The Science of Breath' (http://www.aolresearch.org/pdf/ArtOfLiving.02032014.pdf)

vein, the promotional video 'Meditation Then and Now',[3] published by The AOLF, United States, is meant for its 'Youth Empowerment and Skills Workshop' (YES Plus), for young adults. The animated video begins with the image of a meditator, perhaps a sage, and a voice in the background informs us that some of the world's first scientists discovered secrets about the body, mind and consciousness by keeping their mind really still.

Meditation, the video goes on to suggest, is universal, 'just like you don't need to be Italian to eat pasta'. The video later enumerates certain benefits of meditation like getting good grades, growing smarter, stronger, faster and so on. The video ends with the animated representation of Ravi Shankar, with an invitation to 'dive deeper'. Here again, the assertion, repeated time and again, is that the Indian sages who discovered the benefits of meditation were indeed scientists, though not in the typical way. Much like the pamphlet discussed earlier, the promotional video appeals to the modern day where validation from Western science is enough to garner authenticity.

Counter to such representations, the promotional video[4] of the same Yes Plus programme, in Bangalore, does not deal with such scientific aspect or health benefits associated with the programme. The video features personal experiences of young adults from different countries. While one participant from Denmark talks about 'being alive once again', another from the United States shares how he got more 'clarity' in his life. The participant from India, on the other hand, talks about having been able to overcome depression and highlights the strong community orientation of The AOLF; he observes that even though participants 'live seven oceans across ... still the people are one'. The video ends with glimpses of Ravi Shankar talking about youth being 'global citizens'. More than the health-related aspects of The AOLF courses, the promotional video, meant for the Indian audiences, is concerned with this transnational aspect of the organization: the idea of being able to connect with a 'global' community.

---

[3] See artofliving.org, 'Meditation Then and Now'. https://www.artofliving.org/in-en/video-meditation-then-now?mobile=1

[4] YES Plus Course, Art of Living International Center, Bangalore, India. https://www.youtube.com/watch?v=p4tTNv5pkhg

This contrast is not to suggest that scientific 'proof texting' that is the take-off point to woo a Western audience is simply divested for advances made to the Indian counterpart. What can, however, be more certainly suggested is that while the pressure to assert authenticity is more for a Western audience, for an Indian public, the presentation of arguments in favour of the health-related benefits of yoga takes a backseat when compared to the offer of a 'cosmopolitan rootedness'. Jacobs suggests that 'export' of 'philosophical ideas and yoga to the West not only provided a certain prestige to the cultural heritage of India, but also in the process transformed them' (Jacobs 2015, 208–209).

The rationalization of rituals and their re-dubbing as secular and scientific practices[5] further adds to this prestige element, and, therefore, for the Hindu followers of the organization in India, such 'scientific' aspects further strengthen their faith in the movement, which is additionally rooted in their own tradition. Jacobs associates the Indian middle class's need for being grounded in the ancient Vedic traditions, yet being commensurate with the 'modern', to 'rooted cosmopolitanism', a term he borrows from Kwame Anthony Appiah's 'Cosmopolitan Patriots' (Appiah 1997).

Yoga along with certain routine rituals followed at The AOLF centres puts together an amalgamation which appeals to the members who are convinced that the practices are scientifically relevant and rational, apart from being globally accepted. One, therefore, sees different modes of persuasion actively used for its prospective audiences at the international and the national level. At a local level, however, Indian identity plays a greater role.

AOLF AND THE HINDU IMAGINATION: READING *RISHIMUKH*

The fact that the cosmopolitan dimension of Ravi Shankar's message gets far diluted on the Indian terrain has been voiced by some scholars, for instance Alexis Avdeeff. He says that even though a universal nature of the message propagated by Ravi Shankar has enabled the

---

[5] See Art of Living, 'Significance of Navratri Yagnas'. https://www.artofliving. org/navratri/significance-yagnas

organization to have a large community of transnational followers, nevertheless, 'this inclusivist spirituality with universalistic aims' takes an 'identity turn' in India through the political discourse Ravi Shankar, who 'seems to be inclined to vigorously defend Hindus interests'.

Avdeeff in his study takes into account the various occasions where Ravi Shankar has voiced majoritarian Hindu interests; for instance, his objections to proselytism of Christian missions in South India, his strong indictment of the state government of Karnataka for allocating more money to churches and mosques than Hindu temples, and the supposed purpose of some of the tribal programmes (such as Sri Sri Tribal Welfare) to contain religious conversions to Christianity (Avdeeff 2010, 8–13). Ravi Shankar's public support for the Ram temple in the Ram Janmabhumi/Babri Masjid dispute[6] was also met with criticism from certain sections of the mainstream media (Joshua 2019).

At least a certain section of the Hindu following of The AOLF is captured by the appeal to the archaic sense of belongingness to a primordial Hindu community. This is often reinforced in not-so-subtle proclamation of Hindu cultural supremacy. Some of Ravi Shankar's lectures, despite advocating the equality of all religions, implicitly assert the overarching superiority of Vedic knowledge as a generic umbrella superseding other, more modern religio-cultural traditions. For instance, following is a short analysis of one of Ravi Shankar's talks published in the June 2016 edition of *Rishimukh*. This talk is in the context of the bombings in the Brussels Airport in March 2016. Although the date and venue of the talk are not mentioned in the issue, the picture accompanying the excerpt shows Ravi Shankar sitting in front of an audience with a microphone in his hand, wearing a white robe, bordered by saffron and green colours, symbolizing the Indian flag. He repudiates terrorism and questions the assumptions of Islamic universalism suggesting that such youth involved in the bombings need to be 'educated' about the different traditions and religions of the

---

[6] Ravi Shankar was officially a part of the court-appointed mediation panel for the dispute. This mediation, however, failed, and the final verdict of the dispute was made by the Supreme Court of India in November 2019, whereby it was ordered that the land be handed over to a trust for the construction of the temple.

world. In this process, he debunks religious indoctrination at madrassas. Teaching yoga, he suggests, will be the solution to the problem. He says that there are seminaries and madrassas that need to be 'de-radicalized'. He further mentions a meeting with a professor who told him that the values of non-violence and truth were dear to Prophet Mohammad, who said that 'Hind' was in his heart. These values, Ravi Shankar continues, are the 'principles of Hind'. He concludes saying that the Vedas, which he calls the 'first book of wisdom', were written in India, and it is this knowledge which must reach out to people (*Rishimukh* June 2016).

Even though Ravi Shankar's repudiation of religious indoctrination is in the context of a certain incident involving Islamist terrorism, he distinctly places the Hindu Vedic doctrine above and beyond the Islamic worldview. Thus, in order to refute the claims to universalism of Islamic theology, he, nonetheless, exchanges it for another kind of religious universalism, touting the Vedas as the mainspring of human wisdom. It is, therefore, not surprising to find a similar tone of Vedic universalism in another piece published in the magazine a few months afterwards. The December 2016 issue of *Rishimukh* celebrates the graduation of 41 scholars of the 'heritage school' called the *Veda Agama Sanskrita Maha Pathshala*, dedicated to Agamic Studies. The article reports that the school teaches students from all over the country to 'conduct temple rituals, puja, *abhishekas* and other rituals'. The 'syllabus' the article goes on to inform, 'includes the study of the Veda, Agama, Sanskrit Language, astrology, yoga, music, sculpture and religious epics' (*Rishimukh* December 2016).

It is interesting to note that the 'syllabus' of the special school does not mention anything in the mode of its training, which may help employ its pupil outside the Hindu temple. The rising number of schools training for priesthood has been highlighted by Meera Nanda who argues that such schools are now being associated with social welfare and progressive development, and hence enjoy sanction by the state as well as funds from corporates. Here, the emphasis is on rote learning, correct memorization and the correct reproduction of the sound of Sanskrit verses with no room for critical thinking (Nanda 2009). The inherent contradiction between the indictment of one religious pedagogy and an enthusiastic promotion of another goes curiously unchecked in the talk given by the founder leader. With the Indian flag adorning him, these statements are similar to other voices defending a conflated Hindu-Indian identity, which Manisha Basu (2016, 15) has called 'metropolitan Hindutva'. It is interesting, however, that these contradictory statements and logics continue to be a part of The AOLF portfolio. Avdeeff aptly calls the organization an 'incarnation of two seemingly contradictory logics':

> Incarnation of two seemingly contradictory logics, The Art of Living Foundation appears as a transnational movement participating fully to the process of religious globalisation, but also as a major actor in the enduring phenomenon that is the Hindu revitalisation in contemporary India, providing thereby its contribution 'to the global picture of the politicisation of religion'. (Avdeeff 2010, 13)

Jaffrelot talks about similar instances of opposites coming together in the reformation of Hinduism in the 19th century and the early 20th century. He associates the rise of Hindu nationalism in India with a 'strategic syncretism in ideology building' that brought together cultural values of groups perceived as being antagonistic to each other (Jaffrelot 1993). In a similar vein, a 'strategic syncretism' is visible in The AOLF philosophy as it brings together ideas from opposing worldviews. It envisages the world as one family, adopts the concerns of social unrest in the world and upholds Gandhian values of non-violence, and equality, while also engaging in a particular kind of populist cultural nationalism and Vedic primordialism, and tacitly supporting Hindu hegemony.

PRIMORDIAL NATIONALISM: A CLOSER LOOK AT 'BHARATH GYAN'

This section examines the *Rishimukh* issues published from January 2016 to December 2017 to have a deeper understanding of the organization's day-to-day trappings within India. The magazine is available in Hindi and English, including various other regional languages. It carries regular sections on yoga, meditation, health, psychology, nutrition, latest news about Ravi Shankar's visits in India and abroad, a section on social service initiatives by the name of *Seva*, a regular feature on religious tourism called 'Spiritual Sojourn', covering mostly a South Indian Hindu temple, news about the organization covered in national and regional newspapers, excerpts from Ravi Shankar's talks, and a special section about the knowledge of India, 'Bharath Gyan'.

'Bharath Gyan' is a regular feature in *Rishimukh*, and the contributors, DK Hari and Hema Hari, have authored a book series by the same title. The idea of these books, as the name suggests, is to share knowledge or 'gyan' about India. The AOLF India webpage describes it as a 'research organization that endeavours to bring forth knowledge from the ancient times'. The vision statement itself discloses that the idea behind setting up the organization is 'to offer credible evidences that establish India as a land rich in science and knowledge along with culture and spirituality'.[7]

The founder duo, who had earlier been multinational corporation professionals and software engineers, reportedly quit their careers to write about Indian history and culture (Vijay 2013). A bulk of the literature collaborated by them is not only published as regular features in *Rishimukh* but also as separate book editions running into various volumes. The titles of some of the books published include *Historical Rama, Historical Krishna, Understanding Shiva, Ayodhya—War and Peace* and so on. The 'historical evidence' of their work, they suggest, is established by 'modern methods of tracking time and history'. The 'modern methods', which are not aptly dwelt upon or explained, are put to use to assign exact dates according to the Gregorian calendar to events like the birth of Lord Rama, Lord Krishna, date of the Kurukshetra war and so on. One of the articles, published in December 2017, suggests that the work of 'Bharath Gyan' is to establish the 'historicity of personages such as Rama, Krishna and many other legendary figures of ancient India'. This, the article goes on to suggest, also establishes that the descendants of these religious figures 'would also have been historical' (*Rishimukh* December 2017).

---

[7] See 'Bharath Gyan'. https://www.artofliving.org/in-en/bharathgyan

Likewise, according to the article published in the November 2016 issue, the Bhagavad Gita can be precisely dated. The article thereby says that since Gita Jayanti is celebrated on a particular day of the lunar calendar, the year 2016 marks the Gita's 5,083rd year (*Rishimukh* November 2016).[8]

However contrived this amalgamation of myth and history may be, the larger question arises when documented history is downplayed in favour of mythic tradition. On the exact dating of Bhagavad Gita, for instance, such narratives do not take into account the significance of the oral tradition and transmission processes such as the *smriti* tradition that account for different versions and renditions of the same text.

In this context, historian Peter Heehs' paper, 'Myth, History, and Theory' (1994), throws light on the contestation between myth and history. He identifies that this conflation of myth (mythos) with scientific history (logos) is not restricted to the Indian scenario or the third-world societies; he cites various examples of this amalgamation in countries such as the United States and Greece. While myth and history can easily coexist, each having the legitimacy of its own, the conflict, he suggests, arises when the methods of logos are used in order to legitimize mythos. He says,

> From the point of view of logos, problems involving conflict between logos and mythos could be avoided if each kept to its proper sphere. Conflict arises when proponents of a mythical view use logos methods or institutions to force acceptance of their claims on others. (Heehs, 1994, 14)

The 'Bharath Gyan' series exemplifies the above-mentioned conflict between mythos and logos. For instance, one article (December 2017) suggests that there is an 'inseparable link' between Lord Rama

---

[8] This particular admixture of myth and history, one may argue, is not uncommon to the Indian scenario. The Gita Jayanti Samaroh is a week-long state-sanctioned festival organized by the Kurukshetra Development Board, Haryana. One of the monographs published by the Kurukshetra Development Board (1997) talks about Krishna as a historical administrator dedicated to his country.

and Ayodhya that goes back to more than 7 millennia. The 'Babar–Ayodhya link', on the other hand, is 'just 500 odd years old' (40). It further establishes that the Sikh community 'of the Sodi and Vedi clan are· descendants of Luva and Kusha, the twin sons of Rama respectively' and thereby making the Sikh community a 'joint stakeholder of Ayodhya, Rama and the temple at Rama Janmabhoomi' (*Rishimukh* December 2017).

The above arguments cited by the magazine not only seek to systematically validate the Hindu claim over the disputed Ram Janmabhumi site, they also count the Sikh community as one of the legitimate stakeholders of the dispute. The Muslim claim over the site, on the other hand, is simply ruled out, touting the span of Muslim claim as miniscule compared to the Hindu right to the place. Given that the particular contentious issue of the supposed birthplace of Lord Rama has been associated with violence, the potentially inciting content of the piece is very obvious.

The underlying assumption behind such arguments, as has been stated above, is that India has primarily been a homogeneous Hindu culture, until later occupied by its Muslim invaders. The idea of a homogeneous Hindu identity is discussed in Romila Thapar's 'Imagined Religious Communities? Ancient History and the Modern Search for a Hindu Identity'. She concedes that the usage of the word 'Hindu' in non-Islamic sources is known from the 15th century; even then, the recognition of a religious identity does not automatically establish a religious community. Moreover, as Thapar points out, the notion of a Hindu community does not have as long an ancestry as is often presumed. Even in the normative texts of Brahmanism, the Dharmasastras, it is conceded that there were a variety of communities, determined by location, occupation and caste, none of which were necessarily bound together by a common religious identity (Thapar 1989). What may be called the 'Hindu community' or a 'Hindu way of life' even now is fraught with its own contradictions, as it takes for granted the existence of the diversity within. Historically speaking, therefore, the claim supporting a pan-Indian adherence to a 'Hindu way of life' would be a highly problematic argument to make, something that one finds repeatedly in the Bharath Gyan articles.

Political implications of such writings aside, the above article seeks to delegitimize the inherent diversity of the Indian tradition. Heehs (1994, 10) points out that 'when tradition is invented in the twentieth century, it tends to use the discourse of science, our prevailing cultural "myth"'. In a similar vein, Chetan Bhatt (2001) in *Hindu Nationalism: Origins, Ideologies and Modern Myths*, calls an invention of tradition of this kind as primordial nationalism. Tracing the history of Hindu nationalism through the 19th century, Bhatt identifies a kind of cultural primordialism that played a major part in not only the Hindu nationalist thought, but also the resurgence of cultural nationalism in the light of the existing debates about minorities, secular citizenship, ethics and modernity. *Rishimukh*'s deployment of cultural myths comes very close to the primordialism he describes as a characteristic of the post-colonial Hindu nationalism.

CONCLUSION

Before coming to a conclusion about the various kinds of publics attracted to the organization, one may want to differentiate between the ideas of religious universalism and religious cosmopolitanism, or what Ulrich Beck (2010) in *A God of One's Own: Religion's Capacity for Peace and Potential for Violence,* has called 'cosmopolitan religiosity'. Here, Beck makes clear demarcations between these two categories. Religious universalism, he says, is noticeable for its structural intolerance and is characterized by demonizing unbelievers. It also opens up new abysses between religions and creates potential for violence. Religious cosmopolitanism, on the other hand, may be distinguished from such templates by its recognition of religious otherness as a guiding maxim in thought, action and social existence (Beck 2010, 70–71).

One may thereby distinguish between distinct types of transnational communities of faith-based organizations on the basis of the larger philosophies they endorse. Even though subtle assertions of the Hindu hegemony resonate more with religious universalism than with cosmopolitan religiosity, The AOLF cannot still be strictly categorized as absolutist in terms of its ideological foundation. The organization does not preach or defend a compulsory following of the rules, and participants include people from different religions. In fact, Jacobs in his study of The AOLF (in a fieldwork carried out in the United Kingdom, Germany and India) observes that The AOLF prioritizes yogic technique over doctrine. One of the interviewees says that the 'beauty of AOL is that there is no indoctrination. There are no rules' (87). Similar responses were shared in various other interviews he cites. Most of The AOLF followers, especially in the West, Jacobs observes, do not associate The AOLF with the Hindu religion. Interestingly, a similar argument about AOLF being essentially non-Hindu was offered by one of the German followers of the organization I interviewed as a part of a larger study. The 48-year-old entrepreneur said: 'Gurudev accepts all kinds of religion and wisdom and teaches diversity and multi-religion education'. In fact, she suggested that one can 'practice *pranayamas* without honoring God Shiva, but believing in Jesus Christ for example' (*sic*) (interview dated 28 April 2019, Berlin, e-mail extract).

It will, therefore, be hard to bracket AOLF as an example of either religious universalism or for that matter religious cosmopolitanism. Aspects of rationality, modernity, transnational community orientation, as well as Vedic primordialism, all work together to consolidate The AOLF community within India and worldwide.

In order to understand these disparate sections of its audience, a deeper study of the ethnographies of the organization with a comparative thread, taking both Indian and Western audience, is needed. Nevertheless, it can be definitely said that as a part of its functioning in India, The AOLF, in its many manifestations, shows an ideological inclination towards the retrieval of an imagined historical community, which is based on the primordiality of a uniform Hindu (Vedic) culture that invests in archaic and mythological archetypes as a method of cultural nationalism.

REFERENCES

Appiah, Kwame Anthony. 1997. 'Cosmopolitan Patriots'. *Critical Inquiry* 23 (3): 617–639.

Avdeeff, Alexis. 2010. 'Internationalisation of a Contemporary Hindu Movement: Between Universalist Ambition and Nationalist Orientations: The Case of The Art of Living Foundation (Vyaktivikas Kendra) and Its Transnational Community'. Paper presented at 21st European Conference on Modern South Asian Studies (ECMSAS), Bonn, Germany, July.

Basu, Manisha. 2016. *The Rhetoric of Hindu India: Language and Urban Nationalism.* Delhi: Cambridge University Press.

Beck, Ulrich. 2010. *A God of One's Own: Religion's Capacity for Peace and Potential for Violence.* Cambridge: Polity Press.

Bhatt, Chetan. 2001. *Hindu Nationalism Origins, Ideologies and Modern Myths.* New York, NY: Berg.

Heehs, Peter. 1994. 'Myth, History, and Theory'. *History and Theory* 33 (1): 1–19.

Jacobs, Stephen. 2015. *The Art of Living Foundation: Spirituality and Wellbeing in the Global Context* (Routledge New Religions). New York, NY: Taylor and Francis.

Jaffrelot, Christophe. 1993. 'Hindu Nationalism: Strategic Syncretism in Ideology Building'. *Economic and Political Weekly* 28 (12–13): 517–524.

Joshua, Anita. 2019. 'Sri Sri's Past Views Raise Eyebrows'. *The Telegraph,* New Delhi, 9 March.

Nanda, Meera. 2009. *The God Market: How Globalization Is Making India More Hindu.* Noida: Random House India.

Narasimhan, Bhanumathi. 2018. *Gurudev: On the Plateau of the Peak: The Life of Sri Sri Ravi Shankar.* Chennai: Westland Publications.

Rishimukh. 2016a. 'Meditation and Yoga are Tools to De-Radicalize the World: Excerpts from Talks by Gurudev Sri Sri Ravi Shankar'. Bangalore, June.

———. 2016b. '*Bhagavad Gita*'. Bangalore, November.

———. 2016c. '41 Vedic Scholars Graduate from The Art of Living Heritage School'. Bangalore, December.

———. 2017. 'A note on Ayodhya from Bharath Gyan'. Bangalore, December.

Shri Krishna Sangrahalaya. 1997. *Shri Krishna: Bahuaayami Vyaktitva: A Monograph.* Haryana: Kurukshetra Vikas Board.

Thapar, Romila. 1989. 'Imagined Religious Communities? Ancient History and the Modern Search for a Hindu Identity'. *Modern Asian Studies* 23 (2): 209–231.

Vijay, Hema. 2013. 'History Matters'. *The Hindu,* Chennai, 31 December. http://www.thehindu.com/features/friday-review/history-and-culture/history-matters/article5522782.ece

Waghorne, Joanne Punzo. 2014. 'Engineering an Artful Practice: On Jaggi Vasudev's Isha Yoga and Sri Sri Ravi Shankar's Art of Living'. In *Gurus of Modern Yoga,* edited by Mark Singleton and Ellen Goldberg, 283–307. New York, NY: Oxford University Press.

Williamson, Lola. 2010. *Transcendent in America: Hindu-Inspired Meditation Movements as New Religion.* New York, NY: New York University Press.

Chapter 7

Rethinking Cow 'Protection'
Gender, Caste and Labour at a *Gaushala*

Ridhima Sharma

The initial political and analytical impulse for this chapter comes from a familiar and oft-encountered place—one of discomfort, with historical and contemporary ways of framing and interpreting the 'cow protection movement' or *gauraksha* in India. I argue that the dominant mode of analysing cow politics in India, in its overwhelming association of the cow with Hindu nationalism in both symbolic and material terms, pays necessary but disproportionate emphasis on a certain kind of hyper-visible, spectacular violence. This deeply informs the construction of a purported linear and teleological 'movement' in the name of the cow as if all heightened, finite episodes of cow-related violence, their varied textures notwithstanding, add up to produce a coherent 'cow protection movement'. This conception of the 'cow protection movement' I posit obfuscates not only the everyday process of the mobilizing of the cow into a potent Hindu politico-religious symbol and the intimate relationship between the 'everyday' and the 'event' (of violence) but also obscures the manner in which gendered and caste-marked routinized practices of labour have come to constitute a 'movement' in the name of the cow. Making a departure from the commonly deployed method of analysing spectacular modes of violence such as cow-related 'riots' and 'lynching', this chapter uses an ethnographic engagement with the space of a *gaushala* or cow-shelter as a way of entering the cow protection discourse.

The first section sets the stage for my claim of *gaushalas* as a significant constitutive site in the making of the 'cow protection movement' and introduces the *gaushala* in which my ethnographic inquiry would be located. The second section provides a historical view of the scholarly construction of a linear 'movement' in the name of the cow and its analytical effect in the reading of the 'cow protection movement'. The third section, the kernel of the ethnographic engagement, explores the manner in which gender, labour and caste shape symbolic, material and discursive practices at the *gaushala* to produce simultaneously the figure of the *gau sevak* (loosely translated as 'one who serves the cow') and the *gau mata,* the feminized and revered cow who is at once, the mother, the goddess and the nation. I also reflect briefly here on the politics of my own presence as a researcher in the field. The final section reiterates the political and analytical value of a *gaushala* as a point of entry into the cow protection discourse which I argue can, in fact, enable a feminist retelling of the story of cow protection.

WHY *GAUSHALAS*: INTRODUCING THE SHREE GOPAL GAUSHALA

The story of cow protection in India has conspicuously omitted *gaushalas* as active constitutive spaces in the making of the 'cow protection movement'. While there is some information available on the role played by cow protection societies or *gaurakshini sabhas* that began to sprout in 19th-century North and West India, in the culmination of 'cow-based riots' (Freitag 1980; Pandey 1981; Robb 1986), *gaushalas* are mentioned, if at all, cursorily as mere 'asylums' for cows in the northern parts of the country (Yang 1980). One of the most significant reasons for this cursory treatment of *gaushalas* in the otherwise verbose story of cow protection, I submit, is that the very idea of 'cow protection' is over-determined by the imagination of a certain kind of spectacular violence, leaving little space for a *gaushala* which is presumed to be a benign charitable space engaged in an innocent form of *seva* or charitable service. The *gaurakshini sabhas,* which were explicitly militant and aggressive in their demand to ban cow slaughter and have been held responsible for the cow protection 'riots' of the late 19th and early 20th centuries, fit far more easily into the violence-ridden story of cow protection, than the generous *gaushalas* that 'merely' shelter hapless, old, and ailing cows.

An ongoing pioneering (unpublished) work by Cassie Adcock aims to account for this absence by finally researching cattle shelter institutions from a historical perspective.[1] She argues,

Cow protection is generally regarded as a political outgrowth of Hindu religious reverence for the 'sacred cow'. But cow protectionists have regularly cited scientific and official literature to support their arguments about the importance of draught bullocks for Indian agriculture, the value of cattle manure for maintaining soil fertility, and the need to direct state efforts toward the preservation and improvement of cattle breeds in India. If scholars have often overlooked this overtly 'secular' line of cow protectionist argument, historically it has allowed alliances to form between the state and cow protectionist institutions in the cause of agricultural development.

Adcock here points towards the need to visit afresh those institutions, actors and practices that have been marked as 'secular' or even apolitical in the making of the cow protection discourse. The *gaushala* is one such space which, on the one hand, needs to be brought into the fold of the religiously marked cow protection story while, on the other, also providing the opportunity to explore the more seemingly 'secular' workings of religion that may not necessarily be wholly explained by placing it in the framework of Hindu nationalist violence. What constitutes the bedrock of this chapter is my argument that a *gaushala* can enable us to go beyond the 'exceptional' events of heightened violence (which are arguably becoming a present 'everyday reality'), to capture the makings of the cow protection discourse, helping us understand how the two intimately relate to and construct one another.

---

[1] See https://religiousstudies.artsci.wustl.edu/articles/634 for a detailed description of Adcock's upcoming work.

Part of the current interest in *gaushalas* can be attributed to the investment of the present Hindu nationalist government, which first came to power in 2014, in the setting up and maintenance of *gaushalas*. As per news reports, the Bharatiya Janata Party (BJP)-led government spent ₹5.8 billion on the construction and maintenance of *gaushalas* in the period from 2014 to 2016 (Upadhyay 2016). In mid-2014, soon after coming to power at the Centre, the BJP started the Rashtriya Gokul Mission, a national programme to build 'havens for retired, ailing and barren bovines' (Upadhyay 2016). In May 2016, a national conference was held on *gauvansh* (cow-clans) and *gaushalas* in the national capital which had a 'three-pronged agenda'—to discuss (a) the challenge of increasing cows' productivity, (b) steps to ensure better care of cows and (c) security 'against smugglers and other cruel incidents' (PTI 2016). In the same year, Baba Ramdev's Patanjali Ayurved declared its plan to invest ₹500 crore in four 'mega', 'scientific' *gaushalas* across the country (Dutta 2016). This governmental interest in *gaushalas* at the contemporary moment when cases of cow-related lynching have come to constitute a category of violence in itself, then, presents the need to examine further the linkages between the *gaushala* as a site and a heightened, spectacularly violent event like the lynching.

My ethnographic inquiry is located at the Shree Gopal Gaushala (SGG) in the town of Faridabad, in the north Indian state of Haryana, nearly 30 kilometres from the national capital. SGG is one of the four registered *gaushalas* in Faridabad district. Founded by the Vishwa Hindu Parishad (VHP) in 1995 and run by those principally identifying as VHP *karyakartas* or 'activists', SGG self-identifies as a 'religious organiza-tion', unlike other *gaushalas* in the town which refer to themselves as 'animal shelters' or related variants. Even though the *gaushala* is one of the oldest in the city, it began to acquire visibility only towards the middle of 2015. This is true of *gaushalas* in general in Faridabad; their existence was a rather lesser-known fact before 2014–2015, when the current dispensation first came to power. It was around this time that two trusts, namely the Som Prakash Charitable Trust and the Kailash Devi Trust, started the service of running cycle rickshaws across the city to collect food and other supplies for the cows housed in the *gaushalas* in Faridabad, thereby familiarizing many residents with the existence of the *gaushalas* in the first place. The knowledge of SGG (procured through these very cycle rickshaws) made it convenient for my family to perform the Brahminical ritual of *gaudaan* or 'cow donation' at SGG, upon the death of my long-ailing grandmother. A month before her passing away, a cow from SGG was made to perform *Vaitarani*, a Brahminical ritual where

> a cow is first worshipped and then its tail grasped with both hands ... in preparation for that terrible event after death in which the dead have to cross the fetid river of death on the opposite bank, on which the kingdom of the dead is found. (van der Veer 1994, 87)

Thus, my familiarity with the SGG was mediated by a familial encounter. In a following section, I shall dwell on how this kind of mediation shaped my presence in the field.

Situated at Surajkund Road, Faridabad, SGG, with its stated objective 'to encourage people to respect cows', housed nearly 840 cows as of December 2017. Of these, roughly 150 are milk-producing, 170 are male cows (referred to as *Nandis*), 200 are old, 60 are blind, 20 are accident-stricken and/or are disabled, and the remaining are calves and unproductive cows.

The number of paid workers at SGG, both men and women, all of them from Bhil, Gond and Sahariya tribes who have migrated largely from VHP-mobilized districts of Madhya Pradesh, is around 40, with nearly 30 men among these. All women workers are wives of the men working at the *gaushala*. In addition, there are a few volunteers who visit the *gaushala* regularly and provide financial assistance in times of requirement. The workers reside in the premises of the *gaushala* itself, making the home the same as the workplace. SGG is owned and run by VHP *karyakartas*, men from middle-class Brahmin-Baniya backgrounds, who occupy all leadership roles at the *gaushala*. The members of the leadership and the trustee board are therefore entirely male, dominant caste and middle class. The manager at SGG is a young Jat man in his 30s who also works part time as an insurance agent.

THE COW PROTECTION MOVEMENT: A HISTORICAL OVERVIEW

The relevance of the cow in India has been at the centre of much academic conversation, especially since the 1960s. Anthropologists, economists, ecologists, historians and geographers have engaged with various strands pertaining to the bovine (Korom 2000). An important debate was initiated in the 1960s by Harris' controversial thesis that the sanctity of cow in India must be understood as largely a techno-environmental issue, a taboo grounded in scientific principles which helps maintain a 'low-energy, small-scale, animal-based ecosystem' (van der Veer 1994, 87). Harris argued that the problem of the 'holy cow' is found to unravel itself not in the domain of the religious but the economic–ecological—its functional importance to the Indian peasant farmer. He further upheld the Hindu logic of the cow's sanctity as economically and ecologically sound and asserted that the Hindu practices reflect a level of economizing that is not appreciated by the Western standards of saving and husbandry (Harris 1974). Harris' functional approach was severely criticized for reducing the complex cattle question to a mere 'calculus of calories' (Glucklich 1997). In an attempt to 'correct' the 'imbalance' resulting from a disproportionate emphasis on the economic and environmental, Simoons and Lodrick (1981) placed the 'sacred cow concept in a broader cultural perspective by examining its varied and interesting expressions in Hindu religion, folk thought and everyday behavior' (Simoons and Lodrick 1981, 121).

In the 1980s, scholarly attention shifted to the sacred status granted by Hindus to the cow and the manner in which this 'sanctity', defined in religious terms, affected the socio-political landscape of India. This body of work, most of which came from historians, dates the cow protection 'movement' to the late 19th- and early 20th-century cow-related 'riots' (Freitag 1980; Pandey 1981; Robb 1986; Yang 1980), the formation of cow protection societies or *gaurakshini sabhas* and the efforts undertaken by Arya Samaj's Dayanand Saraswati to prevent cow slaughter and protect the *gau mata*. One of the most rigorously documented aspects of cow protection is the period around the 1880s when a large number of *gaurakshini sabhas* began to emerge and the reformist Arya Samaj's Dayanand Saraswati actively took up this agenda (Freitag 1980; Pinney 1997; Robb 1986; van der Veer 1994). Scholars have held the activities of the *gaurakshini sabhas*, along with the efforts undertaken by an army of *gau swamis,* that is, 'agitators, emissaries, lecturers, paid agents, penniless adventurers, preachers and propagandists' (Yang 1980, 586), who toured different parts of the country (though largely limited to the northern belt), chiefly responsible for a series of 'communal riots' that broke out in almost all of North India in the 1880s–1890s and 1900s.

While this body of work is insightful in its description of the causal mechanisms and structures of violence that erupted in the name of the cow as early as the 19th century, it suggests a linear history of the 'cow protection movement' and conflates the spectacle of violence with the process by which the cow was made to become the charged symbol of the *gau mata*.[2] I seek to caution against this uniform and linear conceptualization of the 'cow protection movement' and argue that the sanctity of the cow draws from a range of symbolic, discursive and material practices, across multiple spheres—economic, ecological, religious and political—and it is these aspects that are called upon discreetly and distinctly at various points in history to (re)cast the cow as *gau mata* and activate 'her' as a powerful politico-religious symbol.[3]

---

[2] Many significant political actors took public positions on the matter of cow protection in the late 19th to early 20th centuries. Since these do not directly pertain to my argument in this chapter, I do not delve into their intricacies here but mention a few examples to indicate certain positions. Gandhi (1909), for example, in line with his belief in non-violence harboured a love for the cow but was against a legislative ban on cow slaughter. Ambedkar (1948) argued that the declaration of beef-eating as sacrilegious was rooted in the tussle between Brahminism and Buddhism. Jha (2009) has shown through archaeological evidence that Hindus, including Brahmins and even deities, consumed beef in ancient India. Interestingly, Savarkar, known for his 1923 work *Hindutva,* was opposed to the notion of the cow's divinity. The Kukas, a millenarian Sikh sect, despite their belief in Hindu–Sikh distinctions thought of cow slaughter and beef consumption as *mleccha* or 'impure' (Oberoi 1992).

[3] I have demonstrated this at length elsewhere by (re)visiting several moments in a rather long period, from the mid-1700s to the 1890s, when the figure of the 'holy' cow had been made to (re)surface at distinct points. I posit that the vignettes

In the following section, I dwell on my ethnographic experience at SGG to understand the ways in which it constructs the notions of *gau mata* and *gau seva(k)*, which I argue are central to the present project of cow protection. Exploring the manner in which the *gaushala* is built and presents itself as a space and place—I examine the spatial organization of SGG; its motivations of founding, structure and organization with emphasis on the division of labour (between the leadership and the workers in general as well as between the men and women workers); the way in which the cow is recast as *gau mata* and the Adivasi worker as her *sevak* and lastly, my own gendered position in the *gaushala* as well as the larger project as a researcher.

THE PRODUCTION OF *(GAU) SEVA(K)*: AT THE INTERSECTIONS OF GENDER, CASTE AND LABOUR

The Spatial Organization of SGG

The spatial organization of SGG exemplifies one of the material practices that order the *gaushala* in specific ways to produce a gendered discourse of *gau seva* and regulate the construction of masculinities and femininities in that space. Underlying this approach is the idea that challenges a static or reactionary conceptualization of space, as if time/history plays itself out against an inert, homogeneous and unchanging space. I intend to show instead that the space of the *gaushala* itself is central to the production of the practice of *gau seva* and the figure of the *gau sevak*, within the rubric of which, we must understand the cow protection movement. 'Space', therefore, is not the background against which the action of cow protection can be plotted; it is the protagonist of the story of cow protection that positions both materially and symbolically, some actors at the centre of the cow protection discourse

---

described at length, some of which can be dated to the 18th century, must not be seen as the components or parts that simply add up together to produce a singular, cohesive 'whole' of the 'cow protection movement'; instead, it would be productive to see them as pieces of varying shapes and textures that are embedded in their own contexts and histories and can tell us only partial and situated stories of cow protection.

as the legitimate *gau sevaks* and marginalizes and vilifies others as *gau hinsaks* (perpetrators of violence against the cow).

Upon entering SGG, the first area to make itself visible is the shed for milch cattle on the extreme left and the office area on the right, with a sizeable parking lot in between. The milch cows' shed is the most valuable section of the *gaushala*, placed right at the front, as it houses the productive female cows. Right next to it is a huge expanse, designated for the construction of the Shani Temple (a temple dedicated to *Shani*, the Hindu god for justice and death), which is likely to be complete by 2020. In the office on the right is the seating area of the manager (and, sometimes, the visiting trustees and other guests) along with a small shop which sells various cow-based products along with neatly-lined Patanjali[4] products and a few books on Hindu religion and culture, most of which are Gita Press publications.[5] Immediately adjacent to the office is a huge, well-maintained temple, where idols of various gods of the Hindu religion reside. This is also where *bhandaras* or 'religious feasts' are held almost on a daily basis, by visitors as part of rituals on occasions such as birthdays, anniversaries, death of a loved one and so on. Behind the temple are more sheds for disabled (mostly, blind) cows, with a shed for bulls and buffaloes adjacent to it. Next to it is the open shed for calves. Removed from the rest of the sheds is a dispensary where accident-stricken and seriously injured/sick cattle are brought, where they are attended to by the in-house vet. Right next to the dispensary, in keeping with the government guidelines, is a separate shed for cattle suffering from various kinds of illnesses, where they are housed during their recovery. Amidst these sheds is a single room, often locked and opened only in the event of need—this is where numerous notebooks are stocked, to be borrowed by visitors

---

[4] Patanjali Ayurved Limited is an Indian consumer goods company with Baba Ramdev at the helm, who started out as a 'yoga guru'. The company claims to rely on the wisdom of using 'native Hindu' ingredients and takes pride in its purportedly Hindu ethos, thus setting itself apart from 'Western' companies and products. Known for its herbal products, the company has also been mired in multiple controversies for not meeting quality and hygiene standards.

[5] Gita Press, set up in 1923 in Gorakhpur in the North Indian state of Uttar Pradesh, is the world's largest publisher of Hindu religious texts.

only to write 'Ram' innumerable times, as they chant the god's name as a sign of their devotion to him and, once done, return the notebooks to be kept in the same room. This room then is an embodiment of Ram bhakti (worship of Ram) demonstrated by the *gau bhakts* (cow worshippers). On the extreme periphery of the *gaushala* are the staff quarters, that I was politely denied access to. This is where the migrant Adivasi workers reside, some with their families. See Figure 7.1 for an illustrative depiction of SGG.

This spatial mapping illustrates the manner in which the *gaushala* is structured and hierarchized on lines of gender and caste. The area of most value is the sheds of the milch cows—the milk obtained from these cows also becomes the chief source of revenue. It is, therefore, not surprising that the milk-producing cows are regarded as *gau mata* and worshipped in literal terms every morning, right before the day starts at SGG. They are, in fact, placed at maximum distance from those who may be a threat to their (re)productive capacity and/or purity—bulls in general and disabled and accident-stricken bulls in particular. The practice of mating is crucial and needs to be regulated. For instance, Mr Tyagi, one of the senior VHP *karyakartas,* would often stress the fact that one of the major strengths of SGG over other *gaushalas* was that it houses only native breeds that are far superior to Western breeds like Jersey, which do not even qualify as the sacred *gau mata*. He stressed, 'We have here many cow breeds that have been referred to in Vedic literature—the *kamadhenu* (the wish-fulfilling cow), *surbhi* and *kapila* cows which cannot be seen in most *gaushalas* around'. He noted further that one of the missions of SGG is to restore the purity of *gau mata* through *nasal sudhaar* or breed improvement. Notably, he dated the emergence of the 'sin' of cross-breeding in India only after the Muslims invaded India. He elaborated:

> Just as there is the concept of the *gotra* or clan among humans, with prohibition of marriage within the same *gotra*, there had been the notion of a *gotra* among cows with stringent injunctions against mating within bulls from the same lineage, or else their quality and productivity is adversely affected. This malpractice of mating of intra-familial cows started with the Mughal rule and it is precisely this sin of the Muslim which has caused a decline in productivity of cows today.

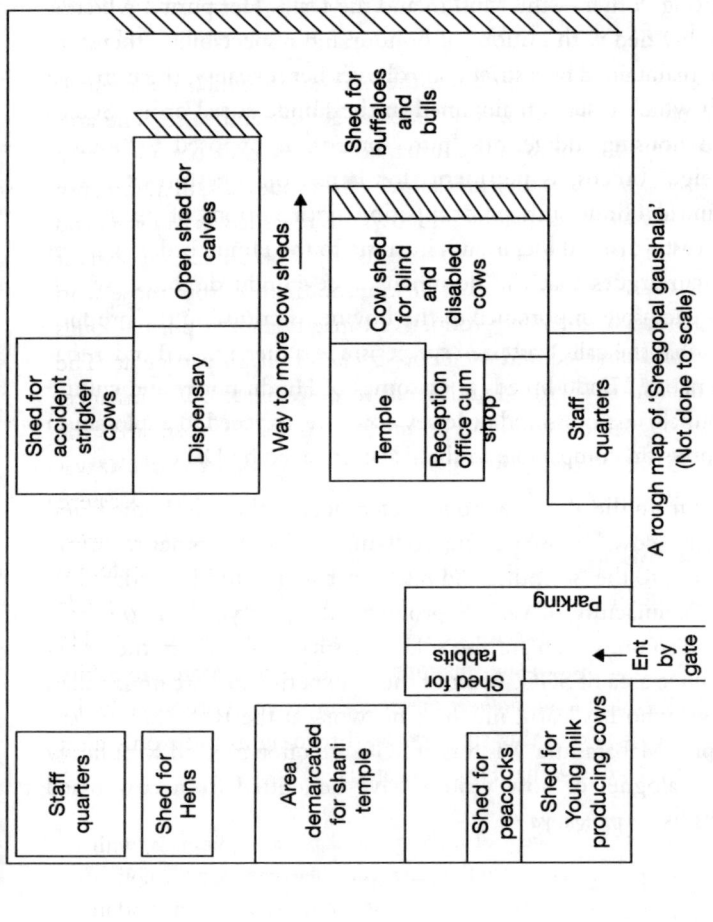

Figure 7.1 *Spatial Layout of SGG*
Courtesy: Sanjay Sharma and Ekata Bakshi

The *gau mata,* therefore, emerges as akin to the ideal Hindu Brahmin woman, another figure carved in the image of the 'mother'—the generous, self-sacrificing woman who nurtures her (Hindu) sons and the (Hindu) nation at large through her (re)productive capacity and her milk; she is, on the one hand, a nurturer, a protector but is also in constant need of protection herself, against the 'cow-slaughtering' or 'beef-eating' 'other'—the Muslim and the Dalit. Her purity, which is inextricably tied with notions of honour and respectability, therefore must be maintained by a strict control over her sexuality, the principle through which caste is maintained in the Hindu social order. SGG's pride in housing indigenous 'pure' breeds, as opposed to 'mixed' or 'foreign' breeds, is pertinent, for it not only gestures towards Brahminical Hinduism's preoccupation with notions of purity but mirrors caste-marked hierarchies intrinsic to the Hindu order. Yamini Narayanan argues that the dominant caste-Hindu discourse which ascribes excessive importance to the bovine, is critical in the production of what she calls 'casteized speciesism'—a hierarchized order that regards native Hindu breeds as epitomes of Hindu purity and culture while buffalo and crossbred or Jersey cows are 'exposed to exploitation and oppression comparable to the situation faced by Dalits'.

Apart from the aforementioned references to the able-bodied, and 'productive cows' housed in the front-most sheds, the other recurring reference is to the 'scientific and research-based' activities undertaken there—manufacture of various products like phenyl, shampoo, eye-drops and so on, which are also sold on a small scale within the front-facing office area of SGG. Most of these 'experiments' are undertaken by Tyagi, who has learnt much of his work at the RSS-run *gaushala* at Nagpur, Maharashtra. Visitors at SGG are often greeted with heavy verbal catalogues of how visitors have benefitted from cow-based products like *panchgavya.*[6]

---

[6] *Panchgavya,* a concoction of cow dung, urine, milk, curd and ghee, is regarded as one of the most significant and beneficial products obtained from the cow. Repeated insistence on the useful properties of *panchgavya* recurs in the cow protection discourse and is one of the refrains at SGG.

Founding and Organizational Structure of SGG

The stories around the founding of SGG are central to understanding its social and political ethos, motivations and proclivities. While more than one version with minor variations were narrated to me, I recount here the broad contours of what was told to me by senior *karyakartas* and the manager:

> After some thinking and assistance from the VHP, Baislaji, one of our *karyakartas* started a small *gaushala* on a piece of land in Sector 8 in Faridabad. The Congress was in power then. We were, very soon, driven out of there and this was when Baislaji, one of senior leaders, inaugurated his own 1.5 acre land, right here, with a *Bhoomi Pujan*. Nearly 240 cows were given to us then by the Municipal Corporation. At that point, we were struggling to make sheds but the lord showed us the path once again. Out of nowhere, a Jain female ascetic came to the *gaushala* one day. She was terribly angry on seeing the state of the *gaushala*, and how much we were struggling with taking care of the cows. She reprimanded us a lot and we listened. After all, she was an ascetic. But then, she emptied a bag of more than 70,000 rupees before us. 'Take this and make use of it to serve *gau mata*', she instructed. That very week, another *bhakt* from the Jain samaj, a businessman, donated another lakh. This amount became the foundation on which the *gaushala* was built and today, we can say with pride, that this is one of the superior *gaushalas* in not just Faridabad but all of Haryana.

Many questions remained unanswered despite my polite insistence on responses. Who informed the VHP *karyakartas* about the transport of cattle and how exactly did they come to know of it? How exactly were the cows 'rescued'? What happened to the *kasai* or butcher who was taking them for slaughter? The question of land for the construction of SGG seemed to have been easily resolved too, just as the question of the initial funding. These absences in Dagras's story are as critical to its construction as the elements that overtly constitute it. In the case of the story of founding, as in the general context of my work, the recovery of an 'authentic truth' is not the motivation this work is guided by; it is, in fact, the self-fashioning of the story of cow protection that I am interested in. It is in this specific regard that this story becomes significant. What emerges most strongly is the continuation and consolidation of the trope of the Muslim 'other', given a material-visual image as the dangerous *kasai* threatening to the *gau mata*. A large part of the verbal interaction and visual representation at SGG builds on the notion of the *kasai* as representative of the entire Muslim community. Even though there is no Muslim presence at SGG, among the leadership, workers or even visitors, the Muslims occupy an important place in the cow protection discourse at SGG, either as the threatening *kasai* or by way of occasional references to the 'good Muslim' who is 'accommodating of and respectful to' Hindu values and beliefs. Mr Tyagi once told me, 'I will welcome Muslims with open arms as long as they are as reverent to the *gau mata* as we are'.

Labour is an important structuring category to understand relationships and networks at SGG. As mentioned earlier, the board of trustees as well as the leadership at SGG is entirely male, Brahmin and Baniya. It is composed mainly of senior VHP *karyakartas*, who supervise the overall functioning of SGG, look into financial matters and serve as the connecting bridge between the VHP and SGG. The physical work is undertaken by the workforce, composed of Adivasi men and some women. The manager is the point of contact between the leadership and the workers. The workers report to the manager. He oversees the three teams of 10–15 persons each, headed by a team head who is always male. An ordinary day at the *gaushala* begins at 4 am with the feeding of the cows followed by milking the cows. The selling of the milk takes place 6.30 am onwards, a process managed by the team heads and overseen by the manager. After this, all the 11 *wadas* or sections are cleaned thoroughly by the women workers. The cows and calves are then separated and placed in different *wadas*. In the evening at around 4:00 PM, this process is repeated, and milk is sold again at 6:00 PM onwards. The entire process is supervised and assisted with by the team heads. Women are responsible for cleaning the *wadas*, the temple in the compound of the *gaushala* and the room of the temple's *pandit* (priest). Among the workers, duties and areas of work are interchanged periodically. When women workers are not doing '*gaushala* work', they are involved in cooking, cleaning, taking care of their children and other household tasks. It is significant to note that men workers are regarded as 'full-time workers' with a wage of ₹10,000 per month, while women workers are given a 'part-time' wage of ₹5,000 per month. This is an exemplification of one of the ways in which women's labour is devalued, compounded at the *gaushala* by the fact that there is a hazy distinction, if any, between 'home' and 'work-place'. My argument is that the deification of the productive cow into the *gau mata,* who must be elevated by ritual worship and protected, is sustained by the simultaneous recasting of the Adivasi *karmachari* or worker into the *gau sevak*. The discourse of *seva* in general and *gau seva* in particular, therefore, becomes important in marking the contours of the current cow protection discourse.

GAU SEVA AND THE MAKING OF THE *GAU MATA*

Dating the emergence of *gau mata* as a loaded symbol of the Hindu nation to the late 19th to early 20th centuries, Gupta argues that the cow had the 'potential to be represented as the mother of all Hindus and of a Hindu identity and nationality, requiring protection from Non-Hindus' because of its transcendent appeal (Gupta 2001: 4295). The *gau mata* was akin to the Brahmin domestic woman as well as the goddess whose chastity and honour needed to be guarded against 'external' penetration, as metonymic of the nation that had to be pro-tected against the non-Hindu invasion (Gupta 2001, Oberoi 1992). This iconography of the cow as mother-nation-goddess was central to her construction as sacred. The association of the cow with the loaded image of the mother was further solidified by giving it a concrete material base—the economic usefulness of the cow in terms of its productivity and capacity to provide milk, curd, ghee and so on was repeatedly emphasized. The *gau mata* then, much like Bharat Mata or Mother-India, is almost always in a fragile position of threat and in need of militant protection against the ever-present danger of violation of her honour at the hands of the 'outsider'. The extent and intensity of the danger must constantly be reinforced to arouse 'her' virile Hindu sons, who must dedicate themselves to the cause of her protection or else face the disgrace of emasculation.

If the dominant discourse of cow protection takes shape through the violent *gauraksha*, *gau seva* with its dual aim of rearing of 'ailing and helpless cattle' and the 'upliftment of the downtrodden Adivasis' is a seemingly more benign project. The political and ideological construction of both is, however, inextricably tied with the gendered project of rescuing the *gau mata* from the villainous *kasai* and/or the filthy beef-eater, thus consolidating communal and caste-based antagonisms. At the *gaushala,* we witness a specific manner in which the practice of *gau seva* enjoins the Brahmin–Baniya leadership and the Adivasi workers or *gau sevaks* in mutually constitutive or even seemingly reciprocal ways—while the leadership can appropriate the workers into a benign project without necessarily having to eliminate them through the violent *gauraksha* as typified in the 'riot' or the 'lynching', the workers are imparted dignity for labour that is otherwise regarded as filthy or dehumanizing through a systematic recasting of working with cattle as the noble, virtuous and sacred *gau seva*. Freitag (1980) has eloquently demonstrated the manner in which 'lower' castes, Chamars for instance, have historically been kept outside the fold of the 'sacred' cow protection while also being assigned the physically demanding and 'impure' labour of working with animals' bodies. More recently, Singh (2017) has also pointed out the irony of the exclusion and vilification of Dalit-Bahujans from the Brahminical fold of cow protection when the labour of cattle rearing has historically been the task of the *Ahir* community. I argue that *gau seva,* therefore, emerges as a relatively more sanitized means of ensuring Adivasi and Dalit-Bahujan cooperation in a Brahminical project with the appearance of granting them a 'better' life while also keeping them in 'their place'.

The appearance notwithstanding, the project of *gau seva* is built on fundamentally unequal terms. Analysing *seva* as a concept and practice, Srivatsan (2014) argues that it has come to constitute one of the most significant strands of voluntary activism. *Seva*, in its very structural mode, encodes beneficiaries of charity bound in a hierarchical relationship with the *sevak*-saviour, where any attempt to criticize or challenge what the saviour has chosen to offer will be marginalized. In other words, *seva* consolidates the hegemony of the elite while also providing them an ethical supremacy. He points out how an activism of this nature is founded on the view of the disadvantaged as the 'sinful wretch' who needs to be uplifted. In the context of cow protection, the 'wretch' is also seen as 'dirty', in need of purification through bodily work that involves coming in contact with *gau mata*, the work that simultaneously dirties and purifies him. This kind of *seva* is fundamentally qualitatively different from a view that looks at entry to schools, libraries and so on as civic rights. Srivatsan's observation of the sevak-saviour's attitude seems especially accurate in the light of the statement made by Dagra, who once casually mentioned to me, 'The workers' children are really not interested in studying or for improving their life prospects in general. They just like to while away their time, sitting around, doing nothing. We ask them to work at the *gaushala*, help around with something or the other so they realize the value of work and learn to do something!' Dagra's utterance makes clear his view of the workers' children who, he posits, are not just in a social and economic crisis but a moral one.

The notion of *gau seva* at the VHP-run SGG is also informed significantly by the VHP's use of *karseva* in the Ram Janmabhoomi movement, in semantic and discursive terms.[7] The idea of *karseva* was used originally by Sikhs in the context of restoration of the Golden Temple in 1984 when it had been damaged in the face of military action by the then Indian government (Chopra 2010). *Kar* (meaning 'hands') and *Seva* (meaning 'service') evokes an idea of 'selfless service' or 'voluntary labour' that is religious in nature—a 'labour of love' performed in service of religion with humility (Virdee 2005). *Karseva*, then, is associated simultaneously with both 'worship' and 'service',

---

[7] In 1984, the VHP and its affiliates launched an agitation to demolish the Babri mosque at 'Ram Janmabhoomi' (the birthplace of the Hindu god, Ram) in Ayodhya in order to erect a Ram Temple instead. The 'Ram Rath Yatra' organized by the BJP and led by its then president, L. K. Advani, was launched in September 1990 to accomplish the mission of building the Ram Mandir at the site of the Masjid. The Yatra triggered serious violence and led to riots across the country, where hundreds lost their lives. Both with regard to the history of Hindu–Muslim relations in the country and the political career of the VHP, the 'Ram Janmabhoomi agitation' marked and continues to be a defining moment.

in ways that sometimes makes them one and the same. In 1989, the VHP appropriated the erstwhile Sikh notion of *karseva* to mobilize Hindu activists to demolish the mosque and build the Ram temple (Jaffrelot 1996). Incitement of violence as a means of protection was an intrinsic part of this imagination of *karseva*. At the centre of this protectionist discourse then was the figure of Ram (imagined as male but also feminized in certain visual and symbolic repertoires of Hindu tradition), metonymic in a larger sense of Hindu religion and nation.[8] In the distinctive couching of *karseva* at SGG into *gau seva* (and its intimately porous relationship with *gauraksha*), the feminized figure of the *gau mata,* who at once embodies the mother, the goddess and the nation, becomes the object of protection, in whose service, the labour of Adivasi men and women must be deployed. The SGG leadership in this specific rehashing of *gau seva* also sees itself as engaged in *samaj seva* (social service) and *desh seva* (service to the nation), not only for the role it views itself as playing in cow protection but also in the 'upliftment' of disadvantaged sections.

In one of my interactions with the manager at SGG, he emphasized repeatedly the 'pious' nature of *gau seva*. This emphasis on piety and religious virtuosity becomes important in the project of the sanitization of the otherwise supposedly 'dirty' labour of working with cattle, which needs to be spiritually elevated in order to be devalued and appropriated. The differentially hierarchized positions at SGG—the Brahmin–Baniya men who occupy leadership roles and the board of trustees; the young Jat manager who supervises the workers; the Adivasi men who are regarded as 'full-time' *gau sevaks* and the Adivasi women, their wives who are viewed as 'part-time' *gau sevaks* with no representation in both the SGG core bodies or the workers' teams—are illustrations of Ambedkar's argument of the caste Hindu order manifesting as not a mere division of labour but the division of labourers. The devaluation of women's work is pertinent to the blurry distinction between 'work' and 'home'. Gopal (2013) has argued that the mechanistic distinction of

---

[8] For a detailed analysis of the various meanings ascribed to Ram through the VHP's organization and ideology during the Ram Janmabhoomi movement, see Datta (1991).

'work' into the compartments of formal, informal and domestic reflects the superficial and artificially imposed distinction charted out between production and social reproduction and that a

> significant aspect of social reproduction, as reflected in the subsistence and socially necessary activities done by women as well as the numerous degraded tasks performed by women/workers in the informal sectors, also fall under the rubric of caste-based labours. Thus, caste hierarchies, as much as gender hierarchies, contribute to the segmentation and devaluation of labours. (Gopal 2013, 92)

While devaluation of labour is central to the production of stigmatized labouring bodies, the *gaushala*'s fashioning of the discourse of *gau seva* through symbolic and material practices stigmatizes as it claims to spiritually elevate—which, as Srivatsan (2014) argues, *seva* as a form of voluntary activism has historically allowed for.

THE POLITICS OF MY PRESENCE AT SGG: A BRIEF NOTE ON METHODOLOGY

Arguably, my own social and political–analytical location informed not only the ways in which I navigated the space of SGG but also what I 'saw' and 'was allowed to see' in the course of my fieldwork.

A large body of feminist scholarship on ethnography has been tremendously useful in challenging the dualisms of the 'subject and object, thought and feeling, knower and known and political and personal' as well as the 'arbitrary boundaries of traditional academic disciplines' (Stacey 1988, 21). At the same time, there has been hesitation to place uncritical faith in the feminist principles of empathy and mutuality as the necessary analytical and ethical frameworks to do ethnographic research, with the fear that purportedly feminist research may actually pose a greater risk of abandonment and betrayal than even positivist research (Stacey 1988). In this context, conversations around the methodological aspects of working with what Nigel Fielding (1993) has termed 'unloved groups' have been especially rich and insightful. As a feminist-identified, dominant caste, university-trained women's study scholar researching a *gaushala* founded and run by a militant Hindu nationalist organization, I grappled with several concerns about accessing the field, performing various roles at SGG (of which that of the researcher was but one) and walking the tightrope between my privilege which gave me access to the *gaushala* as well as my vulnerabilities within that space which invoked fear and at many points, the genuine possibility of threat.

I came in touch with SGG through a familial encounter and my access to it was mediated significantly by my father, who though not from the VHP or its circles in any manner was seen as 'one among us' in certain ways by the *gaushala*'s leadership, given his gender, caste–class and political position. Joseph (1996) has referred to access of this nature, facilitated by figures of authority whose own positions are often oppositional to the researcher's own, as 'patriarchal connectivity'. Further, women researchers have written about the invisibility or even the erasure of their researcher-selves in the field. In her contribution to *Women Fielding Danger* that deals with the methodological challenges faced by women researchers, Schwandner-Sievers notes that, 'as a woman working on my own that the greatest threat was not the violence toward me, but rather not being taken seriously as a researcher' (Schwandner-Sievers 2009, 1). In SGG's view, I was the daughter of a respectable Hindu middle-class man, curiously interested in the cow but largely a politically insignificant actor, given my age and gender, both different from the SGG as a larger constituency. I was also the 'brahmin *beti*' (Brahmin daughter) interested in learning about the SGG's investment in another Brahminized-feminized figure—that of the *gau mata*. While this perception undermined my researcher-self, it is also what facilitated my access to the space. In many ways, I was not a consequential presence by the virtue of not being aligned with their notion of an influential man of power. However, suspicion and distrust were far from completely eliminated. On my very first day at SGG, my father's personal and professional details were noted (mine were not), and reticence and hesitation coexisted with the insistence on transparency and benevolence. The former was at its strongest in the context of my interaction with the workers; all my conversations with them took place in a highly supervised environment and were, therefore, limited in many ways. SGG then would often manifest for me as a disorienting space where rehearsed politeness and a seemingly welcoming disposition would uncomfortably sit with fear, suspicion and strategic revelation and concealment by all parties. As Sehgal (2009) points out in the context of her ethnographic work with the RSS:

> I began to see that my own covertness was matched by that of the Hindu nationalist interlocutors…. [E]ach of us was subtly and covertly 'bargaining' for our interests on the basis of what we perceived to be the identity and social location of the other… I discovered that the Hindu nationalists and myself each held assumptions about, and goals for, the other that were not always totally true and usually not fully explicit. (Sehgal 2009, 11)

I, therefore, build on the suggestion that feminist methodological principles of honesty, trust and empathy cannot be called upon simplistically or worse, eulogized as essential to doing 'authentic' research. Ethnographic identities in the field play out in far more complex ways than the polarities of overt–covert, honest–dishonest, all powerful–subservient, disclosure–concealment can capture or allow for. It is in these complex webs of relationships and networks in the field that various truth-claims are operationalized.

CONCLUSION: JOINING THE DOTS

I have argued in this chapter that the cow protection discourse has been reductively and, in my view, wrongly viewed as a coherent 'movement', with emphasis on spectacular violence that is episodic in nature. The epistemic offshoot of this approach is the production of a linear, uniform cow protection movement that climaxed into the 'riot' in the late 19th to early 20th centuries and the 'bovine lynching' in the contemporary moment. Making a departure from this mode of analysis, I place at the centre an ordinary and benign space like a *gaushala* and examine its everyday symbolic, material and discursive practices to understand the manner in which the 'everyday' and the 'event' are both intimately related and mutually constituted. The fashioning of the discourse of *gau seva* and the making of the *gau mata* at SGG bring to fore the ways in which gender, labour and caste shape and collapse the fine distinction between the violent *gauraksha* and the charitable *gau seva*.

REFERENCES

Ambedkar, B. R. 1948. *The Untouchables: Who Were They and Why They Became Untouchables*. New Delhi: Amrit Book Company.

Chopra, Radhika. 2010. 'Commemorating Hurt: Memorializing Operation Bluestar'. *Sikh Formations: Religion, Culture, Theory* 6 (2): 119–152.

Dutta, Arnab. 2016. 'Patanjali to Spend Rs 500 Crore on Cow Protection'. rediff. com, 14 August. http://m.rediff.com/money/report/patanjali-to-spend-rs-500-crore-on-cow-protection/20160814.htm.

Datta, Pradip K. 1991. 'VHP's Ram at Ayodhya: Reincarnation through Ideology and Organisation'. *Economic and Political Weekly* 26 (44): 2517–2526.

Freitag, Sandra. 1980. 'Sacred Symbol as Mobilizing Ideology: The North Indian Search for a "Hindu" Community'. *Comparative Studies in Society and History* 22 (4): 597–625.

Gandhi, Mohandas Karamchand. 1909. *Hind Swaraj or Indian Home Rule*. Ahmedabad: Navjivan Publishing House. https://www.mkgandhi.org/ebks/hind_swaraj.pdf.

Glucklich, Ariel. 1997. *The End of Magic*. Oxford: Oxford University Press.

Gopal, Meena. 2013. 'Ruptures and Reproduction in Caste/Gender/Labour'. *Economic and Political Weekly* 48 (18): 91–97.

Gupta, Charu. 2001. 'The Icon of Mother in Late Colonial North India: "Bharat Mata" "Matri Bhasha" and "Gau Mata"'. *Economic and Political Weekly* 36 (45): 4291–4299.

Harris, Marvin. 1974. *Cows, Pigs, Wars, and Witches*. New York: Vintage Publishers.

Jaffrelot, Christophe. 1996. *The Hindu Nationalist Movement and Indian Politics*. London: C. Hurst & Co. Publishers.

Jha, Dwijendra Narayan. 2009. *The Myth of the Holy Cow*. New Delhi: Navayana.

Joseph, Suad. 1996. 'Relationality and Ethnographic Subjectivity: Key Informants and the Construction of Personhood in Fieldwork'. In: *Feminist Dilemmas in Fieldwork*, edited by D. L. Wolf, 107–121. Boulder, CO: Westview Press.

Korom, Frank J. 2000. 'Holy Cow! The Apotheosis of Zebu, or Why the Cow Is Sacred in Hinduism'. *Asian Folklore Studies* 59 (2): 181–203.

Oberoi, Harjot. 1992. 'Brotherhood of the Pure: The Poetics and Politics of Cultural Transgression'. *Modern Asian Studies* 26 (1): 157–197.

Pandey, Gyanendra. 1981. 'Rallying around the Cow: Sectarian Strife in the Bhojpuri Region, c. 1888–1917'. In *Subaltern Studies II*, edited by Ranajit Guha, 1–95. New Delhi: Oxford University Press.

PTI. 2016. 'Government to Introduce Special Protection Measures for "Desi" Cows'. hindustantimes.com, 17 May. http://www.hindustantimes.com/

india/government-to-introduce-special-protection-for-desi-cows/story-b6Dbk75ICmv6HyG0QbSaKN.html.

Pinney, Christopher. 1997. 'The Nation (Un)pictured? "Chromolithography" and Popular Politics in India'. *Critical Inquiry* 23 (4): 834–867.

Robb, Peter. 1986. 'The Challenge of Gau Mata: British Policy and Religious Change in India, 1880–1916'. *Modern Asian Studies* 20 (2): 285–319.

Schwandner-Sievers, Stephanie. 2009. 'Securing "Safe Spaces": Field Diplomacy in Albania and Kosovo'. In *Women Fielding Danger: Negotiating Ethnographic Identities in Field Research*, edited by M. K. Huggins and M. L. Glebbeek, 325–352. Lanham: Rowman & Littlefield Publishers.

Sehgal, Meera. 2009. 'The Veiled Feminist Ethnographer: Fieldwork among Women of India's Hindu Right'. In *Women Fielding Danger: Negotiating Ethnographic Identities in Field Research*, edited by M. K. Huggins and M. L. Glebbeek, 325–352. Lanham: Rowman & Littlefield Publishers.

Simoons, Frederick J., and Deryck O. Lodrick. 1981. 'Background to Understanding the Cattle Situation of India: The Sacred Cow Concept in Hindu Religion and Folk Culture'. *Zeitschrift für Ethnologie* 106: 121–137.

Singh, Asha. 2017. 'Cow, Backwardness and Bahujan Women'. Round Table India.

Srivatsan, R. 2014. *Seva, Saviour and State: Caste Politics, Tribal Welfare and Capitalist Development*. New Delhi: Routledge.

Stacey, Judith. 1988. 'Can There Be a Feminist Ethnography'. *Women's Studies International Forum* 11 (1): 21–27.

van der Veer, Peter. 1994. *Religious Nationalism: Hindus and Muslims in India*. Berkeley, CA: University of California Press.

Virdee, Gurmit Singh. 2005. 'Labour of Love: Karseva at Darbar Sahib's Amrit Sarover'. *Sikh Formations: Religion, Culture, Theory* 1 (1): 13–28.

Upadhyay, A. 2016. 'Cow Urine Can Sell for More Than Milk in India'. *Bloomberg*, 18 July. https://www.bloomberg.com/news/articles/2016-07-17/cow-urine-can-sell-for-more-than-milk-in-india

Yang, Anand. 1980. 'Sacred Symbol and Sacred Space in Rural India: Community Mobilisation in the "Anti-Cow Killing" Riot of 1893'. *Comparative Studies in Society and History* 22 (4): 576–596.

Chapter 8

The Nation and the Hero, or the 56-Inch Paradox

Manjima Chatterjee

'*Modi ek insaan nahin, ek soch hai*', says the character Narendra Modi in the hagiographical film *PM Narendra Modi*. Modi is not a human being; he is an idea. In modern India, Modi is considered to be both man and more than man: a *Lauhapurush* (iron man) and a *Yugpurush* (a millennial man). Barely 17 years from being considered the architect of one of the worst massacres in recent history, he is today projected to be the son, the saviour and 'hero' of the Indian nation in the second decade of the third millennium. How did this come to be?

In the course of this chapter, I chart the phenomenal rise of Narendra Modi as a media-led journey by way of newspaper reports and op-ed articles. In the years since his journey to stardom began, there have been several works—critical as well as hagiographic—that have sought to explain the so-called Modi wave. The impact of these works cannot compare with the constant media limelight on Modi, the man. While TV channels and a large section of the print media have been openly fawning, some sections of print and Internet-based news agencies have tried to keep a critical eye on Modi and his cohort, focusing on the impact of his government and his use of media to cover up his numerous gaffes and dreadful decision-making. As I write this chapter,

Kashmir has been under curfew for over a month, with Article 370 repealed and its right to be deemed a state taken away. The impact of demonetization are being felt all around the country, and the steady economic slowdown which has had the country in its grip since 2012 is threatening to reach its nadir, with large industries laying off workers and the automobile industry, particularly on the verge of a total collapse. Yet, in the face of all the joblessness and despair, Modi's star continues to shine brightly.

What is most surprising to many liberals is how a large portion of India's population worships Modi as a 'hero'. This is not the hero of our epics, not the ones we expect to see in the movies, or the comic book superheroes that are increasingly taking over the world of entertainment (although there have been hilarious echoes of both in works by Modi *bhakts*), but rather a home-grown version of the nationalist hero who lives, breathes and speaks for the nation. He is a martyr to the cause of nationhood, having, by his own claims, sacrificed days and nights and a family life for it: this particular aspect endearing him to the masses and reminding them to forgive all his lapses. In India, a society that has traditionally recognized and sought a balanced life between the four aspects of *dharma, artha, kama* and *moksha*, the man who opts out of family life cannot be corrupt, because he has already conquered the *Maya* of earthly desires. In modern India, a society at the brink of overwhelming changes, when such a man speaks with authority, 'daring', so to speak, to lead by the dint of his self-proclaimed immense capability (and his 56-inch chest), he has no trouble becoming the people's, and the media's, hero.

BUILDING UP THE HERO

'Slogans can be uttered by all, but the "punch line" always belongs to only one man—the hero'.

—*Economic Times* (24 December 2007)

While he had been steadily climbing the ranks of the BJP since the mid-1980s, Narendra Modi came into the spotlight when he was appointed chief minister (CM) of Gujarat to handle the mess created by Keshubhai Patel's health-related absences in the face of the earthquake that hit Gujarat in 2001. An RSS man through and through, he had a reputation as a strong organizer and a man with some degree of personal charisma. Less than a year into his rule, in February and March 2002, Gujarat was beset by riots which left up to 2,000 people dead, and a further 3,000 injured or missing. Many stories abounded about the nature of these riots, often denoted as an organized pogrom against the Muslims of the state. As the serving CM of Gujarat, Narendra Modi's career should have suffered a severe blow. Instead, this event became the catalyst that propelled his career in politics, giving him a voice and stature that no RSS man since L. K. Advani had enjoyed.

Soon after the riots, the BJP leadership made a big noise about investigating the events, with its serving prime minister (PM), Atal Behari Vajpayee, advising Modi to uphold 'Raj Dharma' and 'not discriminate on the basis of caste, creed or religion' (Venkitesh 2013) while working on reparations following the riots. Soon, however, the criticism dwindled down in favour of praise for the development work being done by the CM of Gujarat. Even as whispers confirmed the regime's ruthlessness and appetite for vendetta, the government received praise from many quarters for presenting an energetic, pro-development face focussed on ease of business.

One interesting fact about most of the praise coming Modi's way from 2002 up to the present time has been the consistent disregard for facts. At a conference in 2013, as shared by a member of the BJP's partner in the National Democratic Alliance, JD(U), Sivanand Tiwari, Modi talked vigorously about undoing the evil done by several years of Congress misrule in Gujarat and claimed for himself the success of Amul Dairy (established in 1946). This was something of a joke, especially because of the humiliation Modi had heaped on Verghese Kurien, the IAS man who had saved Amul Dairy from closing down due to internal strife, on account of the latter's being widely perceived as a Congress man (Thakkar 2009). Tiwari also talked about the relentless use of Public Relations (PR) machinery, which had successfully managed to highlight the 'Gujarat Development Model' by covering up several facts, such as the following:

how the public health infrastructure in Gujarat is in a shambles; how the rate of decline in Gujarat's infant mortality rate is much lower than the national average; how project implementation has plummeted from 73 per cent in 2003 to 13 per cent in 2011; how Gujarat is lagging behind in per capita income, gross domestic product and foreign direct investment inflows; or the pathetic state of malnutrition and the gender ratio (Venkitesh 2013).

The press also came to recognize that most of the 'punch' in Modi's speeches came not from facts, but from well-constructed punchlines. In December 2007, the *Economic Times* ran an article with a subheading which read: '"Punch dialogue" now will have a new mascot—Gujarat CM Narendra Modi' (TNN 2007). The article went on to give examples of Modi's strategic use of statements that stick within the public domain. In one speech, it quotes Modi as saying: '*Main aaliya, maliya, jamaliya, mafia, tapori/In sab ko Gujarat ki dharti se bhaga doonga*' (roughly, 'I will get rid of all the aaliya, maliya, jamaliya'—all surname endings associated with Muslims—'mafia and rowdies from the land of Gujarat'). In the same speech, he draws attention to his 56-inch chest, which grants him the unique ability to take on his detractors with panache. In other words, he asserts himself as the new strongman of Hindutva, the alpha male all set to teach a lesson to anyone who poses any sort of challenge.

Of all the personal qualities that his supporters and rivals have, variously, admired and criticized, the 56-inch chest seems to hold a special place. First reported around the year 2007, Modi and his supporters have continued to mention this apparently impossible chest size as indicative of his strength and capability. For instance, in response to a challenge thrown at him by Samajwadi Party leader Mulayam Singh Yadav in 2014, Modi said, 'Do you know what making another Gujarat requires? … It requires a *chhappan inch ki chhati* (56-inch chest)' (PTI 2016). In 2016, after the so-called surgical strikes in Uri, Pakistan, Shivraj Singh Chouhan, CM, Madhya Pradesh, said that the 56-inch chest was now 100 inches wide! (PTI 2016). Most recently, in 2019, after the strikes on Balakot by the IAF, Modi's right-hand man, Amit Shah, went on record to say that, by this action, Modi had proven that he was a man with a 56-inch chest (PTI 2019).

THE HERO AS SEX SYMBOL

The magic 56 inches seem to have garnered him an unexpected boost in support from women, who, it is reported, are quite taken up by the attributes of Modi the man. His overt masculinity and tendency to be seen as a man's man seemed to make him even more attractive to the female electorate. Newspaper reports point out that women tend to see him as a powerful man who makes 'tough decisions' (Tewari 2019) and has the strength to withstand their cost or impact. In all his oratory, his decision-making or action, the one thing Modi does not display is doubt. He refuses to question his team's or his own speech or actions, preferring silence in murky areas, and constantly attacking some well-identified opponents. It seems that this 'decisive' posturing works well with female voters, who see him as a man who can be relied upon in crises. This ties in with female preference in the animal kingdom of powerful males who can potentially protect their families (Staff Writers 2011). The conversation around the 56 inches adds to this overall image of machismo. But while the core reasons for Modi's popularity among women may be related to animal instincts, there are various paradoxical aspects of his life which ought to distance the female electorate. By his own admission, he abandoned his wife and maintains a distant, though respectful relationship with his mother (mediated annually by TV cameras). He commands a troupe of loyal female party-members whom he abandons at the slightest sign of trouble and, in a well-known incident, used the heft of state machinery to stalk the young daughter of a friend, apparently at the friend's own request (Simha 2019).

It is possible to argue that, in fact, these very attributes that make Modi attractive to women. They are interpreted as the attributes of a man who is virile, but controlled, and independent of female influence. In a country like India, where patriarchy continues to dominate thought and mediate private and public spaces alike, where women continue to be blamed for inviting rape and turning men gay, among other things, this is hardly a revelation. In a country where, moreover, women are increasingly turning out to vote, with over 65 per cent of women voting in the general elections of 2014 and over 66 per cent in 2019, it makes sense to woo the conservative female voter (Pachauri 2019).

Accordingly, the government since 2014 has put out schemes that target women, particularly in rural areas. The Ujjwala scheme, Jan Dhan deposits in the name of women, the Swachh Bharat toilet-making scheme and land registries in the name of women are all schemes that, effective or not, make a clear pitch to woo women voters. Additionally, a news report from 2013 pointed out, Modi's look, in recognition of the positives to be gained from his unexpected sex symbol status, had undergone a sea change since 2007—'the half-sleeve kurta is of the finest linen, not the humble khadi, Gucci stoles are casually flung around his neck and a suspiciously generous pelt of hair has appeared on Modi's pate' (Hebbar 2013). The 56-inch association was further popularized by songs[1] and even food that celebrated the 'Modi myth'.

Modi's detractors, too, have kept the conversation going on this numerical reference, with ex-minister of the UPA government Kapil Sibal, going so far as to compose a satirical rhyme on Twitter: '*56 inch ki chhati, 58 ka rupaiya; kahan gayee woh chhati, kahan gaya rupaiya*' (The chest is 56 inches, the value of the rupee is 58 [against USD]; where is the chest now, where is the rupee now) (Shekhar 2015). News reporters have sought to demolish the myth by trying to prove that the chest is in fact only 44 inches (Sandhu 2014) or perhaps 50 inches wide (ScoopWhoop Staff 2016). One way or another, it continues to remain newsworthy.

THE HERO AS PERFORMER

A number of the features that make up the 'Modi myth' can be found in hero myths in other parts of the world. The 56-inch chest finds resonance in the stories about the physical attributes or sexual prowess of Alcibiades, or Napoleon, or even Hitler, even though the

---

[1] For instance, see https://littleletterslinked.com/this-election-try-modi-jis-56-inch-thali/ for a description of the 'Deshbhakti Thali' or '56-inch Thali'. The conflation of Modi with *deshbhakti* or patriotism is deeply entrenched within the business class, in particular. The film *PM Narendra Modi*, which sought to present the man as a hero of our times at par with the likes of Gandhi, had a song, 'Namo, Namo', which played on the preferred short form of his name.

last, just like Modi, worked hard to propagate the idea that he was 'married to the state'. The status of a sex symbol is useful as a channel for the adoration that the hero inspires. It further allows for humans of either sex to venerate the hero while allowing him to remain approachable. Like the 56-inch chest, the hero is an imaginable, yet unattainable dream.

In her book, *Heroes*, a study of eight remarkable men who shocked as well as enthralled their societies, Lucy Hughes-Hallett (2006) points out that 'heroes are not required to be altruistic, or honest, or even competent. They are required only to inspire confidence and to appear, not good necessarily, but great.' Alcibiades, Napoleon and Hitler all inspired admiration and disgust in equal measure. All were acknowledged by intellectuals in their time to have committed dastardly acts, and all were known to be unpredictable and wild. All were, almost immediately, forgiven in the light of their hero-worthiness. Having said that, all were acknowledged as heroes in the light of their deeds. Their people's confidence in them arose on the basis of what they had already achieved and, therefore, what they could potentially achieve in the future.

If one looks at Modi's achievements over 13 years of leading Gujarat and 5 years of leading India, one is led to wonder once more at the development of the aura. Sivanand Tiwari was neither the first nor the last of Modi's friends and foes to call attention to his dismal record as CM. Yet, as Salil Tripathi (2013) pointed out in his essay in *The Caravan* magazine (before Modi opened his first innings), the best of Indian minds seemed to be more than happy to praise and validate him even as he gave clear indications of going the way of Indonesia's President Suharto and China's Deng Xiaoping. Like the two East Asian dictators, Modi had a history of repression of the media, hounding of civil rights activists, artists and union leaders that went hand in hand with the acclaimed 'Gujarat Model of Development', which, as shared above, was always highly suspect.

What were the achievements of the 'Gujarat Model of Development'? It was widely acknowledged that the state had good roads, and that there was ease of doing business there. Also, very importantly,

Gujarat's bureaucracy is decentralized, responsive and supportive of innovation. Given the difficulty of working with government offices in almost any part of India, most Indians will appreciate that this is a major achievement. One of the main planks of Dr Manmohan Singh's UPA government was the cleaning up of the bureaucracy and issuing of single-window clearance options wherever possible. However, Dr Singh was widely regarded as a political pushover and was not able to complete this task over two terms. Enter Modi, the *Baahubali* (strong man), who firmly asserted that he was successful because he did what needed to be done and did not allow silly things like the bureaucracy or due process get in his way. He did not seek permission; he did not need to. He hammered his chest and acknowledged that he simply steamrolled anyone who got in his way.

And who decided what needed to be done? Why, Modi himself! He was judge, jury and executioner: a vigilante in the PM's chair. This presented a peculiar conundrum before the ordinary citizen: a PM who claimed to despise and belittle the very institutions he had sworn to protect. Here, then, was a democratically elected leader who had no respect for democracy or its tools and support systems. This was a monarch in the making, a man who allowed his associate, Sakshi Maharaj, to go on record to say that there would be no elections in India after 2019, because there would be no need for them after Modi's second victory (ANI 2019). This refusal to apologize or be seen as apologetic, coupled with a chest-beating flair for the controversial, is a trait we find in a number of world leaders today, most spectacularly the presidents of the United States and Brazil. Interestingly, all have a strong female following, despite (or perhaps because of?) their blatantly misogynistic comments and actions in public.

Here, then, we have a 'hero' whose rise was powered by praise and criticism from his contemporaries by way of a single event—the Gujarat riots of 2002—followed by a development model that was highly suspect. He pushed himself ahead as the decisive saviour India needed, but by itself this was not enough to keep the wheels of the PR machinery turning. Modi was seen as the strong 56-inch chested man capable of brushing everyone aside to achieve his goal, even the democratic process itself, but it was all the more laudable because of his humble beginnings. He claimed to be the son of a humble *chaiwalla*—a tea vendor—who had barely managed to complete his education before dedicating his life to the service of the nation. He represented the aspiration of the regular man on the street to rise to power and achieve his dreams—'*Modi hai to mumkin hai*' (It is possible with Modi). For such a man, of course, the opposition would be offered up by the established powers—the political establishment, the bureaucracy, the literati—all those who sought to uphold the old value system. In the story he likes to tell, time and again, the 'hero' emerged triumphant over a sea of opposition, and had the panache to do this with a wink and a nod for the man on the street.

One needs to watch any one of Modi's public speeches to see how much of his aura derives from his performance. As most Indians, irrespective of social background, will affirm, good leader or not, there is no performer quite like Modi. Even as voices rose seeking reports for the last five years of Modi's rule, the question dominating his re-election campaign was: 'If not Modi, who?' Who else could be as entertaining, as witty, as ruthless in decimating his rivals as Modi was? Who else could be quite as good a storyteller? True, the story was mythical, facts were thin on the ground, the achievements were questionable, but who else could be the hero that India needed? When Modi performs, the facts cease to matter. All that matters is the way in which he uses propaganda to rouse the masses at an emotional level. As Hitler understood only too well, 'the more modest its intellectual ballast, the more exclusively it takes into consideration the emotions of the masses, the more effective [propaganda] will be' (Hitler 1943). Modi has learned at the feet of masters such as Alcibiades and Hitler, and more recently, Vladimir Putin. Here is a hero given birth by a nation that was eagerly awaiting one. Here is not a hero who inspires *bhakti* (devotion) but one who was created by the needs of the *bhakt* (devotee).

GLOBALIZATION AND THE CHANGING FACE OF BHAKTI

In the last few years, the world over, countries have seen a backlash against globalization and the free market economy. Russian President Vladimir Putin, in a recent interview (6 July 2019) with the *Financial*

Times pointed out that one of the major contributory factors to Donald Trump's victory was the disillusionment of the middle classes with globalization, which had benefited only the leading US companies—'the companies, their managers, shareholders and partners'. The middle classes, he said, were 'left out when this pie was divided up'. It was from this group of disillusioned voters that Trump's call to 'Make America Great Again' got the maximum support (Barber et al. 2019).

A similar thing happened in India. Globalization opened up new vistas for the rich and the upper middle classes and created new benchmarks of aspiration for the upwardly mobile youth. It added more glitter and shine to the urban landscape but remained mostly absent from rural India. Where it did enter, it piled up a heap of disasters, from the tragedies inflicted by genetically modified crops to the attempts at forcibly taking over agricultural and forestland for the purposes of industrial manufacture and mining. For those who were already at mid-career or past the mid-point, globalization meant the loss of the familiar and the stripping away of trust in national institutions such as banks and medical and communication services. The marketplace had changed, both literally and figuratively, and, while the promise of more jobs and opportunities available not just nationally but worldwide was tempting, it also brought about a crisis of identity, an empty space that the 'cultural nationalists' were raring to fill.

As we opened up to the world, Indian society also opened up considerably in the last 30 years, with several taboos around sex and gender lifting, female roles within and without the family being queried and overhauled, and the very definition of family changing. While all of this may seem to be movement in positive directions, the seismic shifts caused by these changing attitudes have led to considerable anxiety, reflected in the rise of superstition and the grand performance of rituals (such as *jagrans*) and, predictably, rapes. We are reminded of Erich Fromm's (2013) assertion, in *Escape from Freedom*, of how freedom, though it may bring the individual independence and rationality, 'made [human beings] isolated and, thereby, anxious and powerless. This isolation is unbearable', and the easier alternative facing him is frequently the one that involves escaping into new dependencies and surrendering their choices. This is made easier when a leader steps forward who is assertive and very willing to take choices out of the hands of individuals.

As Romila Thapar has observed, the idea that the religion of a community constitutes its identity is a British colonial one, which swamped the subcontinent and left a bloodbath in its wake, and continues to plague us in the present day (Thapar 2014). In an older time, the definition of a Hindu may have been closer to that of, say, a Greek—imbued with a sense of continuous historical presence within a geographical area over millennia, or with reference to this experience, and a sense of shared culture and what may loosely be termed a texture of living. The Hindus, in this sense, always worshipped a pantheon of gods who fought each other to seek supremacy and struggled to find a place in the caste hierarchy. Allah and Christ soon joined the pantheon, along with others such as Vailankanni (a version of Mary) and various cross-over goddesses such as *Bandebi* and *pirs* such as Manik and Badar Pir. For the longest time (and even now, in many parts of India), 'Muslim' and 'Christian' have been aspects of *jaat* rather than names of different 'national' identities, no matter what the likes of Jinnah and Savarkar would have preferred! When this writer first came to Delhi, she was privileged to be the house guest of a lady who was a Goan Christian, and who referred to herself as a 'Brahmin' on account of having Portuguese blood flowing through her veins. How shocked Aunty Fatema would have been to learn that she did not belong to the Hindu nation and therefore had no right to call herself Brahmin!

What will follow now is a very brief overview of the events I believe have significantly contributed to the creation of the 'Hindu identity' as we know it today and its proliferation, especially in North India. The events are too vast and too many to be handled within the dimensions of a single book, leave alone an essay, and I must therefore beg forgiveness if some of the writing in the next few paragraphs seems facetious.

It was Bhartendu Harishchandra who, in the 1870s, switched from Urdu to Hindi with a vengeance and fought to prove that Hindi was the language of India and of 'Hindus'. The germ of the idea that periodically threatens to overtake the idea of India was implanted only 150 years ago. Despite the years of relentless campaigning, to this day, the language spoken on the streets of Delhi and Lucknow continues to be a mixture of Hindi, Urdu and dialects. The purported 'purity' of languages remains a dream to be achieved by 'nationalists' whose colonial ideal of nationhood, however, has been, and continues to be, drilled into the minds of the Indian public every passing day.

The development of the notion of the 'Hindu' identity, the project of a few business- and literary-minded men inspired by Bhartendu Harishchandra, was initiated in the early 20th century and grew exponentially, inspired as it was by the ideology and imagery of the burgeoning Swadeshi movement. The journey of one iconic institution that played a pivotal role in this project has been studied by Akshaya Mukul in the brilliant *Gita Press and the Making of Hindu India*. Mukul closely examines how the Gita Press, over the 90-odd years of its existence, has been instrumental in laying down the principles that have served to define the identity of the average middle-class person in the Hindi belt—arguably the largest common-language-defined region in India. The works of the Gita Press and others of its ilk, put out with the clear intent of uniting all 'Hindus' within a common moral universe, received approbation and support from M. K. Gandhi and various other political leaders and social reformers and played a role in upholding the Swadeshi movement and the Indian identity. (However, its editors were always connected emotionally and ideologically more with the politics of the Rashtriya Swayamsevak Sangh—a 'cultural nationalist' organization— than with that of the larger independence movement, tending to look at reform that focussed on removal of Islamic influences rather than political independence from the British, who were viewed as a progressive and positive influence.) One of the major tasks that this group of 'Hindu revivalists' set out for itself was the popularization of the Ramayana, and the version written by Tulsidas, *Ramacharitmanas*, was chosen for a very interesting reason—the promotion of the 1938 *Manas Ank*—a special issue of the *Kalyan* magazine published by the Gita Press (Mukul 2015). The *Manas Ank* was a lavish work with gold-embellished paintings, which soon became a coveted family heirloom—over 6 million copies of this issue have been printed so far. The popularization drive for the *Manas Ank* involved regular readings of sections of the Ramayana within mid-sized community gatherings, most popularly the *Sundar Kand*, which prominently featured the character of Hanuman.

The figure of Hanuman, believed by some historians to have been the appropriation into the North Indian Ramayana tradition of a South Indian tribal deity, started gaining a more prominent role in oral retellings around the 10th century, possibly as a reaction to the rise of Vaishnavism in the north. Hanuman, traditionally a Shaivite, came to be seen as the biggest devotee of Ram, the avatar of Vishnu, thus making peace between the two feuding religious groups. The *bhakti* period brought renewed interest in the 'Monkey God' as the epitome of devotion and obedience, and the embodiment of the belief that, literally, faith can move mountains. The *Hanuman Chalisa*, a poem of 40 lines celebrating the qualities of Hanuman and written by Tulsidas, had been popular in parts of the Hindi belt ever since the 16th century. With the targeted popularization of the *Sundar Kand paath* in the late 1930s, the recitation of the *Hanuman Chalisa* on a daily basis became almost mandatory for men and women alike across the Hindi belt. Ram, the *Maryada Purushottam,* was an unattainable ideal. The aim, as reiterated over and over by priests and preachers across the region, was to be like Hanuman—devoted to faith, honest, reliable, brave and strong; a servant and soldier, not a king. The Bajrang Dal, a militant youth group formed by the Vishwa Hindu Parishad to protect its leaders during the Shri Ram Janaki Rath Yatra of 1984, took on this name with the clear intent of positing itself on the side of Ram. To this day, the group aims to support and protect the VHP and the RSS in their works, and anyone with leadership aspirations must move from this group to its parent body, as its stated aim is to nurture workers, and not leaders.

Unless we acknowledge this background of decades of cultural indoctrination, it is impossible to understand the wave of humanity that turned up in support of L. K. Advani's *rathyatra* in 1990, or the Babri Masjid demolition that followed it, or, indeed, the growing support offered to the RSS and its allies, such as the Bajrang Dal and the Durga Vahini. It is with respect to this background that we look at the rise and rise of Narendra Damodardas Modi.

THE IMPORTANCE OF HANUMAN

Before plunging into the modern-day political implications of a myth, it is important to look at the character of Hanuman and its various implications. Interestingly, the only mainstream deity to be worshipped across India and beyond who is, to all intents and purposes, an anthropomorphic animal, Hanuman is also considered to be immortal and, therefore, alive in the present time. This belief has led to the possibility of creating a huge amount of fiction, including cartoons and films centred around the character, which has only added to its popularity, introducing it to new generations of Indians as a fun, friendly character, even as it continued to serve in its primary role as protector.

Stories of the mighty Hanuman may be found, with important focal variations, all across the country. While the Hindi belt as well as many parts of Southern India have had a long tradition of Hanuman worship, in the East, where I grew up, he was always regarded as a character that added humour to the rather sombre Ramayana story. In the annual Ramleela plays, Hanuman would be played usually by a young boy, whose jumping and prancing around would lead to the comic relief in the play. In the early days of television in the 1980s, Ramanand Sagar's *Ramayan* featured the erstwhile wrestler and action movie star of the 1960s, Dara Singh, in the role of Hanuman, played as an imposing, yet kind-hearted figure with a perennial twinkle in his eye. Up until the early 2010s, the benevolent figure of Hanuman could be seen guarding many a street crossing, and 'Sankat Mochan' Hanuman temples were open to all seeking protection from their troubles.

It was around 2016 that the image that came to be known as 'Angry Hanuman' started appearing on posters and car stickers. The young Malayali artist who had created this image claimed to have had no idea that it would take off in quite the way it did; he had, he said, intended to create an image that had 'attitude', but it came to signify aggression: the anger, as it were, of the person on the street (Bose 2018). Almost overnight, Hanuman started to assume his more dangerous incarnation, that of the formidable enemy who defeated magical monsters by sprouting five heads or changing his size at will. This was the almost one-man army that is considered to be the power that brought about *Ram Rajya*.

The one aspect of Hanuman that seems to have always endured is his undeniable maleness. In Hindu stories, the male celibate is considered to have tremendous power, and not everyone is believed to be capable of containing it. *Tapas,* or immersive meditation, is believed to be the only way to contain *tejas,* or the built-up heat of unreleased semen. This seminal energy is then transferred to other parts of the body, all of which become imbued with immense potential. Therefore, despite being a life-long celibate, Hanuman has a son called Makaradhwaja, born of a crocodile living in Lanka's waters which had swallowed a drop of Hanuman's sweat as he flew above. This notion of celibacy as an ideal to be pursued for the sake of heightened masculine energy is one that has influenced, for instance, the training of wrestlers, who worship Hanuman as their guiding deity. It is also an underlying factor in the celebration of men such as Atal Behari Vajpayee and Narendra Modi, who claim to be life-long celibate or to have abandoned their sexual partners in order to be 'married to the state'. Similar parallels exist with the Buddha, who abandoned his wife and child in search of higher truths and was therefore able to dedicate himself in service to a higher cause. These are the parallels drawn, directly and indirectly, by the BJP in the case of the present PM. Modi, so the myth goes, is able to take tough decisions and make the impossible happen because he is dedicated to the nation, has no attachments and has boundless energy, apparently working up to 20 hours a day. A popular lyricist, in a staged 'casual talk' in London, famously asked Modi this difficult question: 'How do you work so hard? Don't you ever get tired?' This purported tirelessness in the service of the nation—a straightforward parallel to Hanuman's dedication to the service of Ram, his self-proclaimed title of Pradhan Sewak or chief serv-ant, the constant claim to hold India in his heart—drawing attention to the image of Hanuman tearing open his chest to reveal Ram and Sita within it—are all strategic socio-emotional triggers planted to direct the populace towards an epiphany: the nation is the body of Ram, the public are His devoted servants, and Modi, as their leader, is Hanuman.

THE *BHAKT* AND THE HERO

The promise of *Ram Rajya* has been the plank on which the BJP has fought every election since the early 1990s. It took the disillusion-ment with globalization, however, to truly rouse the latent *bhakt.* To quote Amit Bhaduri, 'Economic globalisation challenges the political authority which the nation-state had attained by undermining gradu-ally many of the norms of the traditional civil society' (Bhaduri 2000).

The 'sovereignty' of the nation—a neo-Hegelian view of the absolute authority of the state—is seen as being at stake in the face of rapid alterations of urban aspiration and changing lifestyles. Mark Juergensmeyer points out that the increasing porousness of boundaries and acceptance of other identities has led to the nation-state being viewed as a weak institution, and the 'vulnerability of the nation-state, in turn, has been the occasion for new ethno-religious politics to step into the breach and shore up national identities and purposes' (Juergensmeyer 2019). This phenomenon has been steadily on the rise in India since 1992. Increasingly, over the past two decades, the middle classes and small towns have voted in favour of reducing personal liberties and increasing community-based policing. Mob lynching is on the rise, *khap*[2] panchayats are gaining more ground even as the courts condemn their diktats. Hanuman is out protecting the *maryada*[3] of this land.

While the last statement above may be read as ironic, what is even more ironic is that this is the precise statement that has accompanied many a communal march in recent times. As Jawhar Sircar recently pointed out, Ram Navami marches with swords, guns and *trishuls* (tridents) have become the norm in the past few years in areas such as Bengal, where Ram worship has never been practised. Hanuman Jayanti is being celebrated in places which were hitherto quite unconcerned with the circumstances of Hanuman's birth (Sircar 2018). Shivratri celebrations regularly involve *kanwariyas*[4] taking over entire national highways and city arterial roads for a month and more in North India. The more hooliganistic the display of religious fervour

---

[2] *Khaps* are community organizations representing a clan or a group of clans, usually found in rural Western Uttar Pradesh and Haryana. *Khaps* often operate as an alternate power structure to the *panchayat* and issue behavioral diktats to their members, particularly on matters related to marriage and caste.

[3] *Maryada* is another term for honour, though it often relates specifically to the roles of men and the positions of women in society.

[4] The term *kanwariya* literally means 'bearer of the *kanwar*', which is a contraption made of a pair of containers suspended on either side of a pole. This *kanwar* is supposed to be used to carry water from a source sacred to the Hindu god Shiva, and the *kanwariyas* are supposed to follow certain special norms on this journey, such as walking on foot and eating only what is offered to them on their way. Locals who meet them on their route treat them with reverence because they are supposed to be closely aligned with Shiva on this journey.

gets, the more acceptance it seems to receive from a citizenry that is entirely happy to serve the greater cause of 'rescuing' Hinduism from the threat of others. What the BJP did very successfully for over 20 years was to convince the populace to take up the role of *bhakt*. This is interesting because the characteristic of the *bhakt* now is no longer that of a jobless male from a certain socio-economic background and with limited educational opportunities—which was the case generally around the time of the Babri Masjid demolition and subsequent riots. The *bhakt* now may be a blue-collar worker or an entrepreneur, a teacher or a doctor, often employed and upwardly mobile, and frequently female. The fear of the educated 'Other' whose religion purportedly requires them to propagate without control and therefore become a threat to future generations of 'us' is a fear that now plagues many countries across the world and has been successfully used to win elections, notably in the United States, Brazil and India. The fear we speak of is not merely an economic one—'our jobs are under threat'—but more importantly an emotional one: 'the very fabric of the nation and society is in danger.'

The 'Nation in Need of a Saviour' theme, prepared for 20 years, then, became the perfect receptacle for Narendra Modi. This is how, in the face of Gujarat riots, Narendra Modi shone like a beacon for the *bhakt*. Here was a man who refused to apologize for his deeds, who insisted that what he had done was right and he had taught a lesson to all those who needed to be disciplined, and who somehow found a way to slip by the nagging arm of the law. To paraphrase Rebecca Solnit, his patriarchal authority itself was claimed as the solution to disasters, as though his very presence was all the reassurance we needed (Solnit 2019). He lost some of his shine when the United States refused to offer him a visa in the light of the investigations which implicated him for communal crimes, but gained it back soon enough through persistent attempts and a dogged refusal to allow anything to besmirch him. In a world where financial corruption seemed to be the norm, Modi was the one politician who gave the impression that he was not interested in money. This, coupled with his mysterious preening powers that did not allow any allegations to stick, gave him the aura of an invincible survivor. Even those who did not like him felt that they had to admire him. And thus, the hero was born out of the needs of the *bhakt*.

THE NATION AND THE HERO

As we have seen so far, the resistible rise of Narendra Modi bears a close resemblance to the rise of the authoritarian personality that is outlined in the works of Erich Fromm and others. There is a clear relationship based on emotional dependence; I follow Fromm in calling it a sadomasochistic relationship. A popular comic strip depicts the Indian public seeking jobs, food and clothing, while Modi gives them grand gestures—demonetization, Sardar Patel's immense statue, the overnight overhauling of Kashmir's status and rights. In the comic, he finally loses his cool that the public is not appreciative of his grand gestures and keeps whining for staples. A number of people 'liked' the strip but, as it turned out, about half of them claimed to understand the cartoon Modi frustration with an ungrateful public, and sent messages of support to the PM!

Our anxieties and emotional dependence go deeper still. In a country as diverse as India, the importance of asserting the national identity is a widely accepted fact. Even the liberal who questions the need to play the national anthem before the movies agrees that the Indian identity cannot be stressed enough. This makes the liberal deeply uncomfortable in the face of anti-India protests in Kashmir and Manipur, anti-CAA protests in Assam or when faced with a Muslim person who supports the Pakistani cricket team. This is the weak spot that the *bhakt* attacks again and again, relentlessly. When a Modi repeatedly calls out to the 'Hindu within us', or Bolsonaro says 'We Brazilians don't like homosexuals', or a Putin reminds his audience that 'all of us live in a world based on biblical values,' it is comforting to their listeners to be reassured that their world is, indeed, still recognizable, even though it may not feel that way. When Modi calls out to Hindus worldwide, he is reminding Indians that it is not merely the nation-state which is theirs, but that they have a trans-national existence which guarantees that their culture, and the Hindu nation, will persist, and triumph, in the face of all manners of cultural and economic threats. There is not a hint of irony in these speeches, and they are, in fact, delivered with so much confidence, that in the ten years or so that he has spent projecting himself as the saviour, over a third of the voting population has been beguiled by the promise of Modi the Hero. The fact that he hosts no press conferences and refuses to face the public unrehearsed does not seem to have dented his image as a man of wit and wisdom. Fawning interviews, cartoons featuring him as a superhero, films and songs released in his praise: all have gone a long way towards building the 'Modi myth'. The parallels with Vladimir Putin, in particular, are obvious, down to the patented turns of phrase known variously as 'Putinisms' and 'Modiisms'. Even an accusation as serious as the one associated with the Rafale deal seems to have been 'handled' already in the light of the party's victory in the 2019 elections. Modi, in keeping with the tradition of the heroes he seems to have modelled himself after, particularly Putin, is also very clear about ignoring certain things.

In the last few years, incidents of mob lynching have been rising steadily, leading to a slew of protests, at the forefront of which have been artists. National award-winning artists have returned their awards and citations, held protests and demonstrations and supported signature campaigns. This is natural, since the arts can only flourish where there is a certain amount of social stability, and vigilante mobs must be necessarily viewed as a threat to art and artists. For various reasons, the Modi government has an extremely uneasy relationship with the arts, which, in India, are the embodiment of the very intricate connectedness between various religio–cultural strands which the RSS questions. Even in their 'classical' forms, neither music nor dance nor theatre can claim to remember forms from an ancient past free of 'other' cultural influences, and the visual arts positively revel in varied cultural associations. Literature and film have been similarly guilty, even though the film community, conscious of the pitfalls of running a business with many lives depending on it, fawns over the powers-that-be. Choosing to address these discomforts directly would mean putting himself into a questionable spot, the kind of situation which he knows well to avoid. Instead, his publicity group has put together a clever strategy by way of which the questions put to the PM by artists are countered by accusations of anti–nationalism by other artists. Thus, serious, hard-hitting questions in the public space are degenerated into absurd cat-fights where all come out looking bedraggled and sorry, while the PM remains untouched. With Modi supporters having been named to every possible position of power in the country, and TV channels and newspapers having been frightened into submission by the threat of pulling out all government advertisements, now the artists, traditionally the conscience-keepers of the country, have been silenced.

The National Register of Citizens is now a potent weapon in the hands of the present government to determine who deserves to be termed a citizen of the nation. All those who oppose it are termed anti-national, and the Home Minister, Amit Shah, has made it very clear that the NRC will be used against those who are deemed as 'infiltrators', marking exceptions for 'Buddha (*sic*), Hindus and Sikhs' (*The Quint* 2019). This is very much in keeping with the expectations that people have from the party in power. The question, though, is how far are we, the Indian public, willing to go in our celebration of this man whom we have appointed as our hero? How deep does the fear of the Other truly go?

Per the Assam NRC, over 19 lakh people had been declared nation-less. At this juncture of history, it may be worth our while to ponder on the words that Shakespeare gave to Ulysses, as he warns the Greek leaders of the dangers of investing too much in an unpredictable hero:

> Force should be right; or rather, right and wrong,
> Between whose endless jar justice resides,
> Should lose their names, and so should justice too.
> Then everything includes itself in power,
> Power into will, will into appetite;
> And appetite, an universal wolf,
> So doubly seconded with will and power,
> Must make perforce an universal prey,
> And last eat up himself.

> William Shakespeare (*Troilus and Cressida*,
> Act I, Scene 3, 1609)

REFERENCES

ANI. 2019. 'There'd Be No Elections in 2024, Says Sakshi Maharaj'. *Economic Times*, 15 March. https://economictimes.indiatimes.com/news/elections/lok-sabha/india/thered-be-no-elections-in-2024-says-sakshi-maharaj/articleshow/68432071.cms?from=mdr

Barber, Lionel, Henry Foy, and Alex Barker. 2019. 'Vladimir Putin Says Liberalism Has "Become Obsolete"'. *Financial Times*, 28 June. https://www.ft.com/content/878d2344-98f0-11e9-9573-ee5cbb98ed36

Bhaduri, Amit. 2000. 'Nationalism and Economic Policy in the Era of Globalisation'. Working Papers no. 188, WIDER, The United Nations University, July. https://www.wider.unu.edu/sites/default/files/wp2000-188.pdf

Bose, Rakhi. 2018. 'How a Kerala Artist's "Angry Hanuman" Became a Rage on India's Roads'. *News 18*, 9 April. https://www.news18.com/news/buzz/how-a-kerala-artists-angry-hanuman-became-a-rage-on-indias-roads-1711807.html.

Fromm, Erich. 1941/1969 (2013). *Escape from Freedom*. New York, NY: Open Road Media.

Hebbar, Nistula. 2013. 'Sex Symbol Status: Narendra Modi Attracts Female Audience but Need to Show More Tenderness'. *Economic Times*, 29 September. https://economictimes.indiatimes.com/news/politics-and-nation/sex-symbol-status-narendra-modi-attracts-female-audience-but-needs-to-show-more-tenderness/articleshow/23216479.cms

Hitler, Adolf. 1943. *Mein Kampf*. Translated by Ralph Manheim. Boston, MA: Houghton Mifflin Company.

Hughes-Hallett, Lucy. 2006. *Heroes: A History of Hero Worship*. New York, NY: Anchor Books.

Juergensmeyer, Mark. 2019. 'How Globalisation Engenders Ethno-religious Nationalism'. *Zocalo Public Square*, 30 April. https://www.zocalopublicsquare.org/2019/04/30/how-globalization-engenders-ethno-religious-nationalism/ideas/essay/

Mukul, Akshaya. 2015. *Gita Press and the Making of Hindu India*. Noida, India: Harper Collins.

Pachauri, Swasti. 2019. 'Verdict 2019: Why Did Women Vote for BJP?' *Down to Earth*, 12 June. https://www.downtoearth.org.in/blog/general-elections-2019/verdict-2019-why-did-women-vote-for-bjp-65030

PTI. 2016. '56-inch Chest Is Now 100-inch: Shivraj Singh Chouhan'. *Financial Express*, 2 October. https://www.financialexpress.com/india-news/56-inch-chest-is-now-100-inch-shivraj-singh-chouhan/400909/

————. 2019. 'Modi Is the Man with the 56-inch Chest'. *The Hindu*, 28 April. https://www.thehindu.com/elections/lok-sabha–2019/modi-is-the-man-with–56-inch-chest/article26973945.ece

Venkitesh. R. 2013. 'The Modi Myth'. *Frontline*, 27 May. https://frontline.the-hindu.com/cover-story/modi-myth/article4666766.ece

Sandhu, Veena. 2014. 'Who Can Boast about a 56-inch Chest?' *Business Standard*, 31 January. https://www.business-standard.com/article/beyond-business/who-can-boast-about-a–56-inch-chest–114013101063_1.html

Scoop Whoop Staff. 2016. 'PMO Office Exposes Modi's Lie of "Chhappan Inch Ki Chhati"'. Scoop Whoop, 23 January. https://www.scoopwhoop.com/No-More-Chhappan-Inch-Ki-Chhati-PM-Modis-Chest-Measures–50Inches/

Shekhar, Kumar Shakti. 2015. 'When Kapil Sibal Wrote a Poem on Modi's 56-inch Chest'. *Daily O,* 12 August. https://www.dailyo.in/variety/kapil-sibal-trolled-modi-government-56-inch/story/1/5622.html

Simha, Vijay. 2019. 'The Women in Narendra Modi's Life'. *Sify.com*. https://www.sify.com/news/the-women-in-narendra-modis-life-imagegallery-1-features-oeoowCcfdccsi.html

Sircar, Jawhar. 2018. 'Using Ram and Hanuman for Violence and Votes'. *The Wire*, 1 April 2018. https://thewire.in/politics/using-ram-and-hanuman-for-violence-and-votes

Social Dangal. 2019. '"Hitler talk": Twitter Furious over BJP's NRC Plans in India'. *The Quint*, 12 April. https://www.thequint.com/elections/social-dangal/hitler-talk-twitter-furious-over-bjps-nrc-plans-for-india

Solnit, Rebecca. 2019. 'When the Hero is the Problem'. *LitHub*, 2 April. https://lithub.com/rebecca-solnit-when-the-hero-is-the-problem/

Staff Writers. 2011. 'Standing Up to Fight'. *Terradaily*, 23 May. http://www.ter-radaily.com/reports/Standing_up_to_fight_999.html

Tewari, Ruhi. 2019. 'What Makes PM Modi a Hit among Assam's Women: Ujjwala, Toilets and "Tough Decisions"'. *The Print*, 9 April. https://theprint.in/politics/what-makes-pm-modi-a-hit-among-assams-women-ujjwala-toilets-tough-decisions/218887/

Thakkar, Mitul. 2009. 'Verghese Kurien Faces Modi's Wrath, May've to Give Up Basics'. *Economic Times,* 30 January. https://economictimes.indiatimes.com/industry/cons-products/food/verghese-kurien-faces-modis-wrath-mayve-to-give-up-basics/articleshow/4050549.cms?from=mdr

Thapar, Romila. 2014. *The Past Is Present*. New Delhi: Aleph.

TNN. 2007. 'Power of Words That Made Modi Win the Gujarat Election'. *Economic Times*, 24 December. https://economictimes.indiatimes.com/news/politics-and-nation/power-of-words-that-made-modi-win-gujarat-election/articleshow/2646226.cms

Tripathi, Salil. 2013. 'How Some of India's Brightest Minds Have Bought into the Modi Myth'. *Caravan*, 11 May. https://caravanmagazine.in/vantage/minds-modi-myth

Chapter 9

The Question of Minority Citizenship
Shah Rukh Khan as the 'Global Indian'

Sreya Mitra

INTRODUCTION

In January 2010, as Bollywood superstar, Shah Rukh Khan, was touring Britain and North America, to promote his upcoming release, *My Name Is Khan*, incensed protestors back in India were burning his effigies and demonstrating outside his palatial Mumbai home. In the span of a few days, Khan had been demoted from the nation's cinematic idol to a traitor, a vilified figure devoid of any patriotic fervour or national allegiance. The controversy was over the actor's rather innocuous comments on the recent Indian Premier League (IPL) cricket teams' draft. Khan, who is co-owner of the IPL team, Kolkata Knight Riders, had voiced his dismay and disappointment that none of the teams had picked any of the 11 Pakistani cricketers, who were up for bidding. Though there was no official boycott against the players, deteriorating relations between the two countries, particularly in the aftermath of the 26/11 Mumbai terrorist attack, had prompted the IPL franchises to refrain from bidding on them. Describing the entire episode as 'humiliating', Khan had commented, 'We are known to invite everyone, and we should have. If there were issues, they should have been put out earlier so that things could happen respectfully' (*Times of India* 2010a). Although this collective embargo was criticized by many, including the then home minister of India, P. Chidambaram, who termed the non-inclusion of Pakistani players as a 'disservice to cricket' (*Times of India* 2010b), Shah Rukh Khan's public stance earned him the ire of right-wing political outfits.

Shiv Sena, the Maharashtra-based regional, right-wing political party, was quick to denounce the star as a traitor and threatened to boycott *My Name Is Khan* (incidentally a film that examines Muslim subjectivity in post-9/11 America). In a scathing editorial in the party mouthpiece, *Saamna*, Bal Thackeray, Sena's octogenarian supreme declared, 'Shah Rukh was, after all, no ordinary Indian; he was a Muslim' (Raina 2010). Party spokesperson, Sanjay Raut, exhorted: 'This is not Shah Rukh, but the Khan in him that's saying all this. Let Shah Rukh go and stay in Lahore, Karachi or Islamabad. He is not needed in Mumbai' (Bhattacharjee 2010). Other Hindu right-wing leaders also weighed in on the actor's supposed lack of patriotism. Praveen Togadia of the Vishwa Hindu Parishad, argued, 'by favouring the inclusion of Pakistani cricketers, Shah Rukh has proved that he is a Muslim first and foremost and that he will continue to support Pakistan at the cost of our own national interest' (Raina 2010). As Khan promoted his much-awaited Bollywood venture abroad—the picture of the global Indian, urban, suave and cosmopolitan—at home, his religious affiliation was deconstructed as an acknowledgement of his inevitable betrayal. His 'Muslimness' marked him as the Indian subject, incapable of professing loyalty or patriotism to the nation, and consequently, evoked the familiar rhetoric of the (unpatriotic) Indian Muslim's allegiance to neighbouring Pakistan. Though media outlets, social networking sites and Khan's fans rallied to his support, and public sympathy was clearly in his favour, the controversy exposed the vulnerability of both the Bollywood star and the Hindi film industry, and consequently also underlined problematic questions of nationhood, citizenship and 'Global' India's secularist ethos. In my discussion of Shah Rukh Khan's star text, as the 'Global Indian', I analyse how the actor's 'Muslimness' marks him both as the ideal citizen and as the Muslim 'Other', bringing into question his allegiance and loyalty to the national imaginary. In doing so, I also highlight the role of religion in framing questions of nationhood, belonging and minority citizenship in the contemporary Indian public sphere, particularly as it intersects with discourses of popular Hindi cinema and stardom.

Shah Rukh Khan's repeated assertions, 'I am a bloody good Indian', in interviews following the controversy (Khan 2010a), replicates the recurrent and underlying narrative omnipresent in his star text—that of a secular, sophisticated Indian Muslim. Equipped with a middle-class upbringing, a nationalist father and a Hindu wife, the actor not only epitomizes an acceptable variant of 'Muslimness' for post-liberalization India, but also facilitates the global imagining of contemporary India as a secular, modern nation-state. However, Khan's image as the model citizen and that of India as the secular, global entity, are inherently tenuous, fragile and vulnerable. Fraught with fissures and ruptures, the constructs of both the 'Indian Muslim' and 'secular India' expose the schizophrenic character of post-liberalization India, where two decades of economic growth and global visibility have simultaneously been accompanied by sectarian violence and religious strife.

With popular Hindi cinema often being perceived as the nation's cinematic alter ego, employing 'a stock set of tropes, symbols, characters, and narratives that are meant to first air, and then resolve, contemporary anxieties and difficulties' (Virdi 2003, 9), the Hindi film hero functions not only as the films', but also the nation's protagonist. It is this potent relationship between the filmic hero and the national imaginary, coupled with Hindi cinema's embodiment of the nation, which further reaffirms the crucial significance of the Hindi film star (particularly the male star) in the Indian context. Employing Neepa Majumdar's assertion of Hindi film stardom's significant and crucial role (2009) and Richard Dyer's delineation of stars as sites of mediation and negotiation, particularly during moments of transition and change (1998), I argue that the star texts of Bollywood personalities need to be read in the context of the nation's trials and tribulations. Consequently, the inherent contradiction of Khan's persona—as the model citizen as well as the vilified 'Other'—speaks to Dyer's notion of 'structured polysemy', necessitating the need to examine the star image in terms of 'the multiplicity of its meanings' (1998, 63). As Dyer explains, while at times the various elements of signification may *reinforce* one another...In other cases, the elements may be to some degree in *opposition* or *contradiction*, in which case, the star's image is characterised by attempts to negotiate, reconcile or mask the difference between the elements, or else simply hold them in tension. (Dyer 1998, 63–64)

My analysis of Shah Rukh Khan's star text as the Global Indian and the (secular) Indian Muslim attempts to unpack the above-mentioned categories, and map the circulation and consumption of the Bollywood star to the sociopolitical and cultural rumblings of contemporary India. Central to my analysis is Khan's on-screen portrayal of the Indian Muslim in *Chak De! India* (2007), *My Name Is Khan* (2010) and *Raees* (2017), and how his reel *avatars* embody not only the subjectivity of the Indian Muslim, but also underline the susceptibility of Shah Rukh Khan's 'Muslimness' as an Indian citizen and a Bollywood star. Through a simultaneous engagement with the visual imagery of his films, particularly their Muslim protagonists, and Khan's off-screen text, I track the images of the nation and Khan's own articulation of his (Indian) Muslim citizenship and belonging.

GLOBAL INDIA, THE 'NEW HEROIC PROTOTYPE' AND THE MUSLIM SUPERSTAR

In popular Hindi cinema's world of myth, romance and celluloid dreams, Shah Rukh Khan, or SRK, as the star is popularly known, occupies the place of a demigod. Endowed with epithets such as 'King Khan' and 'Badshah of Bollywood' and with a filmography of more than 80 films, including some of millennial India's biggest blockbusters, the actor is phenomenally popular, inspiring fanatical adulation both at home and abroad (Dudrah, Mader, and Bernhard 2015). Khan's star text and media discourse often positions him as the veritable 'Outsider', the middle-class aspirant from Delhi, whose stardom is as much a story of chance and luck as it is of hard work, dedication and perseverance. Prior to his film career, he had been active in Delhi's theatre circuit during his undergraduate years and had even gained a certain degree of success and stardom as a television actor (*Fauji* 1988; *Dil Dariya* 1989; *Circus* 1989). Despite a rather tepid debut as a second lead hero, who makes his appearance only after the interval (*Deewana*, dir. Raj Kanwar 1992), Khan quickly rose to prominence. Shah Rukh Khan's initial rise to stardom was marked by a series of 'psychotic lover' roles, where instead of cavorting with his heroines in picturesque locales, he terrorized and threatened them (*Darr*, dir. Yash Chopra 1993; *Anjaam*, dir. Rahul Rawail 1994), even at times remorselessly murdering them (*Baazigar*, dir. Abbas–Mustan 1993). For the nation's cinematic public, Khan's 'psychotic hero', with its unbridled and all-consuming drive and passion, embodied their own unapologetic embrace of the new consumerist ontology, engendered by the 1990s' economic liberaliza-tion[1] and the utopian possibility of millennial India (Mazzarella 2003; Varma 1998). As Ranjani Mazumdar notes, this new anti-hero 'opened up new possibilities, the least of which is the changed architecture of *desire*, where the psychotic's action holds out the utopian possibility of breaking all boundaries' (Mazumdar 2000, 252).

Shah Rukh Khan's enunciation of the new national ideology would become further consolidated with his popular 'NRI films'—*Dilwale Dulhania Le Jayenge* (*The Braveheart Will Take the Bride*, dir. Aditya Chopra 1995), *Dil Toh Pagal Hai* (*The Heart Is Crazy*, dir. Yash Chopra 1997), *Kuch Kuch Hota Hai* (*Something is Happening*, dir. Karan Johar 1998), *Kabhi Khushi Kabhie Gham* (*Sometimes Happiness Sometimes Sorrow*, dir. Karan Johar 2001), and *Kal Ho Na Ho* (*Tomorrow Might Never Come*, dir. Nikhil Advani 2003). It was in these 'yuppie' roman-tic films, speaking to the cultural aspirations, anxieties and travails of both the non-resident Indian (NRI) abroad and the new (modern) middle-class Indian at home, that Khan achieved his superstardom and iconic fame. In his on-screen 'yuppie' incarnates, as *DDLJ*'s Raj Malhotra, or *Kuch Kuch Hota Hai*'s Rahul Khanna, Khan embodied post-liberalization India's key *mantra*—'Indian values are portable and malleable' (Chopra 2007, 73). His cinematic avatars, with their branded Gap and Calvin Klein apparel, swanky sports cars and high-tech

---

[1] Economic liberalization policies introduced by the Indian government in the early 1990s were instrumental in reducing bureaucratic red-tape, thus encouraging more fiscal growth and foreign investment. Consequently, the earlier emphasis on Nehruvian socialism and Gandhian frugality was replaced by an unapologetic endorsement of consumerism.

gadgets, at once personified the new consumerist ontology of millennial India with its claim on global citizenship, and the emergent ethos of cultural hybridity, where tradition and modernity were expected to exist in complete harmony, devoid of any conflict or contradiction (Uberoi 2006). Signifying spaces that both embodied 'an expanding globalist imagination and where the global and the local encounter one another or are juxtaposed' (Srinivas 2005, 333), Khan's yuppie protagonist, despite the inherent globality, was 'marked as Indian rather than diasporic' (Dwyer 2015, 50), underlining his role as 'the global citizen' while reaffirming an 'uncompromising Indianness' (Dwyer 2015, 63).

What further consolidated Shah Rukh Khan's embodiment of the 'millennial Indian' was his off-screen text, where he repeatedly emphasized his middle-class antecedents and evoked *leit motifs* that were central to the urban (and urbane) Indian middle class, particularly his secular upbringing and educational credentials. As the Bollywood star who personally supervises his son's math homework, teaches his daughter history lessons and attends their taekwondo matches, he is the epitome of Indian middle-class parenthood and values, inculcating in them both the traditional reverence for education and the 'new-age' drive to succeed and, consequently, the aspirational ethos of post-liberalization India. What is more significant than Shah Rukh Khan's espousal of consumerist aspirations in his configuration as the embodiment of millennial India, however, is his religious identity and affiliation—he is a Muslim superstar in a Hindu-majority country. His 'minority' status marks him doubly as the 'ideal' citizen: he validates India's secular credentials and attests to her claims to global modernity.

It is crucial to keep in mind that Khan's on-screen portrayal of the 'new heroic prototype' (Chopra 2007, 138) was inevitably not only Hindu, but also, specifically the Hindi-speaking, North Indian, upper-caste denizen, thus conforming to popular Hindi cinema's tradition of 'centralizing a north Indian hetero-normative Hindu male, upper middle class, and upper caste subject … as national citizen' (Khan 2009, 128). Thus, as a Muslim superstar in a predominantly Hindu nation, embodying the (new) 'Global Indian' who is invariably coded as Hindu, Shah Rukh Khan's star text assumes crucial significance, particularly in the context of the hegemonic narrative of the Muslim 'Other'. Historian Mushirul Hasan has discussed how the exclusionary and violent diatribe of Hindu Extremism 'conjured up the image of a community outside the "national mainstream"', in which Muslims figure as 'aggressive fundamentalists and demonized as descendants of depraved and tyrannical medieval rulers' (Hasan 1996, 185). The slogans of Hindu Extremist political outfits—'Jo Ram ka nahin, wo hamara nahin' ('He who does not worship Ram does not belong to us'), 'Babur ki santaan, jao Pakistan ya kabristan' ('Son of Babur, go to either Pakistan or the graveyard')—reiterate this familiar rhetoric.

While Shah Rukh Khan's (Muslim) religious affiliation marks him as more vulnerable to insinuations and accusations of unpatriotic behaviour, it also positions him, especially in the context of contemporary India's global, modernist ethos, as the ideal (secular) citizen. Khan himself has acknowledged this problematic (and contradictory) duality of his public persona:

> Whenever there is an act of violence in the name of Islam, I am called upon to air my views on it and dispel the notion that by virtue of being a Muslim, I condone such senseless brutality… [And] I sometimes become the inadvertent object of political leaders who choose to make me a symbol of all that they think is wrong and unpatriotic about Muslims in India. (Khan 2013)

In contrast to other contemporary Muslim Bollywood stars (Aamir Khan, Salman Khan, Saif Ali Khan), who maintain a discreet and private demeanour when it comes to their personal beliefs, SRK has been rather vocal and public in professing his faith. Such incorporation of the personal, the real and the off-screen is not only crucial but integral to his star persona. Khan's references to his religious beliefs and his 'Muslimness' function to further authenticate his star image, particularly his subscription to India's secular ethos. As Richard Dyer has mentioned, 'the value embodied by a star is as it were harder to reject as "impossible" or "false" because the star's existence guarantees the existence of the value s/he embodies' (1998, 20). Even though he maintains that he is primarily an entertainer ('Films are for entertainment, messages are for the post office' [Khan 2007c], 'I don't give messages, I try to entertain people' [Khan 2007a]), Khan is aware of the crucial significance of his role as a (Muslim) celebrity in the context of the Indian nation-state's claims of secular credentials and global ethos: 'Just being a movie actor has made me stand for a lot of values and iconic things...one of the things that I suddenly stand for is that I am a Muslim in a Hindu country' (Khan 2007b).

Khan is undoubtedly the perfect spokesperson for millennial India's global persona and its secular agenda. Critiquing Islamic fundamentalists and exhorting the youth to combat communalism and uphold the principles of Indian secularism (Khan 2007a)—'There is an Islam from Allah and ... very unfortunately, there is an Islam from the Mullahs ... I appeal to all of them to please give the youngsters the right reading of Quran' (Khan 2008)—he presents a viable and acceptable variant of 'Muslimness' for the Indian national imaginary. For the Indian (Hindu) middle class denizen, Shah Rukh Khan's sophisticated and erudite demeanour offers a comforting and palatable departure from the dominant images of ghettoized Muslims, insular and illiterate. As he celebrates Hindu festivals, underlining his familiarity with the majority religion, and attempts to clarify the true meaning of *jihad*, the inherent threat of his Islamic affiliation is assuaged, and subsumed by his Indian secularist and pacifist ethos.

> I have read the holy Quran ... Nowhere in the Quran does it say that *jihad* will lead to *jannat* (paradise). (Khan 2008)
>
> One needs to understand the meaning of *jihad* ... (it) means overcoming your own frailities, your own streak of violence ... *jihad* is not about killing other people. *Jihad* is about killing the badness in you. (Khan 2007)

As the liberal, stylish 'Global Indian', Shah Rukh Khan offers a stark contrast to the much-maligned stereotype of the 'barbarian' Muslim and underlines the distinctiveness of the Indian Muslim. In the aftermath of 9/11 and the threat of Islamic fundamentalism, it became imperative for the Indian nation-state to define its 'minority', not as the incompatible 'Other' and 'Outsider', but more significantly, as the resolutely patriotic citizen-subject, whose national allegiance (Indianness) superseded his religious affiliation (Muslim). Indian media rhetoric in the post-9/11 years regurgitated the nation's familiar espousal of secularism. As journalist Barkha Dutt notes, despite a significant Muslim population of 150 million, the country was not besieged by any Al-Qaeda links, and thus, could rightfully claim its 'badge of honour' (Dutt 2007). This new emphasis on the Indian Muslim as the endorser of the nation's secularist ethos is evident in Shah Rukh Khan's contemporary star text. In interviews, the actor often emphasizes his secular credentials—'I would like to believe that I am an educated liberal Muslim, who has a Hindu wife and two kids' (Khan 2008)—presenting himself as the very epitome of a suave, cosmopolitan and urbane *Indian* Muslim.

In the public professing of his faith, Khan presents a rather palatable and acceptable variant of not only 'Muslimness', but also of religious faith and belief for the 'modern', 'global' Indian denizen—

> My religion is sacred to me. I don't wear it on my sleeves. I am not a fanatic, but yes I am God-fearing. And I believe your deeds define you. You get your brownie points and your whiplashes here during your stay on earth. (Sheikh 2006, 231)

However, this rather sanitized version of religion is disconcertingly at odds with the public and social discourse of contemporary India. As the country reiterates its role as an emergent global power, it is also confronted at home with caste politics, ethno-religious strife, gender and class inequities. While the pro-Hindu Right political outfit, Bharatiya Janata Party (BJP), has emerged as one of the major national parties, in the aftermath of the 1990s' divisive rhetoric, the fissures underlying the facade of India's secularism have become even more apparent with the current debates over religious conversions, Love Jihad and cow vigilantism.[2] It is in this context again that Shah Rukh Khan's star text warrants a closer reading, particularly his depiction of Muslim

---

[2] Right-wing outfits such as RSS and VHP vehemently oppose religious conversions of Hindus and have been vocal in demanding more stringent anti-conversion laws. Accusing Muslim men of surreptitiously converting Hindu women by entrapping them in romantic relationships, they perceive Muslims as a threat to the Hindu community. In recent years, cow vigilantism has also been on the rise, with 'cow protection' groups often engaging in violence against those suspected of cow smuggling or beef consumption.

characters—Kabir Khan in *Chak De! India* (dir. Shimit Amin 2007) and Rizvan Khan in *My Name Is Khan* (dir. Karan Johar 2010) and Raees Alam in *Raees* (dir. Rahul Dholakia 2017).

FROM *GADDAR* (TRAITOR) TO *BHARAT KI SHAAN* (THE PRIDE OF INDIA)

Chak De! India (dir. Shimit Amin 2007) was by Bollywood standards, a *hatke* (different) film. With no song and dance sequences, or romantic interludes, or even a lead heroine, the film was a marked departure from Shah Rukh Khan's familiar Raj and Rahul prototypes. Instead, it narrated the tale of the Indian women's hockey team's journey, from the perennial underdog to world champion, under the guidance of their coach, Kabir Khan (Shah Rukh Khan). However, the film was noteworthy for another reason—Shah Rukh Khan's portrayal of hockey coach, Kabir Khan, a liberal urbane Muslim, who presented a stark contrast to popular Hindi cinema's formulaic Muslim stereotypes and reiterated the actor's own liberal politics.

Discussing Muslim representation in Bollywood films, Kalyani Chadha and Anandam P. Kavoori describe the community's cinematic depiction as 'exoticized, marginalized and demonized' (2008, 131–145). Similar to Hindi cinema's other stereotypes (the dissolute and drunk Christian, the Bengali, South Indian and Parsi comic caricatures with their accented speech), the Muslim character also functioned primarily to reiterate and reaffirm the hegemonic value of the Hindu, North Indian (and) upper caste male protagonist's primacy in the narrative world. As Manisha Sethi notes, 'Traditionally, mainstream Bollywood has reserved normalcy for the Hindu hero while encoding minorities with signs of cultural exaggeration… These characters are essential to complete the cinematic tableau of national integration' (Sethi 2002). Consequently, unlike his (upper caste) Hindu counterpart, the Muslim protagonist was rarely accommodated within the cinematic space (with the exception of peripheral characters like the hero's loyal friend or the elderly servant)—signalling, in a sense, the nation's own rather ambiguous and problematic accommodation of its Muslim citizen-subjects. Presented either as remnants of an antiquated culture in the popular 1950s and 1960s' Muslim Social films (Bhaskar and Allen 2009), or more recently, vilified as 'figures of violence, betrayal, inhumanity, bestiality, irrationality, deracination and irresponsibility' (Rai 2003), the Muslim in Hindi films has been traditionally (and still is) designated as the perennial 'Outsider'. The more recent vilification of Muslims conforms to what Charles Ramirez Berg terms as the 'mediated stereotype'—'an agreed-upon vision and a shared sign of the Other in precise and material form', which 'operates by gathering a specific set of negative traits and assembling them into a particular image' (2002, 38–39). Moreover, 'explicit codes' of their attire and religiosity, make the Muslim characters 'emerge as stereotypes represented by well-defined signs of speech, appearance, dress, social and religious practice' (Kazmi 1994, 239). In the aftermath of the 1999 Kargil conflict with Pakistan, increasing sectarian violence and communal strife, and the spectre of global Islamic terrorism in a post-9/11 world, accommodating the Muslim character in the Hindi film narrative became even more problematic and implausible. We need to place Shah Rukh Khan's portrayal of *Chak De! India*'s Kabir Khan in this context.

Unlike the formulaic Muslim stereotypes in Hindi cinema, there was nothing in Kabir Khan's demeanour or appearance that marked him as explicitly Muslim. Apart from his habit of saying *aadab*, the Muslim term of greeting, and his evoking of a Muslim prayer at a crucial moment in the film's narrative, there is little that betrays his religious identity. But in spite of the lack of 'explicit codes' and reiteration of a liberal cosmopolitanism, Kabir Khan's tenuous claims to (Indian) citizenship are underlined, thus implying the Muslim subject's problematic accommodation within the national imaginary. The film begins with the final of the Men's Hockey World Cup, with the host nation, India trailing arch-rival Pakistan by a goal in a game that has at stake more than just sporting laurels. The Indian team is awarded a penalty shoot-out and an opportunity to level the score. In the crucial penalty kick, Kabir Khan (Shah Rukh Khan), the Indian captain and Asia's best centre forward fails to deliver, and India loses to Pakistan. With a Muslim last name, Khan falls an easy prey to media frenzy and a nation desperate for a scapegoat. As angry fans burn effigies and 24×7 news channels hold court on whether the player is to be blamed for his team's debacle, the Indian Hockey Association decides to sack him from the captaincy. The graffiti on his house proclaims him a *gaddar* (traitor); neighbourhood kids clamber to look at the Muslim traitor who betrayed the nation, and onlookers snigger, 'Aise logon ko Partition ke waqt hi Pakistan chale jaana tha' ('Such people should have left for Pakistan at the time of Partition'). The ignominy and shame forces Khan to forsake familiar surroundings and his favourite sport.

As Kabir Khan's fall from grace illustrates, the Indian Muslim is perilously vulnerable to accusations of being a *deshdrohi* (traitor). In the film, Khan's failure to deliver comes to haunt him again and again. The selectors ridicule him and even his players bring it up. Senior player Bindiya Naik, disgruntled with Khan's control, reminds the team of his ignominious past—'Pakistan ka captain tha, India ke uniform mein … World Cup mein desh ko bech diya' ('He was Pakistan's captain in the Indian uniform … he sold the country's honour at the World Cup'). As Khan himself rues,

> Afsoz is baat ka hai ke main apne mulk se haar gaya, jisko mera khoon pasina, dil jaan de ke bhi yakeen nahin hota ke main uske team se khela tha aur zindagi bhar uske team se khelta rahoonga' ('What I regret is that I lost to my country, and in spite of all my blood, sweat, and toil, I cannot convince it that I played for its team and all through my life I will play only for its team').

Thus, Kabir Khan's failure is not merely confined to the arena of sports, but rather embodies his failure to convincingly assert his loyalty and subscription to the Indian nation-state, and consequently, underlines the dilemma of the Indian Muslim. As Saisuresh Sivaswamy points outs, the Indian Muslim 'has to constantly fight two demons: One from the past, of Partition and his/her perspective on Pakistan … and another ghost from the present, when Muslims are usually accused of engineering terrorist plots in India' (Sivaswamy 2007).

Though the film attempts to underline the contentious issues of Muslim citizenship, it also positions Khan as a liberal Muslim and, thus consequently invests him with the ability to articulate the anxieties and hopes of the national imaginary. Kabir Khan is never shown as offering *namaz* or speaking in chaste Urdu; rather, he is always shown dressed in western attire and he never makes any reference to his religious beliefs. Thus, devoid of any explicit markings of his religious identity, the Muslim protagonist now becomes eligible to represent the nation. It is Khan who chides the girls for their regional and linguistic differences and extorts them to perform as a national team. In his first interaction with the team, he drives home the point—not only is he the boss, but they have to conform to his nationalist rhetoric. As each girl rattles off the name of her state, he asks them to leave; they will be allowed to play only when they realize they are playing for their country and not their state. In a country still divided by regional, linguistic, caste and religious fissures, Khan seems to transcend the barriers more effectively than the hegemonic Hindu, Hindi-speaking North Indian protagonist.

However, in spite of his lack of explicit codes, *Chak De! India* still emphatically underlines Kabir Khan's religious identity. After a humiliating defeat at the hands of defending champion Australia, Khan is shown reciting a Muslim prayer—'Nasrum Min Allahe wa fathun qareeb' ('Allah, bring me strength and bring victory closer')—possibly one of the rare moments in the film when his 'Muslimness' is emphasized. However, instead of contradicting his liberal persona, the scene only reaffirms his claims to Indian citizenship and his secular credentials. Khan's recourse to religion is not construed as a sign of his religiosity but rather his fervent desire for the team's victory, for the nation's triumph. Consequently, in the aftermath of the team's victory in the Championship's final, Khan is hailed as the 'sachcha Hindustani' ('true Indian'), 'India ki jaan, Bharat ki shaan' ('the spirit of India, the pride of India'). Khan's embodiment of Muslim citizenship is further underlined in his portrayal of Rizvan Khan in *My Name Is Khan*.

'My Name Is Khan, and I Am Not a Terrorist'

Co-produced by Shah Rukh Khan's Red Chillies Entertainment and Karan Johar's Dharma Productions, distributed worldwide by Fox Searchlight Pictures and starring Bollywood's favourite celluloid couple (Khan and actress Kajol), *My Name Is Khan* (dir. Karan Johar) was one of 2010's most eagerly awaited releases. Johar's films tended to eulogize familial and romantic relationships; his blockbuster *Kabhi Khushi Kabhie Gham* (dir. Karan Johar 2001) was promoted with the tagline, 'It's all about loving your parents'. *My Name Is Khan* was no different;

however, unlike Johar's previous ventures, the film highlighted a pertinent political issue—Islamophobia and discrimination against Muslims in post-9/11 America. Though the focus still remained firmly on the family and romantic relationship of its protagonists, the film examined the 'question of belonging...that plagues the Muslim American and Muslim Indian' (Gill 2015, 123). It also promised to present Shah Rukh Khan in a rather different avatar.

In the film, the actor plays Rizvan Khan, a man with Asperger's Syndrome, a far cry from his usual suave, cosmopolitan, urbane avatar. As the awkward, shy, hesitant Rizvan, who hates physical touch and is reluctant to make eye contact, *My Name Is Khan*'s protagonist was an antithesis of Khan's usual screen archetype—'It was a role without any crutches of stardom. There was no star gaze.... There was no flamboyant walk' (Bamzai 2010). Consequently, as Jaspreet Gill points out, by marking the Muslim male body as 'special' (Asperger's Syndrome), it gives Rizvan 'the license to state what would normally remain unspoken; thus, actively working against a metanarrative of the Muslim terrorist that pervades the global media' (2015, 124). For Khan, who often craved 'something different' from his stereotypical and formulaic romantic roles, *My Name Is Khan* provided the opportunity to showcase his acting prowess. However, it also marked Khan's return to the Muslim protagonist, albeit in a different setting than the critically acclaimed *Chak De! India*.

Contrary to *Chak De! India*'s Kabir Khan, who embodied the problematic accommodation of the Muslim subject within the national imaginary, *My Name Is Khan*'s Rizvan Khan, speaks to the travails of Muslim citizenship in a post-9/11 America. Unlike Kabir Khan, Rizvan is not concerned with questions confronting the national imaginary; instead, his notion of community and citizenship are now articulated in the diasporic realm. Originally from Mumbai, Rizvan moves to San Francisco after his mother's death, where he meets Mandira (Kajol), a single mother with a young son. Despite the objections of his brother to their inter-religious nuptials, Rizvan and Mandira get married and settle down to blissful domesticity in the fictional California town of Banville. In its Hindu–Muslim coupling, *My Name Is Khan* presents one of the rare instances of inter-faith conjugality in popular Hindi cinema.[3] However, unlike the reality of contemporary India, where the transgressions of inter-religious and inter-caste unions are often met with violence and brutality, Mandira and Rizvan, by virtue of their international/global locale, seem to transcend the issues that beset the nation. The couple have a secular wedding ceremony, where references to their individual religions are almost negated, and their marital life seems to reaffirm contemporary India's secular imagining. As Rizvan offers *namaz* and Mandira prays to her Hindu deities, their peaceful cohabitation not only reiterates post-liberalization India's secular ambitions, but also, Shah Rukh Khan's own assertion of his secular and cosmopolitan familial life, where Hindu idols and the Quran are accorded equal respect.

In a talk show on Muslim subjectivity in contemporary India, Khan mentions how the decision to downplay Rizvan's 'Muslimness' was a conscious one—'Can we play him like we play a hero? We don't need to play the religious part of him as the hero. Let it be absolutely *normal*, because I am a Muslim, and I don't wear it any other way' (emphasis added; Khan 2010b). Yet, Rizvan Khan's identity as a Muslim, particularly in a post-9/11 world, is central to the film's narrative, and emblematic of the (Indian) Muslim's global citizenship. As Rizvan greets everyone with a *salaam alaikum* (peace be unto you), offers *namaz* in public, recites verses from the Quran, emphasizes the compassionate ethos of Islam, and reiterates, 'Musalman hona buri baat nahin hain' (being Muslim is not a bad thing), his identity as a Muslim is emphatically foregrounded. While contemporary India necessitated the camouflaging of the Muslim's religious ethos under the cloak of nationalism, the (Indian) Muslim, in the diasporic realm, confronted by the spectre of post-9/11 racial profiling and discrimination, is prompted to reaffirm his distinctiveness.

---

[3] Though Hindi films have occasionally portrayed inter-faith unions, these have tended to be usually Hindu–Christian, with invariably the Hindu man paired with the Christian woman—underlining not only Hindu masculinity's prowess to rehabilitate the (fallen/westernized) Christian woman, but also the spiritual and cultural fragility of the Hindu woman, which deems her as inaccessible for the non-Hindu man (particularly the Muslim). Consequently, Hindu–Muslim romances have also tended to pair the Hindu man with the Muslim woman, where the latter is usually co-opted into the Hindu cultural realm.

As Rizvan and Mandira's idyllic world is disrupted with their son's death in a schoolyard skirmish, and Mandira blames her husband and his religion ('I should have never married a Muslim'), the Muslim protagonist's tenuous sense of belonging is further exacerbated. Taking his wife's angry outburst at face value—'Why don't you go tell the President of United States, 'Mr. President, my name is Khan, and I am not a terrorist'?'—Rizvan embarks on a journey that transforms him into 'a Forrest Gumpian folk hero … (who) attempts to make America see the errors of stereotyping Islam' (Bamzai 2010). As the film's narrative progresses, and Rizvan's quest takes him across America, his repeated assertion, 'My name is Khan, and I am not a terrorist', embodies not only a post-9/11 world, but also the vulnerability of the Indian Muslim's global subjectivity. His allegiance and loyalty to his new homeland is only validated with his acts of 'patriotism'—reporting Muslim extremists to the Federal Bureau of Investigation (FBI) and rescuing the inhabitants of a hurricane-hit Georgia town. In his on-screen narrative of vilification, victimhood and eventual redemption, Khan underlines the binary rhetoric of the 'good Muslim' and 'bad Muslim'. As Mahmood Mamdani argues, the divisive politics prevalent in the post-9/11 milieu not only explicitly linked Islam with terrorism, but also, 'turned religious experience into a political category, differentiating between 'good Muslims' from 'bad Muslims', rather than terrorists from civilians' (2002, 366).

The contentious citizenship of the Indian Muslim, both in the national and the global sphere, is underlined not only in Shah Rukh Khan's on-screen renditions, Kabir Khan and Rizvan Khan, but also in the actor's own star text. While the controversy over his IPL remarks reiterate the Indian Muslim's problematic inclusion within the national imaginary, his repeated detentions at American airports (August 2009, April 2012, August 2016), due to a match with a namesake on the US terror watchlist, are often perceived in the context of post-9/11 Islamophobia. The opening sequence in *My Name Is Khan* is reminiscent of Khan's own experience—as airport officials question Rizvan, viewers are reminded of both Rizvan and his off-screen counterpart's vulnerability as Muslims. In an article titled 'Being a Khan' for *Outlook Turning Points* magazine, Khan mentioned how he gave his children 'pan–Indian and pan–religious' names (Aryan and Suhana) so that they might not encounter discrimination and Islamophobia (Khan 2013).

Khan's response in the media, following the IPL controversy, further underlines the fragility of the Indian Muslim's citizenship. In exclusive interviews to select media outlets, the actor repeatedly emphasizes his allegiance to the nation, making frequent references to his father, who had participated in the country's freedom struggle.

I pay my taxes, I try to be okay law-wise and then, suddenly you are subjected to questioning of this form, and I get very emotional about the things that people say, because my parents gave me nothing else … I'm not saying I'm the most patriotic, but … I'm a good Indian. (Khan 2010a)

In his interviews, Khan also emerges as the voice of the secular, cosmopolitan India, as he questions the undue importance accorded to regional and ethno-religious identities, pointing out the incongruity of such rhetoric with the narrative the modern, emergent global India.

All this (religion, regionalism) is a subset of your country identity, of your national identity. When did subsets become more important than the set itself? And that is something that is unacceptable.

If we are going to talk about regionalism every second, if you're going to talk about religion every two minutes, if you're going to talk about Khans and Kumars and Khannas every 30 seconds… I think nobody should (then) talk about India shining and India becoming bright. (Khan 2010a)

Shah Rukh Khan's own star text, particularly his cinematic portrayals of Muslim subjectivity, reiterates not only the Indian Muslim's tenuous claims to (Indian and global) citizenship, but also, contemporary India's inherent fissures and contradictions. As Khan responded to the Shiv Sena diatribe with repeated assertions of his secular credentials—'I'm a bloody good Indian'—and his legacy as the son of a freedom fighter, the controversy exposed his vulnerability as a Muslim, both within the national and the global space. While incidents involving his detention at US airports are often couched within the rhetoric of his religious affiliation, thus underlining the Muslim subject's vulnerability in a post-9/11 world, the questioning of his patriotism, at home, speaks to the nation's inherent fissures. Post-liberalization's claims of modernity and secularism, thus, are juxtaposed with its recent history of divisive politics, sectarian violence and communal strife. However, Shah Rukh Khan's rendition of the Indian Muslim would undergo a further resignification in Rahul Dholakia's *Raees*.

EPILOGUE: 'BANIYE KA DIMAAG AUR MIYANBHAI KI DARING' ('THE BRAINS OF THE TRADER AND THE DARING OF THE MUSLIM')

In *Raees* (dir. Rahul Dholakia 2017), the audience is introduced to a very different avatar of the Bollywood superstar—a kohl-lined, bare bodied, bloodied Shah Rukh Khan whipping himself with a cluster of blades as he participates in the Muharram *taziya* procession. As Sivaswamy remarks, 'Raees Alam is the most 'Muslim' role Khan has essayed so far...(he) inhabits the world of mohallas, Moharram and maatham, something that Shah Rukh Khan the actor maybe did long ago, but never ever on screen' (Sivaswamy 2017). Essaying the role of the 1980s Gujarati mafia kingpin and bootlegger Abdul Latif, Khan's portrayal of the 'unabashedly Muslim' (Agarwal 2017), *Raees* not only marked a departure from his formulaic role as the romantic 'Global Indian', but also from his previous renditions of the Indian Muslim. In contrast to both Kabir (*Chak De! India*) and Rizvan (*My Name Is Khan*), Raees is 'very much a product of the ghetto' (Agarwal 2017), thus embodying the marginalization of the urban disenfranchised Indian Muslim. The ghettoization of the Muslims in Indian cities underlines not only their significant 'economic deprivation', but also, their 'sense of physical insecurity' and 'increasing socio-spatial segregation' (Gayer and Jaffrelot 2012, 2). Subsequently, the 'ghetto Muslim' is marked as overtly religious, thus further reiterating his inherent extremism as well as his lack of education. In *Raees*, however, we see a more acceptable variant of the *Miyanbhai* (a colloquial term for the Muslim), whose religious subscription is superseded by his business etiquette, the practicality of the *baniya* (trader). A devout and orthodox Muslim, Raees's work ethic is shaped by his mother's constant iteration—'Koi dhandha chota nahi hota, aur dhande se bada koi dharam nahi hota' ('no business is small and no religion is bigger than the business you do'). As the tagline of the film, 'Baniye ka dimaag aur Miyanbhai ki daring' celebrates both his business acumen (*baniya*) and his bravado (*Miyanbhai*), Raees 'allows the otherness of the "Miabhai" to be embraced via the familiarity of the "Baniya"' (Gupta 2017).

Raees might be an orthodox, devout Muslim, but he displays no traces of religious fundamentalism. As an elected political representative, he initiates a low-cost housing project, *Apni Duniya* (Our World), for his constituents, and distributes food to both Hindu and Muslim residents during communal riots, reiterating his motto that humanity trumps religion—'sab hamare log hain' ('they are all our people'). As a cinematic incarnate of the Indian Muslim, particularly the ghettoized lower-class *Miyanbhai*, the film's implicit message is clear—Raees Alam might be devout, but his religiosity should not be equated with extremism or fundamentalism. It is only when he unwittingly smuggles RDX in the guise of gold, which is later used in serial bombings across North India (a reference to the 1993 Mumbai bomb blasts), that he is doomed to an ignominious end. By agreeing to the Mumbai-based don, Musa (a reference to Abdul Latif's own association with Dawood Ibrahim), Raees falls prey to the anti-national Muslim, the antagonist in the narrative of the nation, and consequently, reaffirms the image of the ghettoized Muslim who can never be a true Indian. As he woefully rues in the film, 'mohalla bachate shehar jala diya' ('while trying to save the neighbourhood, I burnt down the city'), it is a clear message that the Indian Muslim needs to think beyond his *quam* (community) or else he will inevitably succumb to the taint of a *deshdrohi* (traitor). What makes such a tragic denouement inevitable is Raees's pronounced Muslimness—his attire, his *tabeez* (religious amulet) and kohl-lined eyes all not only explicitly mark him as the Muslim 'Other', but also deems him impossible to be perceived as an (authentic) Indian citizen. In his on-screen role as Raees Alam, Shah Rukh Khan displays the 'explicit codes' that were absent in his previous portrayals of the Indian Muslim (Kabir and Rizvan). Just as the chaste Urdu, *sherwani* (traditional Muslim attire) and strict observance of religious norms (*namaz* and Haj) defined the 1950s' and 1960s' Muslim protagonist as antiquated and archaic, incapable of embodying the modernistic ambitions of Nehruvian India, similarly Raees's overt (Muslim) appearance makes him untenable for millennial India.

Raees holds particular relevance, not only in terms of enumerating the subjectivity and citizenship of the Indian Muslim, and his role in the national imaginary, but as Gupta asserts, 'it is absolutely important for the optics of this film that this protagonist is a Muslim in a Gujarat where the Hindutva project is on its way to political and social hegemony' (Gupta 2017). With Gujarat being a stronghold of the BJP, a right-wing political party with Hindu-nationalist ideologies (Banerjee 2005), since 1995, the state laid the foundation for the political dynamics on the national front. Since BJP has assumed power at the Centre in 2014, debates over 'Love Jihad,' beef ban and cow vigilantism have become prominent, bringing into question the issue of minority citizenship. With the rise of Hindutva politics and increasing divisiveness, the Indian Muslim now inhabits a place in the margins (Waikar 2018), often ostracized and discriminated against. Though *Raees* seems to evoke the 1980s and 1990s, the period that Latif was active in Gujarat, its relevance in the current political and social environment cannot be disregarded. As Amit Agarwal mentions, 'There is an almost daring foregrounding of Muslim identity … making a passionate case for seeing the community as a victim of rather than the perpetrator of terrorism' (Agarwal 2017). For Arnesh Ghose, 'Relevant, stylish and politically charged, *Raees* is SRK's most important film till date' (Ghose 2017), underlining the significance of the film in the current scenario. Though Raees Alam might seem a departure from Khan's usual oeuvre as well as his previous portrayals of the Indian Muslim, the protagonist, similar to Kabir Khan (*Chak De! India*) and Rizvan Khan (*My Name Is Khan*), embodies the travails and tribulations of the Muslim minority citizenship, an issue which is further highlighted by Shah Rukh Khan's own star text as a Muslim superstar.

REFERENCES

Agarwal, Amit. 2017. 'The Message in the Bottle: Shah Rukh Khan's 'Raees' Is Deeply Political'. Scroll.in, New Delhi, 4 February. scroll.in/reel/828487/the-message-in-the-bottle-shah-rukh-khans-raees-is-deeply-political.

Bamzai, Kaveree. 2010. 'His Name Is Khan'. *India Today*, New Delhi, 1 March, pp. 46–51.

Banerjee, Sumanta. 2005. 'Civilising the BJP'. *Economic and Political Weekly* 40 (29): 3116–3119.

Berg, Charles Ramirez. 2002. *Latino Images in Film: Stereotypes, Subversion and Resistance*. Austin, TX: University of Texas Press.

Bhaskar, Ira, and Richard Allen. 2009. *Islamicate Cultures of Bombay Cinema*. New Delhi: Tulika Books.

Bhattacharjee, Subhadeep. 2010. 'Shiv Sena Threatens Shah Rukh Khan over IPL'. OneIndia Entertainment, 29 January. entertainment.oneindia.in/bollywood/news/2010/shiv-sena-slams-shahrukh-290110.html.

Chadha, Kalyani, and Anandam P. Kavoori. 2008. 'Exoticized, Marginalized, Demonized: The Muslim "Other" in Indian Cinema'. In *Global Bollywood*, edited by Aswin Punathambekar and Anandam P. Kavoori, 131–145. New York: NYU Press.

Chopra, Anupama. 2007. *King of Bollywood: Shah Rukh Khan and the Seductive World of Indian Cinema*. New York, NY: Warner Books.

Dutt, Barkha. 2007. 'Let's Look Inwards Now'. *Hindustan Times*, New Delhi, 7 July.

Dudrah, Rajinder, Elke Mader and Bernhard Fuchs, eds. 2015. *SRK and Global Bollywood*. New Delhi: Oxford University Press.

Dwyer, Rachel. 2015. 'Innocent Abroad: SRK, Karan Johar, and the Indian Diasporic Romance'. In *SRK and Global Bollywood*, edited by Rajinder Dudrah, Elke Mader and Bernhard Fuchs, 49–69. New Delhi: Oxford University Press.

Dyer, Richard. 1998. *Stars*. London: British Film Institute.

Gayer, Laurent, and Christophe Jaffrelot. 2012. 'Introduction: Muslims of the Indian City. From Centrality to Marginality'. In *Muslims in Indian Cities: Trajectories of Marginalisation*, edited by Laurent Gayer and Christophe Jaffrelot, 1–22. London: C. Hurst & Co.

Ghose, Arnesh. 2017. 'Review: Relevant, Stylish and Politically Charged, *Raees* Is SRK's Most Important Film till Date'. *Man's World*, Mumbai. mansworldindia.com/cinema/review-relevant-stylish-politically-charged-raees-srks-important-film-till-date/

Gill, Jaspreet. 2015. '*My Name Is Khan*: Reinventing the Muslim Hero on the Global Stage'. In *SRK and Global Bollywood*, edited by Rajinder Dudrah, Elke Mader and Bernhard Fuchs, 122–137. New Delhi: Oxford University Press.

Gupta, Trisha. 2017. 'Miya–Baniya Bhai Bhai?' *Mumbai Mirror*, Mumbai, 5 February. mumbaimirror.indiatimes.com/opinion/columnists/trisha-gupta/miya-baniya-bhai-bhai/articleshow/56978783.cms

Hasan, Mushirul. 1996. 'The Myth of Unity: Colonial and National Narratives'. In *Making India Hindu: Religion, Community, and the Politics of Democracy in India*, edited by David Ludden, 185–210. New Delhi: Oxford University Press.

Kazmi, Fareed. 1994. 'Muslim Socials and the Female Protagonist: Seeing a Dominant Discourse at Work'. In *Forging Identities*, edited by Zoya Hasan, 226–243. New Delhi: Kali for Women.

Khan, Shah Rukh. 2007a. 'I Don't Give Messages, I Try to Entertain People'. Interview by Saisuresh Sivaswamy and Savera R. Someshwar. Rediff.com, Mumbai, 14 February. specials.rediff.com/movies/2007/feb/14slid1.htm.

———. 2007b. 'Jihad Is about Killing the Badness in You'. Interview with Saisuresh Sivaswamy and Savera R. Someshwar. Rediff.com, Mumbai, 19 February. specials.rediff.com/movies/2007/feb/19slide2.htm.

———. 2007c. 'Films Are for Entertainment, Messages Are for the Post Office'. Interview with Namrata Joshi. Outlook, New Delhi, 22 October. outlookindia.com/article.aspx?235838.

———. 2008. 'Interview: SRK on Mumbai Siege and Terror'. Interview with Rajdeep Sardesai. CNN-IBN, New Delhi, 7 December. ibnlive.in.com/news/islam-does-not-preach-terror-shah-rukh-khan/79834-3.html.

———. 2010a. 'I Am a Bloody Good Indian: SRK to NDTV'. Interview with Barkha Dutt. NDTV, New Delhi, 8 February. ndtv.com/article/india/i-am-a-bloody-good-indian-srk-to-ndtv-15986.

———. 2010b. 'Being Muslim in Today's India'. We The People, NDTV, New Delhi, 8 March.

———. 2013. 'Being a Khan'. Outlook Turning Points, New Delhi, 21 January.

Khan, Shahnaz. 2009. 'Reading Fanaa: Confrontational Views, Comforting Identifications and Undeniable Pleasures'. South Asian Popular Culture 7 (2): 127–139.

Majumdar, Neepa. 2009. Wanted Cultured Ladies Only!: Female Stardom and Cinema in India, 1930s–1950s. Champaign, IL: University of Illinois Press.

Mamdani, Mahmood. 2002. 'Good Muslim, Bad Muslim: A Political Perspective on Culture and Terrorism'. American Anthropologist 104 (3): 766–775.

Mazumdar, Ranjani. 2000. 'From Subjectification to Schizophrenia: The 'Angry Young Man' and the 'Psychotic' Hero of Bombay Cinema'. In Making Meaning in Indian Cinema, edited by Ravi S. Vasudevan, 238–266. New Delhi: Oxford University Press.

Mazzarella, William. 2003. Shoveling Smoke: Advertising and Globalization in Contemporary India. Durham, NC: Duke University Press.

Rai, Amit. 2003. 'Patriotism and the Muslim Citizen in Hindi Films'. Harvard Asia Quarterly 7 (3): 4–15.

Raina, Badri. 2010. 'Constructing Shah Rukh Khan'. Outlook, New Delhi, 3 February.

Sethi, Manisha. 2002. 'Cine Patriotism'. SAMAR: South Asian Magazine for Action and Reflection, 15. http://samarmagazine.org/archive/articles/115

Shiekh, Mushtaq. 2006. Still Reading Khan. New Delhi: Om Books International.

Sivaswamy, Saisuresh. 2007. 'SRK and the M word'. Rediff.com, Mumbai, 13 August. rediff.com/movies/2007/aug/13sai.htm

———. 2017. 'Review: Raees and Fall of the Don'. Rediff.com, Mumbai, 25 January. rediff.com/movies/report/review-raees-and-fall-of-the-don/20170124.htm

Srinivas, Lakshmi. 2005. 'Communicating Globalization in Bombay Cinema: Everyday Life, Imagination and the Persistence of the Local'. *International Journal of Comparative American Studies* 3 (3): 319–344.

Times of India. 2010a. 'IPL's Pak Boycott Humiliating: Shah Rukh Khan'. *The Times of India*, New Delhi, 26 January. articles.timesofindia.indiatimes.com/2010-01-26/india/28117111_1_pakistani-players-ipl-franchisees-australian-players

———. 2010b. 'Chidambaram Slams IPL for Not Picking Pak Players'. *The Times of India*, New Delhi, 25 January. articles.timesofindia.indiatimes.com/2010-01-25/india/28119380_1_pakistani-players-pak-players-ipl-franchisees

Uberoi, Patricia. 2006. *Freedom and Destiny: Gender, Family, and Popular Culture in India.* New Delhi; New York, NY: Oxford University Press.

Varma, Pavan K. 1998. *The Great Indian Middle Class.* New Delhi; New York, NY: Viking.

Virdi, Jyotika. 2003. *The Cinematic Imagination: Indian Popular Films as Social History.* New Brunswick, NJ: Rutgers University Press.

Waikar, Prashant. 2018. 'Reading Islamophobia in Hindutva: An Analysis of Narendra Modi's Political Discourse'. *Islamophobia Studies Journal* 4 (2): 161–180.

Chapter 10

Screening Hindutva
Religion and Television in India

Maribel Elliet Alvarado Becerril

This chapter examines the different narratives of nationalism used in English news channels of India and analyses the intersection between media, especially television debates, and the triumph of the Hindu right with Prime Minister Narendra Modi. It explores the intertwining of the religious/cultural construction of Hindutva with the idea of a perfectly defined nation that allows the association between citizen participation, sense of belonging, as well as individual and collective identity. It argues that the media plays a vital role in shaping and articulating national imaginings by providing a formal and a narrative space for their articulation. It takes the media to be an inherent component of popular culture that has now come to be integrated in formal processes of electoral politics and governance (Jones 2005, 13).

India's rapidly expanding news channels capitalize on the growth of Hindu nationalism, which blends territorial unity with Hindutva. Departing from here, this research focuses on the different symbolic elements and narratives of 'nationalism' used in certain English News

Channels: New Delhi Television (NDTV), Times Now and Republic TV.

The combination of politics, religion, culture and nation has conferred a unique meaning and authority to the parties of the Hindu right. Hindu nationalist agendas, speeches and institutions have gradually penetrated everyday life and have acquired a growing and almost indisputable social respectability in contemporary Indian society (Hansen 1999). The goal of Hindu nationalism, to Hinduize the nation's image using the cultural markers of a 'glorious Hindu past', is increasingly evident.

An inherent element of democracy is the possibility of having a space of interaction, deliberation or communication. Media is a fundamental part of representative governments, helping citizens exercise the rights to freedom of speech and expression, and information. Thus, the interconnection between information message, political reality and public opinion, create a selection of what should be communicated and how it should be done to fit the medium in question (press, radio, television, social networks, among others) or the types of genres and formats (news, reports, interviews, debates, entertainment, advertising and so on).

> Through the relentless communication of the media, a 'commonly
> known reality' is being built, which can then be implicitly assumed as a
> background in all social interactions. This crystallises elements of social
> communication—such as 'knowledge'—and both facts and opinions on
> the facts to create a description of reality, a building of the world and a
> reality that orients the society. The funny thing is that this reality is not
> a mere 'reflection' of what is happening. It is actively built following
> the very logic of the system. (Vallespín 2000, 84)

In this way, popular culture[1] is completely intertwined with political communication. Jürgen Habermas considers that, within political

---

[1] 'Popular culture' has been considered the main component of cultural studies, as it encompasses the set of practices, beliefs and objects that embody the shared meanings of a social system. It includes elements from the media, entertainment and

communication,[2] the deliberative tradition of democracy emphasizes both the political participation of citizens and how public opinion is shaped, that is, political socialization[3] (Habermas 2006). In this process of socialization, media acquire relevance by generating and transmitting messages that help internalize certain political priorities and concepts. At the same time, media—especially television—offer a formal and narrative space for the articulation of particular national imaginations that helps to create the idea that communities have about themselves.

News channels have become one of the main sources of information in India, in a context where news is not merely a media product but a vehicle for engagement in the democratic process, feeding off and into domestic policies and international relations (Thussu 2007, 2). India is a country of 1.339 billion population, of which 836 million have television. In 2018, 298 million households with television were registered, 87 per cent of which are in urban areas and 52 per cent in rural areas. As per Broadcast India Survey, 98 per cent of the 197 million TV homes in the country still have access to a single TV each (Broadcast Audience Research Council India 2018, 1). According to Federation of Indian Chambers of Commerce and Industry (FICCI), in 2019, the average time spent watching television increased to 3 hours and 46 minutes per day, led by megacities, which had 4 hours and 32 minutes and south markets at 4 hours and 14 minutes (FICCI 2019, 37). This consumption tends to increase among the youngest population, and it is mainly carried out in the company of another person in the prime-time zone from 5:00 PM to 11:00 PM. The news genre, including talk shows and debate programmes, claims 8 per cent of total viewership.

---

leisure, fashion, linguistic conventions, among others (Gokulsing and Dissanayake 2009).

[2] 'Political communication' is an interactive process concerning the transmission of information among politicians, the news media and the public (Norris 2014, 318).

[3] 'Political socialization' is the process by which individuals develop conceptions of themselves and their reality, encompassing the political sphere, including direct experiences, judgments and inferences about the knowledge they have at the time (Pinkleton and Weintraub 2001).

Making it the third-largest genre in terms of audience, following the general entertainment channels and movies.

From a cognitive perspective, Doris Graber argues that audio-visual materials are essential in individuals learning about politics, causing the population to be actively involved when they process the transmitted information. The visual nature of television reinforces the degree of reality of the content presented, and increases the credibility of what has been seen. Also, studies reveal that images are memorized better and are accompanied by a greater emotional commitment on the part of the recipients (Graber 2001).

> Broadcasting may be thought of as an 'institution' in two different senses of the term. On the one hand, it is an industry for the manufacture of symbolic goods. It has various institutional sites of cultural production that are characterised by particular professional practices and by specific relationships to the state or the market. On the other hand, at the point of cultural consumption where those symbolic goods enter into the social settings which are inhabited by its audiences, broadcasting can also be understood as what is called an institution in everyday life-part of the social fabric that goes to make up our routine daily experiences. (Moores 2000, 12)

For sociologist Ron Lembo (2000), visual culture includes the formation of attitudes and opinions of people, who correlate what they are see with other aspects of their lives, both textual and 'real'. Audience decide to consciously participate with television when they believe that the stories are plausible, incorporating the speeches into their understanding of the world. This 'voluntary suspension of disbelief' implies the willingness to accept as certain the premises on which the received message is based, leaving aside the critical or rational sense and ignoring possible inconsistencies or limitations (Tomko 2015, 13).

As Sonia Livingstone and Peter Lunt (1994) have pointed out, the audience in front of the public formulation is really based on a series of assumptions of value in competition with the behaviours, practices and state of the spectator, including consumers versus citizens, public versus private, rational versus emotional, disinterested versus biased, participatory versus withdrawn, shared versus individualized, visible versus hidden and so on. As a proof of this, there is what happened following the tweet published by Harbhajan Singh in June 2019.

'Some countries have the moon on their flags... While some countries having their flags on the moon. #Chandrayaan2theMoon' Harbhajan Singh wrote on Twitter after the Indian Space Research Organisation launched its second moon mission from the Satish Dhawan Space Centre at Sriharikota (Andhra Pradesh) on 22 July 2019. He posted the flags of nine countries with the crescent moon and star—Pakistan, Turkey, Tunisia, Libya, Azerbaijan, Algeria, Malaysia, Maldives and Mauritania—and, in the next line, those of four nations with successful space programmes: the United States, Russia, India and China.

Immediately, the former Indian cricketer got numerous compliments for his comment as it reflected pride in the country's achievement. However, others found it to be distasteful and started to call Singh a 'bigot', 'racist', 'communal' and 'Islamophobic'. Harbhajan's tweet became viral with nearly 41,700 retweets and 228,000 likes. It resulted in an extended controversy in the media, mainly television, where many people took it as fun while others criticized it. Arnab Goswami, one of India's most controversial TV anchors, was the first to choose this dispute for the prime-time broadcast of *The Debate with Arnab Goswami* on 23 July 2019.

During this episode, Arnab Goswami attempted to defend the former Mumbai Indians captain from being labelled as a bigot, communal and Islamophobic. Goswami accused those who attacked Bhajji (Harbhajan Singh's nickname) and anyone who is not proud of the country's accomplishments of being 'anti-nationalist'. Even one of the panellists, the filmmaker Ashoke Pandit, called them 'white-collar terrorists, urban-Naxals[4]

---

[4] The term 'urban-Naxal' remains undefined. 'It is best attributed to a book and a few essays by film-maker and social media opinion-maker Vivek Agnihotri. His book, *Urban Naxals: The Making of Buddha in a Traffic Jam*, was released in May 2018'. A few TV news channels and right-wing spokespersons use the term 'urban-Naxal' to label anyone— from academics to activists—who question the policies of the state or are perceived to be anti-establishment. They allegedly are

and *tukde-tukde* gang,[5] as they seem to be working against the country. The anchor ended his debate by declaring 'Harbhajan Singh a nationalist, a patriot and a great supporter of the Indian army, whose heart beats only for India' (Goswami 2019).

These kinds of debates, broadcast on prime-time hours on news channels, are becoming the staple prime time content on news channels. Most of the time they ensure the preference of the viewers and respond only to commercial interests; however, the aggressive campaigning against the supposed 'enemies of the nation' is increasingly linked to the agenda of the Hindu right driven by the Bharatiya Janata Party (BJP).[6] Television channels, or at least some of them, seem to be making a coordinated effort to create a particular scenario and narrative, which adapts to governmental objectives (Bhatia 2019).

In recent years, the growing wave of Hindu nationalism has defied the secularism embodied in constitutional principles, unleashing a debate about the fundamentals of India's political identity. The discourse of Hindu nationalism presents a narrative form at the heart of its operations. That is, it devolved stories that were, in the best instances, enunciated under the governance of the modern, setting up claims of authenticity in line with disciplinary protocols (Basu 2008, 243). Some controversies exacerbated this debate, including the event at Jawaharlal

---

covertly aiding those who are working to break India, such as Naxalite movement (Dutta 2018).

[5] In January 2018, Arnab Goswami coined the phrase '*tukde-tukde* gang' to target people that were out to fragment India (Goswami 2018). The term has been used to justify governmental actions against a range of people considered a threat to the nation.

[6] The BJP was founded in 1980 and emerged from its precursor, the Bharatiya Jana Sangh (BJS). The BJS was founded in 1951 by Shyama Prasad Mookerjee, a member of the Rashtriya Swayamsevak Sangh, organization, which quickly developed into the largest Hindu nationalist movement and was intended not only to propagate the Hindutva ideology, but also to infuse new physical strength into the majority community (Jaffrelot 2007).

Nehru University (JNU) in 2016. On 10 February 2016 during the final minutes of the prime-time broadcast of *The Newshour Debate*, the former editor-in-chief of Times Now channel—Arnab Goswami—addressed to viewers to reflect on this event.

> What we should do with a group of secessionists, anti-nationals, opportunists who masqueraded to be believing into a political ideology. They are simply pro-Pakistan elements and I wonder what the forces are which are behind them... Let us vow never to let something like this happen ever again, not just in a campus or any square inch of our soil. (Goswami 2016)

Weeks before this broadcast, JNU students proposed a cultural event entitled Poetry Reading 'The Country Without a Post Office' to be held on 9 February. The posters presented an event showing solidarity with Kashmiri people's demand for self-determination and criticizing the 2013 execution of Afzal Guru, condemned for his involvement in the attack on Parliament in 2001 (Ray and Singh 2017, 254). Although the respective arrangements were made to carry it out, University authorities cancelled the permission saying that the organizers had not provided detailed information regarding this event.

As a sign of disagreement, the assembled students began shouting slogans, some of which were perceived as 'anti-national', provoking a fight between the Akhil Bharatiya Vidyarthi Parishad (ABVP)[7] and leftist groups present at that time. Demonstrations rapidly intensified, causing police irruption on campus, followed by a chain of events that culminated in the famous address by the then-president of the Jawaharlal Nehru University Student Union, Kanhaiya Kumar. On 12 February, Kanhaiya Kumar was arrested under Section 124A of the Indian Penal Code on charges of sedition. Imposing Similar

---

[7] Akhil Bharatiya Vidyarthi Parishad (ABVP) is a student organization affiliated with RSS, formalized and registered on 9 July 1949. It participates in joint activities with the official youth wing of the BJP, the Bharatiya Janata Yuva Morcha. It is India's largest student organization with more than three million members who, 'inspired by the great culture and traditions of the world's oldest civilisation, wanted to reconstruct India into a powerful, prosperous and proud Nation' (ABVP 2018).

charges were imposed on other students for their organization of, and participation in, an evening of poetry, speeches, talks and song related to the execution of Afzal Guru (Jawaharlal Nehru University Teachers' Association [JNUTA] 2017, 10).

The arrest of Kumar set off a series of strikes, marches and protests, which immediately caught national media's attention. In this extensive media coverage, television played a key role, attempting to address the meanings, stories, experiences and unresolved dilemmas of nationalism. Channels such as Times Now and Zee News were at one end of the spectrum, making value judgments and continuously repeating the dichotomies 'us versus them' and 'national versus anti-national'. NDTV and CNN-IBN were at the other end, trying to broadcast the news as objectively as possible. Among them, the statements of two personalities—Arnab Goswami of Times Now and Ravish Kumar of NDTV—stood out and became the largest source of public opinion formation (Bhushan 2016).

Once again, Arnab Goswami, known for calling himself 'nationalist', was the first to use this topic for his TV show. On 10 February, he invited JNU students to discuss the 'anti-India' slogans raised in the campus. In the course of the debate, he openly called the student panellists 'anti-nationals' and, only a few times, allowed them to defend their stance and articulate their opinions. 'Being a nationalist is a prerequisite for being a journalist' said Goswami (2017), who, in the wake of these events, has contributed to shaping and keeping the 'nationalism' narrative as the central attribute for assessing public life.

A few days later, in his prime-time programme of 16 February, Ravish Kumar broadcasted live from a protest march in New Delhi. Journalists staged the protest against the violence that took place in Patiala House Court on 15 February. A mob of men, wearing lawyers' robe, assaulted some students, teachers, reporters and bystanders when JNU student leader, Kanhaiya Kumar, was to be presented before Metropolitan Magistrate Loveleen. Without taking names, Ravish lashed out at some presenters who, from his perspective, were not only suppressing freedom of expression but were polarizing the audience. While walking, he conducted some interviews and expressed: 'It is good to see journalists showing solidarity and coming together but the problem is that there are still many journalists who have not united to fight against this' (Kumar 2016).

Extensive media coverage of the event highlighted different narratives of nationalism; TV presenters had supporters and detractors who, from this moment on, placed at the centre of the general discourse the terms 'nation', 'nationalism', 'national' and 'patriotism'. It also demonstrated the manner in which the narratives on social media and traditional media intersect with and reinforce each other.

In the political and cultural communication process, some news channels—through rhetoric and reason, performances, debates and public discourses, images and ideas—have been actively participating in spreading Hindutva ideas. Therefore, this chapter also queries if television has reshaped the context in which religion is symbolized, screened and understood. News channels, or at least some of their primetime shows, seem to be making a coordinated effort to create a particular environment and narrative that aligns with the government's goals.

TELEVISION IN INDIA

Television was introduced in India on 15 September 1959 as a project that aimed to speed up the development process. The project—financed by the United Nations Educational, Scientific and Cultural Organization (UNESCO) and Ford Foundation—was launched as a public broadcasting model committed to informing, educating and entertaining people. The then prime minister, Jawaharlal Nehru, gave the state governments full control of these media. All India Radio handled the initial broadcasts, which consisted of educational programmes twice a week for half an hour.

Daily transmission service began in Delhi in 1965 and, subsequently, spread to cities such as Bombay (1972), Calcutta (1975) and Chennai (1975). With the separation of radio and television in 1976, the Ministry of Information and Broadcasting created Doordarshan, the public television company, whose goal was to increase coverage at the national level. In 1982, India achieved this goal with the broadcast of the Ninth Asian Games, which were transmitted, for the first time, in full colour and via the INSAT 1A satellite.

Television in India developed as a medium whose educational purpose was supplemented by its utilization as a spokesman for the central government and the ruling party. Promoting 'national integrity' was one of Doordarshan's most important purposes and, as a result of movements in Punjab and Assam in the late 1970s and 1980s, this purpose became increasingly significant; any information that was transmitted about these regions was treated from the perspective of 'threats to the nation'.

However, the project had a crucial contradiction produced possibly by the very form of mass media dissemination, the compulsive direct address to the people, and the onus of 'representation' through a 'visual' medium. The programmes were mainly compartmentalised fragments addressed towards different segments of people: agricultural programmes for farmers, news in English for the urban elite, quiz programmes for urban school-going children, literacy and awareness programmes particularly for the rural illiterate, folk performances from various parts of India. (Roy 2008, 31)

Furthermore, in January 1987, the secular character of television changed utterly with the national broadcast of a Hindu epic series, *Ramayana*. On Sunday mornings from January 1987 to July 1988, around a hundred million Indians watched this 78-episode series directed by Ramanand Sagar (Kumar 2006, 38). The *Ramayana*'s broadcast coincided with the strengthening of the Hindu nationalist movement, causing unexpected expressions of devotion 'with viewers performing purification rituals before the programme began and adorning television sets with flowers and incense, consecrating them as altars' (Mitchell 2005, 2).

Ramayana, along with other series, such as *Mahabharata* (1988) and *Sri Krishna* (1993), made the Hindu gods extremely popular figures. In all these serials, a particular set of similar symbols was used to denote the Hindu religion, which had several implications. First and foremost, other practices were marginalized, and, within the national image, these were perceived as deviant and non-Indian. This situation resulted in a struggle that was no longer restricted to questions of specific religious rituals but was manifested in political struggles (Mitra 1993, 147).

Hindu nationalist parties cashed in on the success of these epics. The actors of these serials tried to bring this popularity from television to politics, joining parties such as the BJP. Even, 'the BJP's *rath yatra*, or grand tour in 1991, was in imitation of the chariot wheeled in by the god Krishna to war in the Mahabharat epic' (Pasricha 2014). Gods and goddesses were present in almost every political discourse of Hindu nationalism that would trigger the Ram Janmabhoomi[8] movement and end with the destruction of the Babri Masjid in 1992. After this event, television's influence on Indian politics became increasingly apparent.

In the 1990s, the central government, led by Prime Minister Narasimha Rao, implemented a series of economic and social reforms that allowed private and foreign broadcasters to enter the country. After three decades of state monopoly, television went from being a highly centralized one-way communication system, with a limited number of broadcasters' networks, to a more diversified and decentralized broadcasting system. By 1992, the first private channels, local (Zee TV and Sun TV) and foreign (CNN and Star TV), began their satellite broadcast.

It was not until 1998 that the first private channel began broadcasting news 24 hours a day; since then, the number of private satellite

---

[8] The campaign for demolition of a historic mosque constructed in 1528 was spearheaded politically by Hindutva forces to gain power. According to Hindu tradition, Ayodhya (Uttar Pradesh) is the birthplace and capital of the god-king, Rama (Ram Janmabhoomi). Supposedly, in this site was a temple dedicated to the god Rama, which was destroyed in the sixteenth century on the orders of Babur, the first Mughal emperor, and replaced by a mosque, the Babri Masjid. In the summer of 1989, with the logistical support of the RSS, the Rama Shila Pujan festivals were organized, which involved the worship of bricks (*shila*) printed with Rama's name. These sacred bricks would be used to rebuild the Ayodhya temple (Jaffrelot 2007, 20). See also the writings which contest the mythologization of Ayodhya such as 'Ram Janmabhoomi': Sharma (1990), Sharma et al. (1991), Ratnagar (2004) and Thapar (2010).

channels has considerably increased, reaching 869 in 2018, of which 382 broadcast news in 24 languages and 54 of them are in 24×7 format (Ministry of Information and Broadcasting 2018). Within the programming of these channels, different temporal and spatial relationships with the audience developed; the popularity and multiplicity of their debate programmes quickly excelled and 'constituted a space in which new discursive practices are developed in contrast to the traditional modes of political and ideological representation' (Jones 2005, 53).

Competition in the private channel market required the use of distinctive stylistic markers to create a new and more meaningful relationship with the viewers. Debate programmes offer alternative spaces to make sense of political reality 'while directly and indirectly questioning the vaunted place of journalism as the primary arbiter of political truth' (Jones 2010: 64).

POLITICAL STRATEGY OF HINDU NATIONALISM

According to Christophe Jaffrelot (2010), the Jana Sangh,[9] and later the BJP, has maintained a policy that ranges between two strategies. One is a moderate line, which involves positioning itself as a patriotic party in defence of national unity, often with populist connotations. The other is a more militant strategy based on ethno-religious movements and the promotion of an aggressive form of 'Hinduness', symbolized by the campaign to elevate Hindi to the level of India's national language, and the protection of cows, as well as the mobilization around Ayodhya.

One of the main features of Hindu nationalist militancy is the presence of highly disciplined organizations, which promote different facets of the Hindutva. Daily attendance at *shakhas* is considered the core of the RSS activities and is a clear indicator of the organization's spread. A report presented by RSS general secretary Suresh Joshi at the ongoing Akhil Bharatiya Pratinidhi Sabha notes that 58,967 *shakhas* operate in 37,190 locations across the country. In addition to *shakhas*, the RSS

---

[9] The Jana Sangh formed in 1951 as the political arm of RSS, the most prominent Hindu nationalist volunteer organization, aimed at propagating Hindutva ideology.

also has weekly and monthly meetings, as well as training camps for its volunteers (Pathak 2018).

Although the militant strategy was more in line with the wishes of the RSS, the Jana Sangh faced constitutional barriers, which prevented it from expanding and establishing alliances with other parties. This strategy changed in the 1970s when it partnered with the Janata Party. With the creation of the BJP in 1980, the original ideology of the Jana Sangh was gradually diluted to become more acceptable in the party system and was able to find valuable allies (Jaffrelot 2010, 20). After winning the 1996 elections, Hindutva certainly did not disappear, but the coalition arrangement suggested that the BJP deemphasize those controversial social issues that might cause problems for its friends and partners. Once in power, the BJP's programme included some of the traditional elements of Hindu nationalism programme but found it was 'no longer in their interest to stoke communal fires' (Friedlander 2016, 77).

The National Democratic Alliance ruled from 1998 to 2004, when it was surprisingly defeated and replaced by a coalition led by the Congress Party. Most members of the Sangh Parivar[10] considered the defeat a consequence of Prime Minister Atal Bihari Vajpayee's moderate line. For them, the BJP-led government had betrayed the Hindus by not building the Rama temple they so longed for in Ayodhya. The coalition's political decisions hampered Hindutva's agenda, prompting its division. Until May 2014, for the first time in more than 30 years, the BJP achieved, without any coalition, a majority in Parliament and Narendra Modi became prime minister. The election broke a record

---

[10] The Sangh Parivar, the 'family of the [Rashtriya Swayamsevak] Sangh', refers to the collection of Hindu nationalist organizations, led by the RSS. The core group of the Sangh Parivar represents significant areas of the public sphere—the Bharatiya Janata Party in the political domain, the Rashtra Sevika Samiti (women's wing of the RSS), the Vanvasi Kalyan Ashram (for welfare of tribal groups), the Sewa Bharati (for the socially and economically weaker sections of the society), the Vidya Bharati (for a national system of education) and the Swadeshi Jagran Manch (for the economic area).

in terms of the number of voters, candidates, political parties, partici-pation and election expenses. Data from various surveys showed the enormous popularity of the new prime minister, calling this the 'Modi phenomenon'.

Satish Misra (2018) acknowledges that the BJP has been able to expand its political base in the country because of various elements, including (a) financial resources, (b) expansion of mass base, (c) cen-tralized decision-making and (d) emphasis on young and Hindutva hardliners. Television becomes significant in the context of this last point. The debates broadcasted by news channels have been instrumental in animating the impulse of militant nationalism and the narrative of defending the fundamental interests of the majority community.

SCREENING HINDUTVA ON TV NEWS CHANNELS: NEW DELHI TELEVISION (NDTV), TIMES NOW AND REPUBLIC TV

As the Hindu-right strategy seems set to embrace a more militant Hindutva agenda as a part of its core electoral strategy, TV news chan-nels are increasingly used and play a significant role in the formation of public opinion. However, any evaluation of the influence of Hindu nationalism in politics should take into account that it is a set of ideas or beliefs that are located in a much wider space than that represented by the BJP. With a growing need of an identity, belonging, representation and participation, Hindu nationalists seek to attack, in the name of the nation, any perceived weakness in and from faith.

Some news channels—through rhetoric and reason, performances, debates and public discourses, images and ideas—have been spread-ing this Hindutva ideology, playing a pivotal role in the political and cultural communication process. News channels, or at least some of their primetime shows, have reshaped the context in which religion is symbolized, screened and understood. More than ever, they seem to be making a coordinated effort to create a particular environment and narrative that suits the government's goals.

NDTV, Times Now and Republic TV are the three most-watched English-language channels in India.[11] In addition to providing news, they broadcast numerous talk shows and debates that have strongly influenced public opinion and even politics. NDTV, founded in 1988 by Radhika Roy and Prannoy Roy, has pioneered Indian television, producing the first uninterrupted 24-hour news channel. At the Indian Television Awards (ITA), NDTV was named 'Most Popular English News Channel' in 2015 and 'Best English News Channel' in 2017. Its show *We the People* also won the prize for 'Best English Debate Show' in 2016 granted by the Indiantelevision.com Awards.

NDTV in its prime time, from 07:30 PM to 10:30 PM, apart from presenting national and international news, has segments of business, finances, sports, climate, interviews, researches and debates, where experts discuss and opine about current issues. Their commitment is always to provide their viewers with reliable, honest and impartial programmes. 'NDTV is today the most-watched, credible and respected news network in India and a leader in Internet' (NDTV 2019).

Similarly, Times Now is a leader in 24-hour English news broadcasting. The channel was launched by The Television Division of Bennett Coleman & Company Limited in January 2006, with Arnab Goswami as editor-in-chief. The channel won several prizes, at the Exchange4media News Broadcasters Awards of 2012, and also received 'News Channel of the Year Award', while Arnab Goswami won 'Editor-in-Chief of the Year Award'. In 2015, Goswami won the Red Impact 'Editor of the Year' Award, conferred by The Press Club in Mumbai. 'It is a channel that stands for credibility and unbiased approach in bringing news and reportages to the viewers. Sharp, incisive and direct, Times Now is the nation's voice in the news' (*The Times of India* 2017).

---

[11] Broadcast Audience Research Council (BARC) is responsible for providing data on the rating of television channels through the measurement of 'impressions', that is, the number of individuals of a target audience who viewed an 'event', averaged across minutes. BARC published that, during the 52 weeks of 2018, Republic TV tops its lists as the most-watched English news channel, followed by Times Now and NDTV (BARC 2019).

On 1 November 2016, Arnab Goswami resigned from his position at Times Now, broadcasting his iconic show *The Newshour Debate* for the last time on 14 November. A few months later, Goswami founded Republic TV in May 2017. Since its opening week, Republic TV has ranked as one of the most-watched English news channels in India. The channel has nationalism as the core element, the search for truth as its guiding principle and responds to the need to investigate, dig up and transmit that truth to millions of viewers. 'Being home to the youngest and most insatiable news team in India, Republic has broken the norms of traditional newsrooms and journalistic setups' (Republic TV 2019).

The rapid rise of 24-hour news television suggests that these channels play the role of mediators on contemporary political issues of great interest, especially for middle classes. News television's prominence has become influential in every aspect of an Indian's life as the medium has grown to be the primary source of information. Despite the transition to digital media, the print and television news industry in the country has continued to grow although at a sluggish pace. According to the India Digital News Report, with much of the population still offline, hundreds of millions of Indians still turn to newspapers, television and radio as their main sources of news.

Among respondents over 35 years, online (38%) and television (34%) are about equally widely named as the main source of news, and print (27%) still more widely relied on than social media (19%). But among respondents under 35, online generally (56%) and social media specifically (28%) are named as the main source of news by many more than print (16%) and even television (26%). (Aneez et al. 2019, 12)

As time goes by, news television has been engaging with several dominant ideologies. In recent decades, the Hindutva ideology has been a dominant force in Indian politics, and its engagement with news television has been visible in the media narratives on various sociopolitical and cultural issues. NDTV, Times Now and Republic TV have numerous programmes in which religion, nationhood and identity are questioned and come into the debate. In programmes, such as *The NDTV Dialogues: Has Hindutva Replaced Secularism?*, *The*

Newshour Debate: The Hindutva Identity and *Sunday Debate with Arnab Goswami: What Is Secularism?*, the spokespersons of Hindu nationalism attempt to redefine the Indian nation as Hindu, constructing audio-visual narratives that exalt the 'glorious' common past of the Hindus and heavily relying on the discourse of demonizing the 'other' (Mankekar 1999).

Further, the simultaneous use of 'Hindu nationalism' and 'Indian nationalism' has blurred the difference between the two and has given a certain amount of legitimacy or credibility to Hindu nationalism. The interaction between the media and religion, leading to the greater influence of religion in the public sphere, remains a crucial topic of investigation in a society in the age of new media (Dwyer 2006). In this intersection, television constitutes spaces of cultural and social practices integrated into the cultural discourse, wherein identity is not a variable separate from religion (Galal 2014, 97).

Several authors have indicated that television can be fundamental to the nation-building process (Barker 1999; Drummond et al. 1993; Louw 2005; Schlesinger 1991; Van den Bulck 2001). Television offers a formal and narrative space for the articulation of specific national imaginations, helping to integrate the idea that communities have about themselves. Their discourse ideologically guides the construction or reinforcement of the sense of identity, belonging and collective identification with the 'nation', through the idea that 'the nation needs us'. Television in highlighting and glorifying Hindutva sensibilities, has created a favourable environment and has provided the ideological support for the movement's sustenance.

For Hindu nationalism, media play a crucial role in articulating Hindutva as the country's 'national identity' and the 'thread of unity' running through its diversities. In TV programmes—for example, *Left, Right & Centre: Is India Moving Towards a 'Hindu Rashtra'?*, *The Newshour Debate: Is BJP Appropriating Hinduism in Hindutva's Name?* and *The Debate with Arnab Goswami: Should Religion Be Kept Out of Indian Politics?*—members of BJP define their national identity, through their religious identity and in so doing combine the religious with the cultural practices and values. Thus, viewers engage in the process of (re)identifying their own cultural bonds in relation to the 'others', enforcing a collective identity which evokes memories of shared history.

In a crisis or during social or political change, 'nationalisms' appear as a powerful agitation of feelings (Cullingford 2003, 22). In this regard, by analysing television discourse in the symbolic construction of 'nationalism', it is possible to identify the channelling of emotions and feelings towards daily social attitudes or behaviours. Nationalism consistently uses beliefs, representations, assumptions and practices to reproduce nations as the predominant form of political organization in today's world (Jenkins 1995). Further, Grossberg et al. (1998) argue that the media have penetrated identity formations based on traditional understandings of location, profession and religion, among others.

At the same time, the sense of unity among people, created by such powerful identities as were defined by religion, nationality, and work, have themselves been increasingly undermined by the powerful representations of difference that have come to define the media's cultural content, even as the media has come to shape social life. Ultimately, the media's ability to produce people's social identities, in terms of both a sense of unity and difference, may be their most powerful and meaningful effect. (Grossberg et al. 1998, 206)

In turn, ideologies, collective representations, habits and social practices forge identity. They are elements that help to reproduce the way of being in the social world and make it seem natural, ordinary and banal. In the words of Anderson (1983), with the information obtained from television, viewers can identify how, where and when they can be recognized and built as a community, as an imagined community. Likewise, the culturalist approach emphasizes on how the individual actively uses media as an integrated part of their social and cultural life. Television participates in the structuring of social consciousness through style, genre, schedule, images and language. When people interact with it, they become involved in a process that simultaneously connects them with different cultures, with remembered and imagined pasts and with sources of insight and meaning (Hoover 2006, 72).

The use of media and their integration in people's daily lives involves a number of parameters, material, social and individual elements. Although media do not determine identities, they do contribute in the creation of symbolic communicative spaces (Schlesinger 2000) that either include or exclude, thereby affecting audiences' lives and discourses about their identities. Audiences use media to negotiate religious, national, regional and many other forms of identity. As an inevitable aspect of television's participation in the mediatization of identities, it takes part in collective processes of inclusion and exclusion. Hence, media becomes a tool for performing cultural and social ways of life, which become symbolic of belonging. These processes emphasize how religious identity intersects with ethnic and national belonging, and more importantly, how these intersections are inscribed with negotiations of power relations.

The excessive style of the television debates of these three channels is more than just a visual phenomenon; it is a mechanism to develop a permanence in the minds of viewers through its distinctive appeal. These images are consumed/decoded within the viewers' frame of reference constitutive of their own cultural and social values. Besides, anchors—for example, Arnab Goswami, Sonia Singh, Sarah Jacob, Rahul Ravishankar, among others—are chosen on the basis of their personality and public reputation, not just by the genre of the show. The regular broadcast of debates around 'religion', 'nation', 'nationalism' and 'patriotism' is not merely a business-oriented tactic, but it is in tune with a broader strategy involving not only TV channels, but also social media, fake news, troll armies[12] and bots.[13]

---

[12] 'Trolling' refers to a specific type of malicious online behaviour, intended to disrupt interactions, aggravate interactional partners and lure them into fruitless argumentation. A media troll is someone who creates conflict on sites like Twitter or Facebook by posting messages that are particularly controversial or inflammatory with the sole intent of provoking an emotional response from other users (Coles and West 2016, 233).

[13] A bot (short for 'robot') is an automated application that runs over the Internet, used to perform simple and repetitive tasks that would be time-consuming, mundane or impossible for a human to perform. Bots can be used for

News channels focus on the immediacy and proximity of any event. In most instances, the television is the only point of access to politics; it is the place for political meetings that precede, shape and sometimes determine greater participation. This medium does much more than provide information about political ideas, problems, events or participants; it is a container of images and voices, heroes and villains, sayings and slogans, facts and ideas that audience turn to make sense of politics. It also provides the constituent components of the narratives that viewers build to organize, interpret, explain, understand and mediate the realities and illusions found in their daily lives. News channels are melting pots with public life that help us know who and what we are as individuals, as a community, as a public and as a nation (Jones 2005, 23).

Arvind Rajagopal (2004) argues that the media reshape the context in which politics is conceived, enacted and understood. He suggests that Hindu nationalists in recent times represented an attempt to create a populist language of politics, even on television, appealing to authoritarian rather than democratic values. This allows Hindu nationalism to fashion a range of different rhetoric outside the political sphere proper, and to suggest a homology between forms of consumption and voting behaviour, and between cultural identification and the requirements of electoral affiliation.

CONCLUSIONS

The euphoria that surrounded the elections in 2014 remains unaltered; indeed, Hindu nationalist sentiment has intensified, especially during election campaigns for the state assembly and the 2019 general election. However, any assessment of the influence of Hindu nationalism in political terms must take into account that it is a set of ideas that are located in a much wider space than represented by the BJP. These ideas overlap and blend with other critical discourses on society, religion,

---

productive tasks, but they are also frequently used for malicious purposes (Dunham and Melnick 2008).

culture and identity, which are manifested in a wide range of actions and political articulations.

The media have a role to play within representative democratic governments, but they also respond to a market logic that contrasts with the information principle. Religion has been a recurrent topic in the media. However, how the media address religion differs widely among nations and across public and private media. With a growing need to identify themselves, Hindu nationalists seek to attack a perceived weakness in and from the faith, the same vulnerability that many believe resulted in Islamic rule and British colonization of the subcontinent. Through this broad vision, this nationalism presents a Hindu identity, which apparently offers a supposed unity, but which in reality remains deeply fractured.

Considering that popular culture is one of the most widely used areas for informing and discussing any topic, television has become an integral component of politics, incorporated into the formal processes of the electoral and governance policy. In the debates, news channels often purposefully construct an intensely dramatic narrative, particularly in the time of national conflict or crisis, which has a positive relation with audience approval, reflected through consistently high rating points (Pandit 2018).

The news television has emerged as the main source of information in India. While trying to keep its momentum with the market demands, news channels have not been immune to sensationalism. The debate programmes have taken the public sphere and the 'imagined community' to a new level. The mystification, glorification and romanticizing of value systems of the past amply prove that the media can be biased or can be used as a consolidating tool for empowering communal norms. The growth of the Hindutva movement was catapulted by the media explosion, which helped them to form transnational Hindutva communities. The recent history of the Hindu nationalist movement in India provides a good illustration of how modern media technology qualitatively changes the politics of religious diversity and mobilization (Eisenlohr 2011).

Television forges the relation between audiences and politics; through its narratives, political action is given meaning when discussing, reflecting or working on the information provided. When television gives visibility to the members of the Hindutva public sphere, which is firmly rooted in sociopolitical structures, it leads to its further expansion and extension of the Hindutva outfit. Television, in giving visibility to the Hindutva ideologues, helps them in their attempt to compel the state to act in favour of their ideology. News television does not *explain* political changes as such, but, in electoral democracies like India, it functions as a conduit for leveraging political ideology.

REFERENCES

ABVP. 2018. *History*. Mumbai: ABVP. https://www.abvp.org/history

Anderson, Benedict. 1983. *Imagined Communities. Reflections on the Origin and Spread of Nationalism*. London: Verso.

Aneez, Zeenab, Taberez Ahmed Neyazi, Antonis Kalogeropoulos, and Rasmus Kleis Nielsen. 2019. *Reuters Institute: India Digital News Report*. Oxford: Reuters Institute for the Study of Journalism/University of Oxford.

Barker, Chris. 1999. *Television, Globalization and Cultural Identities*. Buckingham: Open University Press.

Basu, Anustup. 2008. 'Hindutva and Informatic Modernization'. *Boundary 2* 35 (3): 239–250.

Bhatia, Sidharth. 2019. 'Indian TV Media's Blatant Endorsement of Hyper-nationalism Is Shameful'. *The Wire*, 28 February. https://thewire.in/media/indian-tv-medias-blatant-endorsement-of-hyper-nationalism-is-shameful

Bhushan, Sandeep. 2016. 'How Television Media Uncritically Reproduced the Sangh's Narrative of "Nationalist" versus "Anti-nationalist"'. *The Caravan*, 27 February. https://caravanmagazine.in/vantage/media-uncritically-reproduced-nationalist

Broadcast Audience Research Council India (BARC). 2019. *TV Audiences. Weekly Data*. Mumbai: BARC. https://www.barcindia.co.in/statistic.aspx

———. 2018. *Impact of Co-viewing on TV Viewership*. Mumbai: BARC.

Coles, B. A., and M. West 2016. 'Trolling the Trolls: Online Forum Users Constructions of the Nature and Properties of Trolling'. *Computers in Human Behavior* 60 (1): 233–244.

Cullingford, Cedric. 2003. *El prejuicioen los jóvenes. De la identidad individual al nacionalismo* [Prejudice in young people. From individual identity to nationalism]. Madrid: Alianza Editorial.

Drummond, P., R. Paterson, and J. Willis, eds. 1993. *National Identity and Europe: The Television Revolution*. London: British Film Institute.

Dunham, Ken, and Jim. Melnick 2008. *Malicious Bots: An Inside Look into the Cybercriminal Underground of the Internet*. Florida: Auerbach Publications.

Dutta, Prabhash K. 2018. 'Urban Naxals: Know the Original Naxals'. *India Today*. 30 August. https://www.indiatoday.in/india/story/urban-naxals-know-the-original-naxals-1327316-2018-08-30

Dwyer, Rachel. 2006. 'The Saffron Screen? Hindi Movies and Hindu Nationalism'. In *Religion, Media and the Public Sphere*, edited by B. Meyer and A. Moors, 273–289. Bloomington, IN: Indiana University Press.

Eisenlohr, Patrick. 2011. 'The Anthropology of Media and the Question of Ethnic and Religious Pluralism'. *Social Anthropology* 19 (1): 40–55.

Federation of Indian Chambers of Commerce and Industry (FICCI). 2019. *A Billion Screens of Opportunity. India's Media & Entertainment Sector, March 2019*. Kolkata: FICCI/Ernst & Young LLP.

Friedlander, Peter. 2016. 'Hinduism and Politics'. *Routledge Handbook of Religion and Politics*. Abingdon: Routledge.

Galal, Ehab, ed. 2014. *Arab TV Audiences. Negotiating Religion and Identity*. Frankfurt: Peter Lang Academic Research.

Gokulsing, K. Moti, and Wimal Dissanayake. 2009. *Popular Culture in a Globalised India*. London: Routledge.

Goswami, Arnab. 2016. 'Tribute to Afzal Guru at JNU—Students Crossed All Lines?' [TV show]. *The Newshour Debate*. Times Now, Mumbai, 10 February.

———. 2017. 'Arnab Is Back!' [TV show]. Republic TV, Mumbai, 6 May.

———. 2018. 'Republic TV Exposed the Tukde-Tukde Gang' [TV show]. *The Debate with Arnab Goswami*. Republic TV, Mumbai, 5 January.

———. 2019. 'Lobby Goes after Harbhajan Singh over Chandrayaan 2' [TV show]. *The Debate with Arnab Goswami*. Republic TV, Mumbai, 23 July.

Graber, Doris A. 2001. *Processing Politics. Learning from Television in the Internet Age*. Chicago, IL: University of Chicago Press.

Grossberg, Lawrence, Ellen Wartella, and D. Charles Whitney. 1998. *Media Making Mass Media in a Popular Culture*. Thousand Oaks, CA: SAGE.

Habermas, Jürgen. 2006. 'Political Communication in Media Society: Does Democracy Still Enjoy an Epistemic Dimension? The Impact of Normative Theory on Empirical Research'. *Communication Theory* 16 (4): 411–426.

Hansen, Thomas B. 1999. *The Saffron Wave. Democracy and Hindu Nationalism in Modern India*. Princeton, NJ: Princeton University Press.

Hoover, Stewart M. 2006. *Religion in the Media Age. Media, Religion and Culture*. London: Routledge.

Jaffrelot, Christophe. 2007. *Hindu Nationalism. A Reader*. Princeton, NJ: Princeton University Press.

Jaffrelot, Christophe. 2010. 'Hindutva's Politics of Denial'. *The Caravan*, 31 August. https://caravanmagazine.in/perspectives/hindutvas-politics-denial

Jawaharlal Nehru University Teachers' Association (JNUTA). 2017. *What the Nation Really Needs to Know: The JNU Nationalism Lectures*. Noida: HarperCollins Publishers India.

Jenkins, R. 1995. 'Nations and Nationalism: Towards More Open Models'. *Nations and Nationalism* 1 (1): 369–390.

Jones, Jeffrey P. 2005. *Entertaining Politics. New Political Television and Civic Culture*. Lanham, MD: Rowman & Littlefield Publishers.

———. 2010. *Entertaining Politics Satiric. Television and Political Engagement*. Lanham, MD: Rowman & Littlefield Publishers.

Kumar, Ravish. 2016. 'Journalists March to Protest against Attacks on Media Personnel' [TV Show]. *Prime Time*. NDTV, New Delhi, 16 February.

Kumar, Shanti. 2006. *Gandhi Meets Primetime: Globalization and Nationalism in Indian Television*. Chicago, IL: University of Illinois Press.

Lembo, Ron. 2000. *Thinking through Television*. Cambridge: Cambridge University Press.

Livingstone, Sonia, and Peter Lunt. 1994. *Talk on Television: Audience Participation and Public Debate*. London: Routledge.

Louw, Eric. 2005. *The Media and Political Process*. London: SAGE.

Mankekar, Purnima. 1999. *Screening Culture, Viewing Politics Television, Womanhood and Nation in Modern India*. New Delhi: Oxford University Press.

Ministry of Information and Broadcasting. 2018. *Master List of Permitted Private Satellite TV Channels as on 30.09.2018*. Delhi: Government of India. https://mib.gov.in/sites/default/files/Master%20List%20of%20Permitted%20Private%20%20statellite%20TV%20Channels%20as%20on%20%2030.09.2018.pdf

Misra, Satish. 2018. 'Understanding the Rise of the Bharatiya Janata Party'. *Observer Research Foundation Issue Brief No. 258*. New Delhi: Observer Research Foundation.

Mitchell, Jolyon. 2005. 'Christianity and Television'. *Studies in World Christianity* 11 (1): 1–8.

Mitra, Ananda. 1993. *Television and Popular Culture in India*. New Delhi: SAGE.

Moores, Shaun. 2000. *Media and Everyday Life in Modern Society*. Edinburgh: Edinburgh University Press.

New Delhi Television. 2018. *Annual Report 2017–2018*. Delhi: New Delhi Television Limited. https://www.ndtv.com/convergence/ndtv/corporatepage/images/AnnualReport2017-18R.pdf

Norris, Pippa. 2014. 'Political Communication'. In *Comparative Politics*, edited by Daniele Caramani. Oxford: Oxford University Press.

Pandit, Sushmita, and Saayan Chattopadhyay. 2018. 'Coverage of the Surgical Strike on Television News in India'. *Journalism Practice* 12 (2): 162–176.

Pasricha, Anjana. 2014. 'Hindu Mythologies Rule Indian Television'. *Al Jazeera,* 30 January 2014. https://www.aljazeera.com/indepth/features/2014/01/hindu-mythologies-rule-indian-television-20141179558915889.html

Pathak, Vikas. 2018. 'RSS Reports Sharp Rise in Shakhas in 2018'. *The Hindu.* Nagpur, Maharashtra, 9 March. https://www.thehindu.com/news/national/rss-reports-sharp-rise-in-shakhas-in-2018/article23009796.ece

Pinkleton, Bruce E. and Erica Weintraub Austin. 2001. 'Individual Motivations, Perceived Media Importance, and Political Disaffection'. *Political Communication* 18 (3): 321–334.

Rajagopal, Arvind. 2004. *Politics after Television. Religious Nationalism and the Reshaping of the Indian Public.* Cambridge: Cambridge University Press.

Ratnagar, Shireen. 2004. 'Archaeology at the Heart of a Political Confrontation: The Case of Ayodhya'. *Current Anthropology* 45 (2): 239–259.

Ray, Shovana, and Jitendra Kumar Singh. 2017. 'Discourse Analysis on Nationalism Debate Reported in India Print Media During Feb–Mar 2016'. *International and Multidisciplinary Journal of Social Sciences* 6 (3): 251–280.

Republic TV. 2019. 'About Us'. Mumbai. https://www.republicworld.com/about-us

Roy, Abhijit. 2008. 'Bringing up TV: Popular Culture and the Developmental Modern in India'. *South Asian Popular Culture* 6 (1): 29–43.

Schlesinger, Philip. 1991. *Media, State and Nation. Political Violence and Collective Identities.* London: SAGE.

Schlesinger, Philip. 2000. 'The Nation and Communicative Space'. In *Media Power Professionals and Politics,* edited by Harold Tumber, 99–115. London: Routledge.

Sharma, R. S., Athar Ali, D. N. Jha, and Suraj Bhan. 1991. *Ramjanmabhumi–Baburi Masjid: A Historians' Report to the Nation.* New Delhi: People's Publishing House.

Sharma, Ram Sharan. 1990. *Communal History and Rama's Ayodhya.* New Delhi: People's Publishing House.

Thapar, Romila. 2010. 'The Verdict on Ayodhya: A Historian's Perspective'. *The Hindu.*

The Times of India. 2017. 'Times Now Marks Its Presence in 100 Countries'. 28 March. https://timesofindia.indiatimes.com/brandwire/media-entertainment/tv-radio-ooh/times-now-marks-its-presence-in–100-countries/article-show/57036050.cms

Thussu, Daya Kishan. 2007. *News as Entertainment. The Rise of Global Infotainment.* London: SAGE.

Tomko, Michael. 2015. *Beyond the Willing Suspension of Disbelief.* London: Bloomsbury Publishing.

Vallespín, Fernando. 2000. 'La Crisis del Espacio Público' [Crisis of public space]. *Revista Española de Ciencia Política* (3): 77–95.

Van den Bulck, H. 2001. 'Public Service Television and National Identity as a Project of Modernity. The Example of Flemish Television'. *Media, Culture & Society* 23 (1): 53–69.

Chapter 11

Sacred Spaces and Gendered Sites
The *Daikho* of the Dimasa

Prithibi Pratibha Gogoi

INTRODUCTION

Landscapes are dynamic social constructions that reflect the workings of historical processes and contextual experience in their changing configurations. They assume significant symbolic meanings on account of their complex interrelations with culture, political and ecological processes that have profound sociocultural implications (Baker cited in Adger et al. 2009, 248). Landscapes provide ample scope to understand the entwined articulations of meanings and values assigned to certain objects and spaces. Landscape is a way of seeing (Cosgrove 1985). Landscape, at the same time, is widely taken to be what we see and perceive, know and interact with.

Indeed, landscape is a broad category that encompasses various physical entities, such as hills, mountains, land mass, streams, rivers as well as elements constructed through human involvement, such as buildings, bridges and roadways, in a particular given frame. Arguably, this broad category has its own variations, and 'cultural landscape' is almost always the result of active human intervention. As early as

1931, P. W. Bryan had indicated how cultural landscapes emerged from modifications of natural landscape in accordance with human desires and adaptive measures. In addition to expressing the needs and aspirations of particular groups, societies or communities, cultural landscapes can also reflect specific techniques of sustainable land use that take into account the characteristics and limits of the natural environment in which they are located, and/or a specific 'spiritual' relation of communities to nature.[1] Cultural landscape is the site where humans ascribe meanings and value to nature, moulding it in a particular way to suit their purposes.

This chapter looks into a 'traditional' institution—the *Daikho*—of the Dimasa community/people.[2] *Daikho* offers a lucid illustration of a cultural landscape.[3] Drawing upon Cosgrove's (1985) idea of landscape as a way of seeing, I attempt to explore the intricacies of cultural landscape wherein the notions of dynamicity, sacredness, pure, impure and gender overlap and negotiate at varied levels. This effort to explore the internal dynamism of the *Daikho* and its interaction with external impulses, such as that of the free-market, expansion of transport and communication, puts into question the influential structural-functional analyses within anthropology (for instance, Malinowski's 1922), which regarded traditional communities and institutions as static and unchanging except for change coming from the outside. Early ethnographies of the region, the colonial ones in particular, classified the Dimasa and other communities as 'primitive', remnants of the past, and described their institutions as changeless. While these writings have been heavily

---

[1] The definition of cultural landscape is taken from the site of World Heritage Centre of UNESCO (2018).

[2] Dimasa is an ethnic group residing in the north-eastern part of the Indian subcontinent. This ethnic group belongs to Tibeto-Burman linguistic and ethnic community. They are recognized as Scheduled Tribes by the Constitution of India. The term 'Dimasa' literally means the children or descendants of a big river, in this case 'the Brahmaputra' (sons of Brahma). 'Di' means water, 'Ma' means big and 'Sa' means children (Bordoloi 1984; Danda 1978).

[3] I use 'institution' in the sense of an important social organization closely related to the sacred, whereas 'cultural landscape' encompasses all elements, such as the rivers, streams, reserved forests, roadways as well as sacred spaces. I use 'space', however, only to refer to the now-confined sacred space of the Daikho.

criticized by recent ethnographies (Ramirez 2014), the communities, intriguingly, are drawing upon colonial conceptualizations of their institutions and belief systems as 'traditional', in order to cope with and counter the severe pressure being put by the developmental imperatives of the state and conserve their 'sacred' institution. Through a focus on the *Daikho*, I also wish to study the importance of 'nature' and geographical spaces in the culture of a particular people and examine the evolving relationship of the Dimasa with *Daikho*. The increasing encroachment by the state into the Dimasa territory, the shifting spaces that were marked out as *Daikho* in particular, has induced the Dimasa to reconfigure their relationship with space and 'faith', offering a lucid illustration of the making and unmaking of 'cultural landscape'. A focus on the long-held belief system of the community of Dimasa will enable an understanding of how geographical spaces offer a crucial point of entry into the culture of a particular people, while an examination of the evolving relationship of the Dimasa with *Daikho*—critically moulded over the recent decades by the imperatives of the modern state and changing ideas pertaining to 'faith'—will throw light on the making and unmaking of 'cultural landscape'.

The concerned ritualized space is, in most cases, located in a remote place deep in the forest (the areas mostly fall under the reserve forest area) or near the banks of rivers, or at the threshold of a village secluded from everyday life. In earlier times, a well-defined and permanent space was not allocated to the *Daikho*. However, developmental processes (construction of roadways and laying down of railway tracks) have posed a threat to the mobility and significance of this institution. With the shrinkage of forest cover owing to the measures of the state and increase in human habitation, a vital change has begun in the way the Dimasas perceive and relate to the *Daikho*. Continual encroachments upon the shifting spaces that were earlier assigned to the *Daikho* have forced the community to devise new modes of conserving it.

THE INSTITUTION OF *DAIKHO*: AN OUTLINE

According to the census report of 2011, 99.1 per cent of the total population residing in the district of Dima Hasao are Hindus, but a small percentage of them have embraced Christianity as well (Census of India 2011).[4] The last Dimasa king is believed to have converted to Hinduism before the Kachari kingdom was annexed by the British colonial state (Hasnu 2017). Even though the majority of the Dimasa population profess Hinduism, they have retained their indigenous rituals and religious practices and continue to relate to them closely. The tradition of *Daikho* is one of those; it constitutes a significant aspect of their social life.

Dipali Danda's *Among the Dimasa of Assam* (1978) was among the first ethnographic accounts of the Dimasa. It offered a short description of *Daikho* under the category of 'Area God'. Danda (1978) mentioned that there were 12 non-structured sanctuaries in different localities inhabited by the Dimasa and they were called *Daikho*.[5] Since then, scholars such as B. N. Bordoloi (1984) have also provided brief descriptions of the *Daikho*, but they are very similar to Danda's narrative. The most recent work on *Daikho* was carried out by Philippe Ramirez in 2006. He defined the *Daikho* as a religious institution and noted that they are specific territorial units of the Dimasa where collective rituals are organized by members of patri-clans. The term *Daikho*, it bears mention, refers to the space/place reserved for a higher omnipresent being. People of the community interviewed during fieldwork roughly equated *Daikho* with a mandir (temple), abode of God (*Dai/Madai*, meaning god/deity/higher/omnipresent being and kho/bokho signifying place/house). Several scholars have associated *Daikho* spaces with sacred groves since they are rich in biodiversity (Chatry 2001; Medhi et al. 2013; Sharma 2000 cited in Malhotra et al. 2001; Thaosen 2017).

---

[4] The district of Dima Hasao is taken in account because the Dimasa constitutes the majority in this district.

[5] Although the number of the Daikhos is reported to be 12 by Danda, during my fieldwork, I found more than 12 Daikhos were mentioned by the people. Another Daikho (13th Daikho) was set up in Doyapur village of Dimapur, in order to bring back the Dimasa girls who were married to non-Dimasa men, and it opened the possibility for non-Dimasa men marrying Dimasa women to come within the fold of Dimasa social life. But this Daikho was reportedly discarded by the community in 2018 since it was felt that its establishment had brought ill fate to the villagers and the community.

A *Daikho* is normally the abode of more than one deity, that of the clan and of the nearby village (area), that is, the abode of both 'area god' and 'clan god', not one or the other. Collective rituals are organized annually at the *Daikhos* in the month of *Fagun* (mid-February, mid-March) or in early April to appease the deities, to ward off disease and bad omen and to conserve the well-being of the Dimasa. They include prayers and sacrifice of small animals such as goat, hen, pigeon and duck.[6] The prayers are offered by the officiating priest (*jonthai*) of each *Daikho* and members of the associated patri-clans. Helpers, normally two in number, clean, prepare and sacrifice the animals. The 12 *Daikhos* are scattered over the districts of Dima Hasao and Karbi Anglong, along the Assam–Nagaland border.

Daikho, generally regarded as a traditional sacred institution of an ethnic group, allows ample scope to broaden the understanding of it beyond its religious significance. Drawing upon my recent fieldwork and data collected in Nagaland (Dimapur) and Assam (Dima Hasao,[7] Karbi Anglong), as well as findings of relevant research, literature and other secondary sources, I will trace how constant negotiations propelled by the continuous restrictions imposed upon the *Daikho* by the state have encouraged varied assertions of identity in North-East India and occasioned vital changes in the institution itself.

DAIKHO AS A GENDERED SPACE

The Dimasas practise a system of double descent where lineage is traced from both the parents simultaneously (Bathari 2011; Bordoloi 1984; Danda 1978; Marak 2012). This was one of the peculiarities of the Dimasas that drew my attention and encouraged me to learn more about them. The Dimasas are among the very few communities in India that follow such a system of descent. In principle, such dual

---

[6] I was told by an informant that earlier large animals such as buffalos were sacrificed but not any longer.

[7] Formerly known as North Cachar Hills, but it was renamed as Dima Hasao on 30 March 2010 (Government of Assam 2010). This district comes under the Sixth Schedule area of the Constitution of India. The Dimasas are the dominant group in this district (Barbora 2002).

descent from the father and the mother allow Dimasa men and women to have an equal position in society. In reality, however, Dimasa society is patriarchal where the offspring takes up the name of the father.

The irony of the whole double descent gets reflected in the practices associated with the *Daikho*. Only male members of a patri-clan participate in the rituals conducted at each *Daikho*; female members of the patri-clan are not allowed. Similarly, sacrificial meat is cooked and consumed within the *Daikho* and never allowed to leave the *Daikho* premises to be shared by others. This paradox indicates an adherence to the normative gender codes.

WOMEN, PURITY AND THE SACRED

In the initial phase of my research, I faced several difficulties in conducting fieldwork. In addition to being an 'outsider', my gender restricted my access to the *Daikho*. When I insisted, I was frankly told that women are not allowed entry into the space designated as *Daikho*.[8] The reason behind such restriction is to maintain the 'purity' of the assigned space. Non-Dimasa men and women, and women in general are considered as threats to the sanctity of the *Daikho*. Indeed, the term used for 'sacred' among the Dimasa is *gathar*, which translates both as pure and holy. Its antonym, *gusu*, on the other hand, connotes only impurity. Women in general are categorized as *gusu*, and the officiating *jonthai* has to take care to lead a secluded life away from contact with women (and non-Dimasas) in order to maintain his purity/holiness. In addition, the *jonthai* also has to follow dietary restrictions, such as abstaining from taking pork and beef. This applies in particular to the priests of the Hansu clan. While for Ramirez, the strict rules and elaborate procedure that are followed in the selection of a *jonthai* offer valuable insights into the institution of *Daikho* (Ramirez 2006, 14), for Bathari (2011), the rules of purity and pollution followed by the Dimasas is

---

[8] In my recently concluded fieldwork (May 2019), one of my acquaintances took me to show the *Daikho* situated in Manja, Karbi Anglong (Assam). Though I got the opportunity to observe the *Daikho* from proximity but I was still asked not to enter the marked sacred site. I had to stand away from the site along with other female companion who accompanied me.

a result of their conversion to Brahmanical Hinduism. The taboo on eating beef, if particular, is a direct consequence of their Hinduization.

The prohibition of women entering 'sacred' spaces is neither new nor particular to the Dimasa.[9] The recent clashes over the entry of women to the Sabrimala temple offer an example. The Supreme Court of India had to intervene to persuade the temple authorities to stop restricting the entry of women of menstruating age (*The Wire* 2017). While in the Sabrimala case, women of a particular age group are sanctioned, in the case of the *Daikho*, all women are prohibited entry. When I tried to enquire why such restrictions exist for Dimasa women, I got varied responses: menstruation undoubtedly featured most prominently. Unlike the neighbouring Assamese community that celebrates the girl attaining puberty, the Dimasas do not have any particular rite of passage ascribed to the attainment of womanhood. Menstruating women are debarred from attending rituals, entering temples (or places of worship) and the family hearth. Men, elderly men in particular, do not consume any food prepared by a menstruating woman.[10] Clearly, such restrictions pertain to most Hindu households; the degree to which the restrictions are followed varies from one individual Dimasa family to another.

According to Mary Douglas (1966), the prescribed rules and restrictions with regard to dirt and pollution inherent in different societies, and the construction of purity in relation to such norms and taboos are indications that make up the structural body of the society.

At par with other double descent societies of Africa and Australia, Dimasas practice some clan-based taboos; but they are heavily

---

[9] The term 'sacred space' is borrowed from Mircea Eliade's work *The Sacred and the Profane*. Eliade discusses the differential marking of space by 'religious' and 'non-religious' individuals. While a non-religious individual perceives earth's surface as a homogenous space, a 'religious' man demarcates space as sacred and profane making space non-homogenous. In this regard the Dimasa territory also attains the non-homogenous topographical expression of space (see Eliade 1987).

[10] According to many informers, a menstruating girl/woman is considered impure and is not allowed to participate in rituals relating to marriage nor is she allowed to touch the bride. In addition to it, a girl who has lost one of the parents is also considered impure.

influenced by Brahmanical notions of purity and pollution. The hierarchy of the clans, moreover, is determined by such notions. In Kolb's (2017) analysis, purity is of utmost importance in the everyday life of the Dimasas.

While the rigid codes of behaviour outlined for women in Brahmanical texts are hardly imposed on tribal Hindu women (Ghosh and Choudhuri 2011), women are not given free access to the *Daikho* space on the pretext that such entry constitutes a threat to the sanctity of the space. As already mentioned, the priest is not allowed to have any kind of intimate interaction with women. He lives in a place away from all kinds of impurities—the presence of animals, such as pigs and dogs, and of women. Evidently, women pose a threat very different from that posed by dirty animals, but they are bunched together with them as impure.

Both men and women justify such restrictions, but they were unable to state the exact reasons behind those practices and their justification. An acquaintance narrated to me an instance where one group of women defied the rules and entered the *Daikho* space. This resulted in bringing bad omen for the whole society. According to the narrative, there were incidents of death, accident and poor harvest: the villagers came to ascribe such unfortunate happenings entirely to the transgression of norms relating to the *Daikho* by women. This story graphically depicts the fear of perilous repercussions that inhibit the breaking of rules and norms in societies and communities.

The seclusion and segregation of women from the space of worship also tell us that men of the society control the movement of women.[11] The space of *Daikho* becomes a contested site where women are excluded. Access to the ritualized space of *Daikho* is given to the male members of the patri-clan; women members are barred entry. Along with women, non-Dimasas and Dimasa Christian converts are not allowed. The men marrying outside the community are also prohibited. At the same time, they are given the option of undergoing a rite of purification (*therba*) and consuming holy water (*dther*). This

---

[11] Seclusions and segregations are regarded as the most potent instrument of control (Dube 1997).

rite, conducted inside the *Daikho*, makes the *Daikho* accessible to the male member of the patri-clan. Significantly, a Dimasa woman marrying a non-Dimasa man is not shown any such consideration. She is ex-communicated and loses her clan membership. Women, therefore, appear to have almost no say in the articulation of the hopes and aspirations of the community in moulding their cultural landscape. This is ironical: *Daikho* as a mobile space and not a static entity evokes fluidity and flexibility. The total and constant exclusion of women from it, however, constrains its dynamism and makes it inflexible.

CONTESTATION AND NEGOTIATION OF SPACE

As discussed above, the *Daikhos* in most cases are located in areas a little away from human habitation.[12] Their relative inaccessibility and remoteness constitute the community's way to preserving their purity by guarding them from any 'foreign' intrusion. The stone house in Maibang of Dima Hasao district (Figure 11.1), for instance, was abandoned when railway tracks were laid close to it. The increasing encroachment by the state, with its developmental projects of construction of roads and the marking of forest areas as 'reserved' zones, is making it increasingly difficult for the Dimasa to maintain the *Daikho* as a sacred space in motion. As the fine line separating state-owned and community-owned lands gets blurred more and more, the *Daikho* acquires greater significance as the key element of Dimasa identity in the context of the growing 'ethnic' politics in the North-East region of India.[13]

In such a situation, the notion of a fluid space extending into forests with no fixed boundaries gets transformed into a well-marked-out

---

[12] Damadi *Daikho* in Manja, Karbi Anglong, Assam is now located near the main road. I visited this *Daikho* in the month of May 2019.

[13] North-East India is an administrative unit which comprises eight states: Assam, Arunachal Pradesh, Nagaland, Manipur, Mizoram, Tripura, Meghalaya and Sikkim. It is one of the most diverse regions of the world (Haokip 2018; Pachuau 2014; Ramirez 2014).

Figure 11.1 *Photograph of a Stone House in Maibang, Dima Hasao District of Assam*

Source: Author.

Note: It is believed to have been a *Daikho* previously. It is situated next to river Mahur. It housed Ranachandi, the goddess of war. This *Daikho* was discarded when railway lines were laid and roadways were constructed near its location.

place that constitutes a vital element of the community's identity.[14] At present, the Dimasas tend to build concrete walls around the space assigned to the *Daikho* to prevent further encroachments. The Damadi[15] *Daikho* is one such example where a demarcated boundary confers a 'concrete' reality to the space. It is important to mention, however, that the money to build the walls was sanctioned by one of the executive

---

[14] This change was visible in the course of fieldwork conducted between February and March 2018 and May 2019 in the Dimasa-inhabited areas of Assam and Dimapur. In May 2019, I got the opportunity to observe Damadi *Daikho* from proximity. The boundaries of this *Daikho* are marked by concrete walls to restrict encroachment of any sort.

[15] Damadi is the name of the deity who is believed to reside in the Damadi *Daikho*. This *Daikho* is one of the 12 Daikhos of the Dimasas.

Figure 11.2 *Photograph Showing the Wall That Has Been Built around the Space of the Damadi Daikho*
Source: Author.

members of the district council who took the initiative in bringing this change in the nature and meaning of the *Daikho*. He also wanted to build temple like structures (shrines) within the *Daikho*, but the presiding *jonthai* and elders of the community prevented him from carrying it out.[16] The construction of the boundary walls (Figure 11.2), however, was allowed because the elders realized that the constant reduction of lands under Dimasa jurisdiction is making it very difficult to continue with the shifting sacred space. Such depletion is occasioning other changes within the community.

Changes Introduced by the Community

The changes made by the community are primarily for survival and for ensuring livelihood. In the context of depleting resources, the

---

[16] According to the priest and the community elders, Dimasas' deities do not reside in shrines.

shifting, *jhum* (slash and burn) cultivation, still prevalent in few hilly areas of North-East India, is coming under tremendous pressure. *Jhum* cultivation requires individuals and groups to move from one place to the other depending on agricultural needs. But in recent times, there has been a major change in the pattern of land use. The land which was used for *jhum* is being handed over to corporate bodies, such as the Coffee Board for coffee plantation (Barbora 2002). Earlier, the entire community had access to such land marked as commons. But once the commons are allotted to organizations, such as the Coffee Board, the access of the community is denied immediately, as local 'encroachment' is deemed illegal. The free movement of villagers get restricted and they are often compelled to clear forested areas (restricted areas) for cultivation.

State Initiatives

The Forest Department of the state has been very active in bringing more and more forest lands under the purview of reserved forest.[17] The Indian Forest Department established under the colonial regime in the year 1864 continues to exert control over one-fifth of the country's land area. The Forest Department in this sense is the biggest landlord that has the power to virtually affect the lives of every inhabitant of the countryside (Gadgil et al. 1995). The claiming of forest land by state institutions can be traced back to the colonial regime when laws and policies restricted the free movement of inhabitants by marking out the peoples of the hills/forests from the peoples of the plains. The Department of Forest in colonial India virtually redefined the notion of space and spatial identity. The first Forest Act declared that the state owns all forest land thereby scraping the rights of the people over the forests. More detailed laws for forest management were formulated by colonial administrators in 1877 (Prasad 2003, 31). These laws allowed the colonial state to govern the forest cover and they had very clear ulterior motives behind them. Apart from this, annual forest reports were printed by the colonial state. This tradition of annual reports

---

[17] Interview with a key informant in February 2018, Dima Hasao.

still exists in independent India. The re-mapping of space engineered by colonial cartographic imagination and imperatives is still persistent among the citizens of India. In such a scenario, the Dima Hasao district offers an interesting site of enquiry as it falls under the Sixth Schedule area of the Indian Constitution. In such areas, the allotment, occupation or use of land for residential or non-agricultural purposes remains under the purview of district or regional councils except for the reserved forest (The Sixth Schedule of Indian Constitution).

THE SPECIAL PROVISIONS

The Government of India grants special provision to 'tribal' areas to protect the rights of 'tribal' people. The district of Dima Hasao as a part of the area under the Sixth Schedule gets a few assured special provisions under which the land belongs to the community. Such special provisions include the formation of a district council, a corporate body constituted by the representative members of a tribal group within the allocated area. The council is vested with powers that allow them to make few laws regarding the allotment of lands, management of forests, regulations of shifting cultivation and appointment of village chiefs. But the main power remains in the hands of the governor who oversees the composition of the council, its term of office and other related issues. As a consequence, the special provisions for the community get severely constrained. The district council has no power to block the acquisition of land by the government of the state or nullify its claims (Barbora 2002). Ironically, the state simultaneously grants special provisions to people who inhabit certain specified areas marked in the Sixth Schedule to protect their community rights and their land, and also takes away such rights to claim ownership over certain areas within the same scheduled territory.

Under such circumstances, the space associated with *Daikho* becomes the site of multiple contestations and negotiation where various actors claim ownership. During my fieldwork, I got different versions where one section claimed that the *Daikho* is usually situated at the edge of a village and is under the jurisdiction of the community, while the others affirmed that that *Daikho* is located in the forest, near a river or by a stream in the 'reserve forest' zone and hence belongs to the state. This induces conflicts over jurisdiction. The district of Dima Hasao, currently, has three reserve forests: the Langting–Mupa Reserve Forest (497.55 sq km), the Krungming Reserve Forest (124.42 sq km) and the Barail Reserve Forest (89.93 sq km) (Northeast Now 2019). These reserve forests do not come under the jurisdiction of the district council but that of the state. The sacred space of *Daikho* which in most cases fall near or within the reserve forests becomes the contesting ground where the tussle between the state and the community gets reflected on the ground.

To cite one instance, members of the Dimasa community filed a case against the Department of Forest that was trying to place a garbage dump near a *Daikho*, since a dumping ground was to desecrate the sanctity of the *Daikho*. The Forest Department yielded to the community's request and changed the location of the dumping ground. Such instances demonstrate that the state recognizes the *Daikho* as a 'sacred space' of the tribal community, even while it encroaches upon it.[18] In addition, the state also recognizes the *Daikho* as a religious institution.

Though the encroachment is not a new event, the demarcation of the *Daikho* space is a recent development among the Dimasas that has important implications. Increasingly, gates are being built to mark the entrance to a *Daikho* and fences constructed to mark its contours. The inclination of the community towards the concretization of space[19] is radically changing the notion of the earlier mobile space. At the same time, such moves can also be viewed as Dimasa community's effort to compete with the growing number of churches, temples, mosques in urban and rural areas by laying claim to 'their' land and establishing their identity. The cultural landscape is changing as it is becoming more and more static.

---

[18] The field visit conducted in Dima Hasao district during March 2018.

[19] Concretization of space is an idea that the researcher is trying to work on based on Mcduie-Ra's (2018) work Concrete and Culture in North-East India.

Clearly, the space associated with *Daikho* is negotiated and contested at different levels—that of the individual, the community and the state. This constant contestation and negotiation redefines the whole idea of the spatial map of the *Daikho*, which holds significant importance in the Dimasa social life. The cultural territory of the community does not fit the political map of the state. State intervention has radically altered the fluid nature of the cultural landscape and led to the confinement of the *Daikho* space to few specific localities.

CONCLUSION

So far, few detailed studies have been carried out on the institution of *Daikho*, which forms an integral part of the Dimasa community's life and belief system. Existing works are primarily descriptive, and they present the *Daikho* as only a 'religious' institution. Here, I have attempted to break away from the clear separation of the religious, the secular and the political by trying to unpack the multiple meanings of the *Daikho* as the crux of the Dimasa social life, its gendered implications, as well as its changing significance on account of its intertwined interactions with state demands. I have traced the evolution of a 'traditional' institution of a 'tribal' community through the lens of territoriality, imagined landscape, and social belonging in contemporary times where boundaries are built and rebuilt to conserve and assert the presence of an ethnic identity. This traditional institution showcases how the religious territoriality is revoked in a district where special provisions are attributed to its inhabitants by the very state which issues such special powers.

With the appropriation of space by the state, the movement for *jhum* cultivation gets limited; this led an individual to encroach restricted government spaces. Apart from the encroachments at the community level, there are numerous state-initiated projects to administrate spaces and bring more land under their purview. The recent declaration of the sixth National Park of Assam in the district of Dima Hasao can be stated as one such motive where the state has added more land mass under it.

In the context of the *Daikho* 'public sphere', exclusive participation rights are conferred to Dimasa men while women are kept away from it. This restriction is imposed on the basis of the gender of an individual. In addition to it, such restrictions create segregated spaces where the access gets confined to only certain section of the society. It displays the uneven power equation within the society with regard to the *Daikho* institution. The fluid intersections of sacred, gender and impurity within the space of the *Daikho* showcase the problems to define this traditional institution of the Dimasas under the banner of 'traditional religious institution', rather there is convergence of various entities.

REFERENCES

Adger, W. Neil, Suraje Dessai, Marisa Goulden, Mike Hulme, Irene Lorenzoni, Donald R. Nelson, Lars Otto Naes, Johanna Wolf, and Anita Wreford. 2009. 'Are There Social Limits to Adaptation to Climate Change'. *Climatic Change* 93 (3–4): 335–354. doi:10.1007/s10584-008-9520-z.

Barbora, Sanjay. 2002. 'Ethnic Politics and Land Use: Genesis of Conflicts in India's North-East'. *Economic and Political Weekly* 37 (13): 1285–1292.

Bathari, Uttam. 2011. 'Double Descent and Concept of Purity'. In *Religion and Society in North East India*, edited by D. Nath, 204–218. Guwahati: DVS Publishers.

Bordoloi, B. N. 1984. *The Dimasa Kacharis of Assam*. Guwahati: Tribal Research Institute.

Bryan, P. W. 1931. 'The Cultural Landscape'. *Geography* 16 (4): 273–284.

Census of India. 2011. Dima Hasao Census. https://www.census2011.co.in/census/district/150-dima-hasao.html

Chatry, Kailash Kumar. 2001. 'Ecological Significance of the Traditional Belief Practices of Dimasa Kachari Tribe'. *Indian Journal of Theology* 43 (1–2): 63–69.

Cosgrove, Denis. 1985. 'Prospect, Perspective and the Evolution of the Landscape Idea'. *Transactions of the Institute of British Geographers* 10 (1): 45–62.

Danda, Dipali. 1978. *Among the Dimasa of Assam: An Ethnographic Study*. New Delhi: Sterling.

Douglas, Mary. 1966. *Purity and Danger: An Analysis of Concepts of Pollution and Taboo*. London and New York: Routledge.

Dube, Leela. 1997. *Women and Kinship: Comparative Perspectives on Gender in South and South-East Asia*. Tokyo: United Nations University Press.

Eliade, Mircea. 1987. *The Sacred and the Profane: The Nature of Religion*. Translated by Willard R. Trask. San Diego, CA: Harcourt Brace Jovanovich.

Gadgil, Madhav, and Ramachandra Guha. 1995. *Ecology and Equity: The Use and Abuse of Nature in Contemporary India*. London: Routledge.

Ghosh, Biwajit, and Tanima Choudhuri. 2011. 'Gender, Space and Development: Tribal Women in Tripura'. *Economic and Political Weekly* 46 (16): 74–78.

Government of Assam. 2010. Sixth Schedule. https://dcha.assam.gov.in/portlets/sixth-schedule-0

Haokip, Pauthang. 2018. 'Clans, Tribes and Unions of Tribes: Nomenclature of North East India'. *Economic and Political Weekly* 53 (35): 61–66.

Hasnu, Santosh. 2017. 'Colonial Archives and the Representations of Pre-colonial Dimasa Pasts'. In *Studies on Dimadasa: History, Language and Culture* (Vol. 1), edited by Monali Longmailai, 41–55. Guwahati: DVS Publishers.

Kolb, Michael R. 2017. *Attitudes towards Religious Culture among the College Educated Dimasas* (Unpublished PhD Thesis). Department of Northeast Studies, Assam Don Bosco University, Guwahati.

Malhotra, Kailash C., et al. 2001. *Cultural and Ecological Dimensions of Sacred Groves in India*. New Delhi: Indian National Science Academy & Indira Gandhi Rashtriya Manav Sangrahalaya.

Malinowski, Bronislaw. 1922. *Argonauts of the Western Pacific*. Long Grove, IL: Waveland Press.

Marak, Quinbala. 2012. 'A Note on Kinship Studies in North-East India'. *South Asian Anthropologist* 12 (1): 61–69.

Mcduie-Ra, Duncan. 2018. 'Concrete and Culture in Northeast India'. In *Raiot: Changing the Consensus*. http://raiot.in/concrete-and-culture-in-northeast-india/

Medhi, Promod, and Sachin Kumar Borthakur. 2013. 'Sacred Groves and Sacred Plants of the Dimasas of North Cachar Hills of Northeast India'. *African Journal of Plant Science* 7 (2): 67–77.

Ministry of External Affairs, Government of India. 1950. The Sixth Schedule of Indian Constitution. https://www.mea.gov.in/Images/pdf1/S6.pdf

Northeast Now. 2019. Assam to Get Its Sixth National Park. https://nenow.in/environment/assam-to-get-its-sixth-national-park.html

Pachuau, Joy L. K. 2014. *Being Mizo: Identity and Belonging in Northeast India*. New Delhi: Oxford University Press.

Prasad, Archana. 2003. *Against Ecological Romanticism: Verrier Elwin and the Making of an Anti-Modern Tribal Identity*. Haryana: Three Essays Collective.

Ramirez, Philippe. 2006. 'A Few Notes of Ritual Geography'. In *Traditional Systems of the Dimasa*, Vivekananda Kendra Institute of Culture, 6–15.

———. 2014. *People of the Margins: Across Ethnic Boundaries in North-East India*. Delhi: Spectrum Publications.

Sharma, B. R. 2000. *Sacred Groves and Their Role in Social Life in Himachal Himalayas*. Abstract National workshops on community strategies on the management of natural resources, Bhopal.

Thaosen, Humi. 2017. 'Semkhor Daikho: Outlining the Sacred Groves of Semkhor'. In *Studies on Dimasa: History, Language and Culture* (Vol. 1), edited by Monali Longmailai, 145–157. Guwahati: DVS Publishers.

The Wire. 2017. Sabarimala Temple Case: Should Regressive Religious Arguments Be Constitutionally Protected? https://thewire.in/gender/sabrimala-temple-case-women-entry-regressive-religious-arguments

World Heritage Centre of UNESCO. 2018. Cultural Landscapes. https://whc.unesco.org/en/culturallandscape/

About the Editors and Contributors

EDITORS

Avishek Ray teaches at the National Institute of Technology Silchar, India. He has earned his PhD in cultural studies from Trent University, Canada. He is interested in intellectual histories and works on issues concerning travel and mobility. He has edited a Bangla anthology on religion and popular culture, and published in reputed journals such as *Inter-Asia Cultural Studies*, *Multicultural Education Review*, *Canadian Journal of Comparative Literature*, *Journal of Human Values*, among others. He has held research fellowships at the Indian Institute of Management Calcutta, The University of Edinburgh (UK), Purdue University Library (USA), Centre for Advanced Study Sofia (Bulgaria) and Pavia University (Italy).

Ishita Banerjee-Dube is Professor of History at the Center for Asian and African Studies, El Colegio de México (The College of Mexico). She has held the DD Kosambi (Visiting) Chair of Interdisciplinary Studies in Goa University, and has been Fellow at the Max Weber Kolleg, Erfurt University, Germany. She has been a Visiting Professor at the Universidad Andina Simón Bolivar, Quito, Ecuador; the University of Syracuse, New York; and the School of Women's Studies, Jadavpur University, Kolkata. She has also been Fellow at the Indian Institute of Advanced Study, Shimla, among others. Her research explores issues of religion, law and power, time and temporality, language and identity, gender and nation, food and emotion, and democracy and social justice. She has authored four books: *A History of Modern India* (2015), *Religion, Law, and Power* (2007), *Divine Affairs* (2001) and, in Spanish, *Fronteras del Hinduismo* (Borders of Hinduism) (2007).

CONTRIBUTORS

Maribel Elliet Alvarado Becerril holds a master's degree in Asian and African studies with a specialization in South Asia from El Colegio de México. Her Master's thesis, 'Media and Nationalism in India: NDTV, Times Now and Republic TV', is a study about how television has been an active element in the material and symbolic reproduction of 'nation', 'nationalism' and 'patriotism'. She has been an adjunct professor of contemporary international politics and human development courses at UNAM. She did an internship at the Mexican Embassy in India and was affiliated as a visiting researcher at the Centre for Historical Studies/School of Social Sciences, Jawaharlal Nehru University.

Manjima Chatterjee is a drama explorer, teacher and occasional writer. Manjima studied English at St Stephen's College, Delhi University, and Sociology at the Delhi School of Economics. She has a postgraduate diploma in drama in education under Maya Krishna Rao from Shiv Nadar University, Dadri, Uttar Pradesh. Her articles have appeared in *Arts Praxis*, the Arts-in-Education journal of NYU Steinhardt, as well as *The Hindu, The Hindu Business Line, Education World* and *Hindustan Times*. She was shortlisted for the BBC's International Radio Playwriting Competition and won *The Hindu Metro Plus* Playwright Award in 2013. Her book, *Two Plays on Hunger*, was published in 2018, and her play, *Mountain of Bones*, was published in December 2019 in *Disparate Voices of Indian Women Playwrights: Creating a Profession*, an anthology of works by female Indian playwrights.

Sayori Ghoshal is a PhD candidate at the Department of Middle Eastern, South Asian and African Studies, Columbia University, New York. Her dissertation traces the construction of the minority identity for Indian Muslims, from the late 19th century to the early postcolonial period. She has a BA degree in English Literature (Jadavpur University), an MA degree in English Studies (Christ University) and MPhil in social sciences (Centre for Studies in Social Sciences, Kolkata). She has published in the *Economic and Political Weekly*.

Prithibi Pratibha Gogoi is a PhD candidate in the Department of Sociology, Tezpur University, Assam. She did her graduation in anthropology from Hans Raj College, University of Delhi. She did her masters in anthropology (specialization in social anthropology) from Miranda House, Delhi University. Currently, she is working on the Dimasa, and her research interrogates the Dimasa ecology and lifeworld.

Anne Hartig is an Art Historian specializing in Indian architecture, religion and culture, travelling and researching South and Southeast Asia for nearly 20 years. Her PhD, from Jawaharlal Nehru University, concerns temple architecture in Delhi, offering new insights into the dynamics of temple patronage from the early 20th century to the present. In 2018, as a scholar-in-residence at the Alice Boner Institute, Varanasi, Uttar Pradesh, she researched about modern temples in Varanasi, Sarnath and Kushinagar. She completed her magister degree in Indian art history, Indology and European art history from the University of Bonn, where she also taught a course on modern Indian art. She was also part of the Angkor Inscription Survey at the ancient temple city in Angkor, Cambodia.

Mark Juergensmeyer is Professor of global studies, Professor of sociology and Affiliate Professor of religious studies at the University of California, Santa Barbara, where he was the founding director of the Global and International Studies Program and the Orfalea Center for Global and International Studies. He is an expert on religious violence, conflict resolution and South Asian religion and politics and has published more than 200 articles and 20 books, including the co-authored *God in the Tumult of the Global Square: Religion in Global Civil Society* (2015; co-authored with Dinah Griego and John Soboslai), *Terror in the Mind of God: The Global Rise of Religious Violence* and *Global Rebellion: Religious Challenges to the Secular State*.

Himani Kapoor is currently pursuing doctoral studies, in the area of guru-led faith movements in India, from the Department of English, University of Delhi. She holds an MPhil in comparative Indian literature, where she studied different renditions and translations of the

Bhagavad Gita. Her research interests include translation studies, disability studies and new religious movements in India.

Tabinda M. Khan received a PhD in political science from Columbia University, in 2015. She was a Postdoctoral Fellow at the Gurmani Institute for Languages and Literature, Lahore University of Management Sciences, where she taught a class on Liberalism and Islamism in Pakistan. Currently, she is completing a book manuscript on the conflict between liberals and Islamists in Pakistan.

Sreya Mitra is Assistant Professor at the Department of Mass Communication, American University of Sharjah, UAE. Her research focuses on South Asian media, popular culture, stardom, globalization, diaspora and culture industries. She has presented her research at various international conferences, and her work has been published in the edited collections such as *Reorienting Global Communication* (2010) and *Transnational Stardom* (2013), and in peer-reviewed journals such as *Journal of South Asian History and Culture* (2012), *Journal of South Asian Popular Culture* (2020) and *Celebrity Studies Journal* (2019, 2020).

Shobna Nijhawan is Associate Professor at the Department of Languages, Literatures and Linguistics, York University, Toronto. She is the author of *Women and Girls in the Hindi Public Sphere: Periodical Literature in Colonial North India* (2012), *Hindi Publishing in Colonial Lucknow: Gender, Genre and Visuality in the Creation of a Literary 'Canon'* (2018) and the editor of *Nationalism in the Vernacular: Hindi, Urdu and the Literature of Indian Freedom* (2010). She has published on Indian feminist movements and South–South encounters in the *Journal of Asian Studies*, *Journal of Women's History* and the *Indian Journal of Gender History*. Her most recent work is on text–image relationships and on advertising in colonial India.

Ridhima Sharma has completed her MPhil from the Centre for Women's Studies, Jawaharlal Nehru University, New Delhi. Prior to this, she completed her masters in media and cultural studies from Tata Institute of Social Sciences, Mumbai. Her research interests include feminist theory and methodology, politics of nationalism, ethnography, sexuality and masculinity studies, and social and political movements.

Index